San Pedro River Water Wars in the Post Drew's Station Era
By John D. Rose

Table of Contents

"SAN PEDRO RIVER WATER WARS IN THE POST DREW'S STATION ERA."
By John D. Rose.

Dedication. This book is dedicated to my wonderful wife Stephanie, who made all my dreams come true, and her parents, John and Shirley Ray, who never allowed their many triumphs to cause them to lose sight of humble beginnings, which they turned into tremendous successes.

Acknowledgments. I would like to thank veteran Cochise County Recorder Christine Rhodes, a good friend mine of nearly two and a half decades, who is always enthusiastic in guiding me and all other researchers through her all-important archives. Special thanks also to Kevin Pyles, whose expert leadership has made the Cochise County Archives a key destination for researchers. I refer to this archive as the "Kevin Pyles Archive Center," though this is not an official title. Kevin truly understands the records that he tends to so well, and in his free time, he has done the cover design and image layouts for this entire book, just as he did for my second book, *On the Road to Tombstone: Drew's Station, Contention City And Fairbank.*

I would be remiss if I did not acknowledge the continuing support and access to family information and archives of the Drew family, the descendants of those who those who built and once lived at Drew's Station. Having contact with them and seeing first hand their generosity and openness is a humbling honor. I could not have imagined it so many years ago when I first read the story of a family who owned a stage stop that became part of Arizona history for all time.

Much gratitude is due to my wife Stephanie Rose who spent countless hours proofing this book, and studying testimony with the goal of annotating and clarifying maps herein so that the reader can better understand the location of these heretofore unknown ranches.

INTRODUCTION

Recorded impressions of the San Pedro River occur only intermittently in the periods prior to and after the major settlement and development of the mill towns connected to the Tombstone mining boom. Some notices appear in the Weekly Arizonian which offer insights, and accounts exist by others who came through the area, even if only for a brief time. James Bell was such an example, bringing a herd of cattle through Arizona on the way to California in the summer of 1854. "The valley through which the San Pedro passes is a desirable location for ranches. The hills on either side are covered with timber…and a good quality of grass; some portions of these hills are verry [sic] pretty…Upon the whole this is the most habitable place seen since I left San Antonio." [1]

I too am enchanted by this area. Its rugged aesthetic still appeals to me, and it challenged me to learn more than just locations of the sites that settlers left behind. I wanted to know who they were, and learn as much as possible about their lives while living there. It led me to many discoveries and many publishing breakthroughs. I was honored to be the first to publish excerpts from Cora Drew's account of her life at Drew's Station, as well as unknown photos generously shared with me by the Drew family. Their generosity has contributed to my greater understanding of the river, which has been a focus for me of decades of travel and research. It has been a privilege and a thrill to work with them. I find writing about towns and settlements along the San Pedro River a unique challenge, wondering if enough information can be found even for short articles. Persistence rewarded me with the research that comprised my first book, *Charleston and Millville, A.T.: Hell on the San Pedro*.

After searching through the Charleston area, I began to look at the area north of Contention City. I was in search of the stage road that completed the final leg of the journey from Tombstone to Contention to Benson. I envisioned not only the remains of a dusty roadway that thousands once traversed, but also accompanying home sites scattered at or near its path across the high Arizona desert. The most famous of these sites was Drew's Ranch and Drew's Station. I was not disappointed in my explorations, and have many times visited the roadway and ruins of home sites nearby this historic route.

The Drew's site was key to the story of Wyatt Earp, Tombstone, and Wells Fargo, as the shooting deaths of driver Bud Philpot and passenger Peter Roerig set in motion a series of events that led in part to the gunfight near the O.K. Corral. Popular culture has placed a great premium on such sites that relate to the Earp story, which can be of particular use and benefit to overall history when it is used as an introduction to the much larger body of records of the remarkable history of the San Pedro River Valley. Doing less of a service to the history of the area is the idea that little else matters outside of the Earp story. It is my hope that in some way this brief window into the past can offer a broader scope to such views. I find of great interest the pioneers who assumed enormous risks in coming to these lands and settling them, and in their own way, helping to develop each successive area of the Great American Southwest.

In my second book, *On the Road to Tombstone: Drew's Station, Contention City and Fairbank*, I also published for the first time William Drew's testimony in a lawsuit against Robert Mason, along with Drew's hand drawn map of this memorable area. Drew, in his sworn testimony, gives the specific mileage which clearly delineates the location of his homestead, confirming the same site that I have identified for years as Drew's. There exist two other sets of foundational remains located north of Drew's ranch. I also published conclusive proof that the northernmost foundation, proposed to be the actual site of Drew's Station by Mrs. Nancy Sosa and a group called TTR, cannot possibly be Drew's Station. But the unanswered questions remain—to whom did this northern site belong? When was it first acquired and built upon? What was its use?

The discovery of the Hill vs. Herrick case is a major breakthrough in the historical study of the San Pedro River and the San Pedro River Valley. The case offers much insight into the day to day lives of so many who toiled up and down the river as teamsters, construction and mill workers, and residents of Contention City, Fairbank, Charleston and Millville, and all of these near forgotten ranches and farms that dotted the banks of the San Pedro in between and beyond those points.

They have faded from the historical record that is often overly influenced by today's interest in "Blood and Thunder" events that imply to some that most men in the old west were lawmen or outlaws, and most women in the west were employed in trades of ill repute. Such stereotypes only serve to remove the humanity and reality of ordinary people who chose to insert themselves in extraordinary times and remarkable places. This lost history is of great importance to the understanding of key sites that relate to the Tombstone and Earp story, as well as more current matters.

The era of settlements and small ranching/farming operations along the San Pedro was not destined to be a long one. Many settlers thought they were on public lands, or at least said so, but it was in the press many times that there was an issue that much of the San Pedro River lands south of Benson and nearing the Mexican border were actually situated on two Mexican land grants. Those who made their livelihoods there, paid taxes there, and endured hardships such as drought conditions, flooding, and a dwindling supply of the overburdened and limited flow of San Pedro River surface water, would later find that these land grants were of real consequence, as is discussed toward the end of this book.

Old myths sometimes have been joined by contemporary ones. The Hill vs. Herrick case disproves a recent claim that by 1881 when George Hearst and James Howard had gained control of the San Juan de Boquillas y Nogales land grant, the entire area, over 17,000 acres, became an outdoor "time capsule" frozen in time, with no one living in the area unless they had Hearst's blessing, making for a sparse population. In reality, this area remained vigorous and vital with substantial settlements and agricultural commerce well through the 1880's and into the 1890's. It wasn't until 1899 that this dynamic would see its underpinnings stripped away as the new owners of the grant began to enforce their property rights in a way that George Hearst had never chosen to.

In addition to accurately identifying historic ranches and their owners, the Hill vs. Herrick case brings to light an issue that is currently pressing to residents of my home town, Sierra Vista, Arizona. It was a surprise to many of us when a slew of lawsuits against the future of Fort Huachuca began to emerge in the 1990's. These suits argued that the water use of the Fort and the city created in its wake had reduced water in the San Pedro River, threatening the river and its rich riparian area. Plaintiffs in some of the suits would have the missions of the fort significantly reduced, diminishing the economic engine of Sierra Vista and the surrounding area. When the fort reopened in 1954, the area on which Sierra Vista now stands was a scattering of minor settlements and ranching areas, a far cry from the modern and thriving community that is the most prosperous in all of Cochise County today. Some in the area began to speculate that if such lawsuits were successful, could the area that is home to so many return to such a depopulated state?

But is it true that the population center that Sierra Vista had become is a threat to the San Pedro River, its majestic stand of cottonwood trees and the opportunities they provide for migratory birds and so many others species that grace the area? It was for reasons of history, current water issues, and my own curiosity that I wrote this book, to answer these questions for myself. It is my hope that this book will be illuminating not only to those interested in historical discovery, but also to those who are debating the future of Sierra Vista and the San Pedro River.

Accounts featured in this book are by those who were alive and witnessed the development of the San Pedro River Valley in the 19th Century. The sparse accounts of such areas are prized in research, as they are rare. There was no press churning out newspapers in any town or settlement along the San Pedro from Charleston to the Drew's Station area. Benson, Arizona would later have a functioning newspaper, but it came too late to record the key events of the area north of Contention City during its heyday, when the opportunities seemed to abound from the very land on which settlers began their years of toil, only to learn that they never had solid legal claims to the very places where their children were born, their elderly passed on, and they called home.

Wintertime near the San Pedro River. Photo by John D. Rose.

CHAPTER 1

A WINDOW INTO THE 19TH CENTURY SAN PEDRO RIVER

"A vast marsh, a cienega, spread out miles and miles ringed with hardwoods." -Excerpt from a 2012 article regarding the San Pedro River.

19th Century image of cattle in the San Pedro River. Copy photo from the collections of John D. Rose.

It was within the last ten years that the branch campus of Cochise College, located in Sierra Vista, Arizona, asked me to drive a tour down to Cananea, Sonora, Mexico. It was an opportunity that I readily accepted. The chance to walk through Colonel W. C. Greene's home which still stands there, as well as visit the mining operation, was one I could not refuse. I also wanted to purchase authentic Mexican made tortillas, as they are a weakness of mine, and to learn more if possible about the San Pedro River, the water way that originates near Cananea, and then flows into the US. On this very worthwhile visit our guide knew well the issues that related to the river, as well as the international implications of water use on the Mexican side and its effect on the amount of water that reaches Arizona after originating in Mexico.

I've long found it ironic that some in the U.S. complain about Mexico's use of San Pedro River water, arguing that they have an unfair advantage over its use before it reaches the U.S. Those individuals may want to reacquaint themselves with another waterway well known to Arizonans, the Colorado River. 19th Century photos and countless documents prove that this once was a substantial body of flowing water, and further, unlike the San Pedro River, it supported steamers moving people and commerce up and down this once navigable river. The American use of the Colorado River water has greatly diminished what now arrives in Mexico today, thus bringing full circle the issue of which nation is depriving which of the greater amount of water.

Among the sites we took in on our day trip was a city street with a fountain. The area that the street traversed was not level, and our guide noted that water drainage flowing down one side of the street headed to a wash that led to the San Pedro River, and the water flowing down the other side went to a different destination. He jokingly added that the fountain nearby was a reminder to Americans that those in Mexico had first access to the waters of the San Pedro. He was of course correct. "See, we're using water that would have gone to the San Pedro to fill that fountain," he said. It was all in good nature, but a point of truth had been well made by our guide. The San Pedro is an international waterway, affecting the lives of the citizenry of two neighboring nations, and we in the U.S. have to acknowledge the obvious. These waters do not originate on our lands, so we don't own it at its inception. This lazy little river originates from many tributaries in the Sierra Madre Mountains, meeting to form the San Pedro just fifteen miles south of the US/Mexico border. It slowly wends its way north, both above and below the ground, till it reaches the Gila River near Winkelman, Arizona.

THE SAN PEDRO RIVER OF A DIFFERENT ERA

On any given day in the 1880's, a horseback ride along the San Pedro River would offer a visual experience that today is hard to imagine. In the spring and summer along the San Pedro one would still see acres of golden brown grasses turned to green, mesquite, willows, and other trees here and there having bloomed for the season, just as one would see today. But this is where the like comparisons would come quickly to an end.

Interspersed between large patches of grass and mesquites would be acres of corn, alfalfa, orchards and garden crops with rows of melons and potatoes in production up and down the San Pedro, often on both sides of this overburdened water way. One would see a steady traffic of wagons filled with vegetables headed for market, farmers and their helpers toiling in the fields, and smoke rising from wood stoves inside the small and often primitive cabins that many along the river called home. Earthen dams and connecting irrigation ditches would guide water flow to distant crop fields. It was a dynamic population that often traveled north and south along the river, heading easterly to Tombstone for banking, shopping, and entertainment only when such errands were required. These farmers often qualified as ranchers as well, tending to stock. The stereotype that ranchers were one group of people, and on the other side farmers were an opposing group, is overplayed. Rather, the portrait of such entrepreneurs shows those who are eager to earn for their families in whatever way the land would allow.

These small settlements would see children playing along the river and attending school. Those folks located in the rural settings also rubbed shoulders with mill men and saloon keepers at river centers such as Contention City and Charleston. Jobs were fluid as mill men became ditch diggers and farm workers and repair men.

These people would also meet a different breed of wage earner first at Contention City, and later Fairbank - the railroad man. It was a very different form of employment, riding the rails for a day's wage, and being a part of the most advanced form of public transportation of the day. It is indeed ironic that the Iron Horse traversed easements purchased from area farmers/ranchers who plowed their fields as passengers viewed them working from the comfort of their seats as the train took them to other destinations. It was an area occasionally plagued by troublemakers and outlaws who sought refuge in the hinterlands that these river settlers called home. This era along the San Pedro has long since faded from view. Today the land grant portions of the river are no longer home to any similar human activity, just to what was left behind. So many of these settlers' stories have never seen the light of a 20th or 21st Century day, until the recent discovery of the Hill vs. Herrick lawsuit, a groundbreaking discovery bringing to life a history heretofore unknown.

A RIVER OVERFLOWING WITH MYTHOLOGY AND LACKING IN WATER

Today's mythology of the San Pedro River has reached unprecedented levels of acceptance in the public discourse. The river has often been referred to as "One of the last great places," as indeed any source of self-sustaining water found in the desert must be considered special. It has also become a rallying point for environmentalists who reside locally, and others who are far removed from the region that such a debate affects.

Hill vs. Herrick and earlier accounts of explorers passing through the area further disprove the fables of paddle wheel steamers and barges floating up and down a once mighty San Pedro River (as I was taught in local schools as a child). It illustrates instead a surface flow of the river 130 years ago and earlier that is similar to the flow of today. This is drawn into sharp focus in repeated testimony that documents a number of dams up and down the river, built in attempts

4

to corral the scant surface flow of the river and send it into ditches that transported it to nearby crop fields. When working properly, any extra or waste water was sent back into the river via a return ditch to continue its northward meandering so that others could use the same. But increased settlement as the 1880's progressed, and reduced rainfall, stressed this already meager supply, turning neighbor against neighbor, and busying a court reporter from Tucson whose duty it was to type well over 1000 pages of testimony on which this book finds its greatest window into a past that otherwise would be lost to the ages.

This important case is not the only source of information about San Pedro water flow. On July 25th, 1880, Tombstone diarist George Parsons headed for Millville and Charleston with friends. They asked him to join them "to go swimming with them at Charleston or near there…At Charleston are the Gird and Corbin Mills - both stopped for lack of water. The San Pedro is anything but a mighty stream. One can jump across most of the rivers of Arizona and California I guess…"

After visiting Millville Parsons added that "on we went several miles to the dam which we found had given way. No chance for a swim." [2] The scarce surface flow that Parsons noted even when the dam was absent proves false today's conventional belief that the San Pedro River had far greater flow in the 1880's than it did in the 20th Century.

George Parsons, Courtesy of Roy B. Young

Six years later in the summer of 1886 Parsons was conducting a trip which included a leg along the San Pedro River. Reports of

Indian sightings were common at this time; Parsons was hoping to dodge any chance meetings with Apaches and Geronimo. On June 15th, he "lunched at St. David" noting that "The Mormons treated us well…I left others here and went to Benson for promised military escort." On Thursday, June 17th, a jumpy Parsons needed a bath and his horse was in need of a rest. "Good bath in [the] San Pedro River this afternoon. Water didn't quite cover me lying down, but had a good wash meantime keeping lookout for Indian." [3] It is noteworthy that prior to the summer rainy season, water flow in the river was scant, barely able to cover someone lying down in it.

NO WATER AT THE SAN PEDRO STAGE STATION

The Weekly Arizonian would also record in 1859 which stations, along what is now commonly referred to as the Butterfield Stage route, had water and which did not, for the benefit of travelers. They reported that the San Pedro Station, which was built so close to the river that the waterway later consumed the site, was without water in 1859, long before Tombstone was even discovered and major settlements sprang up along this key, but very limited, water way. But travelers arriving in Tombstone sometimes told of having to wait to cross the river during its flooding, which only occurs after a substantial rainfall. [4]

Table of Distances.

For the benefit of travelers, we give the fol
lowing table of distances between the stations
on the Overland Mail Route from San Francis
co to St. Louis, via Arizona:

San Francisco to Clark's 12, Sun Water 9;
Redwood City 9, Mountain View, 12, San Jose 11,
Seventeen Mile House 17, Gilroy 13, Pacheco Pass
18, St. Louis Ranche 17, Lone Willow 18, Temple
Ranch 13, Firebaugh's Ferry 15, Fresno City 19,
Elk Horn Spring 22, Whitmore's Ferry 17, Cross
Creek 12, Visalia 12, Packwood 12, Tule River 14,
Fountain Spring 14, Mountain House 12, Posey
Creek 15, Gordon's Ferry 10, Kern River Slough 12,
Sink of Tejon 14, Fort Tejon 15, Reed's 8, French
John's 14, Widow Smith's 24, King's 10, Hart's 12,
San Fernando Mission 8, Canuengo 12, Los Angeles
12, Total 462 miles; time 80 hours.

Los Angeles to Monte 13, San Jose 12, Rancho
del Chino 12, Temascal 20, Laguna Grande 10, Te-
mecula 21, Tejungo 14, Oak Grove 12, Warner's
Ranch 10, San Filipe 10, Vallecito 18, Palm Spring
9, Carisso Creek 9, Indian Wells (without waer)
(without water) 22 Pilot Knob 18, Fort Yuma, 10.
Total, 282 miles; time, 72 hours and 20 minutes.

Fort Yuma to Swiveler's 20, Fillibuster Camp 18,
Peterman's 19, Griswell's 12, Flap Jack Ranche 15,
Oatman Flat 20, Murderer's Grave 20, Gila Ranche
17, Maricopa Wells 40, Socatoon 22, Picachio 37,
Pointer Mountain 22, Tucson 18. Total 280 miles;
time 71 hours 45 minutes.

Tucson to the Cienega 35, San Pedro (without
water) 24, Dragoon Springs (without water) 23,
Apache Pass (without water)40, Steen's Peak (without water) 35, Soldier's Farewell (without water) 42,
Ojo de Vaca 14, Mimbres River 16, Cook's Spring
18, Picachio (without water) 52, Fort Fillmore 14,
Cottonwoods 25, Franklin 22. Total 300 miles;
time 82 hours.

Weekly Arizonian March 31, 1859. The final paragraph shows
that the San Pedro Stage Station, which was near the banks of
the San Pedro, was without water.

Today the San Pedro River still travels from the south to the north just as it always did, inspiring present day myths from romantics who divine a more dramatic history of this waterway. In 1858, James B. Leach of the Department of the Interior was enlisted to supervise the construction of a roadway through southern Arizona. "Leach and his companions had a surprise in store for them as they traveled down the San Pedro about 35 miles below Tres Alamos [north of present day Benson, where Billy Ohnesorgen had a stage stop. This places Leach in the area of Lewis Spring, just south of Charleston, which has been a long term source of water on the San Pedro] on September 12:

"'The train was ordered forward at 7 a.m. Exceedingly to the surprise of every member of the expedition who had passed over this route in the months of March and April it was discovered after a march of a few miles that the waters of the San Pedro had entirely disappeared from the channel of the stream. The discovery was first made by Col. McKinnon, Paymaster, who returned to Camp reporting according. So incredulous were many of those who were on the April Expedition that heavy bets were offered that Col. M. was mistaken. A thorough examination proved his discovery correct much to the astonishment of many. Where the present reporter took quantities of fine trout in March and April 1858 not a drop of water was to be seen. The same circumstance (the sinking of the waters of the San Pedro) however, is referred to in Lt. Parkes journal of his expedition through this country.'" [5]

It is further asserted that the grand stands of cottonwood trees that so majestically line the river at present are of ancient origin, ignoring the fact that photos taken in the historic period contradict some of these claims.

Mary Wood, wife of an important mining executive, would leave behind a credible account, her dates and figures standing up well against historical scrutiny. She recalled only one cottonwood tree in the Charleston and Millville area, and made note of it: "My first view of Millville in the fall of 1880 was a pleasant surprise for their nestling against the hills which closely circled it on the north and east was a lovely alfalfa patch of several acres. On the western edge on the banks of the San Pedro River was a very large cottonwood whose leaves were still a vivid green…It was the first green I had seen since leaving California."

The arrow notes the large Cottonwood at Charleston that Mary Wood recalled. Copy photo from the collections of John D. Rose.

The lone Cottonwood at Charleston marked with an arrow from the opposite direction, looking toward the Huachucas. Cropped from the original stereoview in the collections of John D. Rose.

Assertions that the massive stands visible today were there, and Tombstone and Charleston settlers cut them down for housing or to burn in stamp mills is an attempt to extrapolate "facts" from information that does not exist. Photographic evidence from the day conclusively proves Mary Wood right, as there is one cottonwood visible in the early 1880's at Charleston, and nothing else. That is not to say that there were no stands of cottonwoods in the San Pedro River Valley.

At first glance, eye witness historic accounts of the flora of the San Pedro may appear contradictory. Some explorers speak of stands of willows and cottonwoods, while others searched to find a line or stand of trees to guide them to the river, only to practically fall into the river without that benefit.

But in reality, it may well be that such accounts are not contradictory at all. Once the Tombstone District gained momentum, settlers began dotting the map with sites such as Charleston, Millville, The Boston Mill, Fairbank, Ochoaville, Contention City, Drew's Station, and intermittent ranches and farming operations. From such known locations references were made to stands of trees, or the lack thereof, along the river. But prior to such settlements, less markers existed on the ground, giving such accounts a more general reference in some cases. The founding of the Tombstone District marked the first major development of the San Pedro River Valley, an area largely untouched prior to that, as incessant Apache raids ran off the preceding attempt to colonize the area under the banner of Northern New Spain.

What is clear is that an eye witness along one portion of the river may well have seen plant life that another eye witness in another area of the river did not. That there were pockets of cottonwood and willow trees in given areas along the San Pedro River is clear. What is equally established, not only through written accounts but also through late 19th Century photography, is that the uninterrupted stands of cottonwoods following the river for miles did not exist.

This idea that the cottonwood stands of today are centuries old has become established as fact in the minds of many, gaining press as they continue to be propagated, resulting in the impression that these stands of trees will become endangered as Sierra Vista continues to pump ground water and aquifer waters from the Huachuca Mountains. Many already assert that the city and fort's use of water has diminished the flow of the San Pedro River, which presents a danger to the wildlife which both lives there and migrates through, and to the trees.

THE PRESS OF TODAY AND THE SAN PEDRO RIVER

The University of Arizona press has published "The San Pedro River A Discovery Guide" by Roseann Beggy Hanson. In promoting the book, this prestigious press notes that "It's little wonder that the San Pedro was named by the Nature Conservancy as one of the Last Great Places in the Northern Hemisphere, and by the American Bird Conservancy as its first Important Bird Area in the United States. Roseann Hanson has spent much of her life exploring the San Pedro and its environs and has written a book that is both a personal celebration of and a definitive guide to this, the last undammed and unchanneled river in the Southwest."

It is always of value that authors have enthusiasm for their subject, as it often makes for a more energetic and interesting read. But it is of great importance that such genuine enthusiasm does not hinder an academic study of the issue at hand. Just the statement alone that says the San Pedro is "the last undammed and unchanneled river in the Southwest" confuses the facts of the river's history. It is true that as of the date of Hanson's book in 2001, and as of this writing in 2013, the San Pedro River is undammed and unchanneled. But it may leave the reader with the mistaken impression that part of its status as "One of the Last Great Places" is that it was never dammed, and therefore it remains in an untouched, pristine state.

This troubled promotional article continues, "In addition, the river supports one of the largest cottonwood-willow forest canopies remaining in Arizona." This may well be true, but it should also be pointed out that this canopy as it exists now is not of an historic nature.

I was asked in the 1990's to give a lecture on the history of the San Pedro River to a group of volunteers who would be guiding tours along the river for those who wished to know in-depth, accurate information. At one point, the facilitator of the lecture interrupted, asking me to explain how the Tombstone settlers cut down the cottonwood trees to help build homes in Tombstone, and to burn in the mills at Charleston. Historical records show the locations and operations of wood mills in the Huachuca and Chiricahua Mountains, as well as in the Dragoons, for those purposes, but indicate no wood cutting along the river. Paul De Martini owned a farm on the Babacomari, and later farmed on the San Pedro River just above Fairbank in the 1880's. He spoke of willows on his San Pedro property, and described building a home on that land. In order to build his log house, he brought lumber and other wood from the Babacomari (not the San Pedro). If there were trees along the river more suitable for building the type of structure he had in mind, one would suppose he would cut them there rather than hauling them back from the Babacomari. T.S. Harris hauled lumber from the Huachuca Mountains for use in building the mills along the river. H.C. Herrick went to the Chiricahuas to buy lumber for the construction of his flume.

A much earlier account speaks of the flora around the vicinity of where Charleston would be located. "The Mormon Battalion was still marching north of December 11 [1828] when an encounter took place with bulls close to the present location of the ruins of the mining town of Charleston…'The land on each side of the Pedro River bottom is a dense thicket of bramble bush, mostly muskeet, with which millions of acres are covered.'" [6] Mr. Keysor, who wrote that observation within his broader description of the "Battle of the

Bulls," was probably exaggerating with "millions of acres," but he did not name any cottonwoods. Robert Upton, a teamster in the 1880's, described large and dense thickets of willows in the area of the narrows by Charleston.

Other early accounts describe the river landscape in varying conditions long before the era of settlements. Colonel Stephen Kearney of the California column created the first accurate map of the region between the Rio Grande and Pacific Ocean. In 1848, his Lt. William Emory described the valley at the mouth of the San Pedro where it empties into the Gila River. "'The valley of this river is quite wide, and is covered with a dense growth of mesquite, cottonwood, and willow, through which it is hard to move without being unhorsed...The San Pedro [is], an insignificant stream a few yards wide, and only a foot deep.'" [7] James Leach confirms this report with his own observation of the San Pedro at Aravaipa (just south of Winkelman on the lower San Pedro): "'The waters...were found full of fish, large numbers being taken daily, during our stay on the stream...Extensive forests of Cottonwood and ash lined the banks of the river and the adjoining Mesas and arroyos were natural pasture fields for countless herds and flocks. (Leach 1858)'" [8]

Leach commented on the landscape at Tres Alamos: "'A forest of heavy mezquite timber about one mile in width extends from the river...Leaving the forest it [the river] enters upon a tract of the bottom lands of the San Pedro...In March 1858 the entire body of these lands were covered with a dense growth of sacaton grass averaging four feet in height and dry as tinder. Fire was communicated to it at a point about 20 miles below the site of Camp No. 14 [no specific location is given] and the entire length of the Valley of the San Pedro was traversed by the flames consuming every vestige of this once luxuriant growth. A much to be regretted attendant circumstance of this conflagration was the destruction of large quantities of Cottonwood, Ash and willow timber with which the banks of the river were densely overgrown. In three weeks after the occurrence of the fire it may be remarked that the Sacaton grass had grown up and covered the entire valley with a beautiful carpet of verdure (Leach 1858).'" [9] Cottonwood are mentioned, but only in general terms in the area of the fire, which travelled the river for miles.

In September of 1851, John Bartlett was travelling west, "...crossing north of the Dragoon Mountains into the San Pedro Valley, probably following Dragoon Wash. [This would put him somewhere between Tres Alamos and present day Benson.] Bartlett wrote: 'On emerging from the arroyo, we entered a plain, thickly overgrown with large mezquit bushes, but destitute of grass. We looked in vain for a line of trees, or of luxuriant vegetation to mark the course of the San Pedro – when all of a sudden we found ourselves upon its banks. The stream...was here about twenty feet across, about two feet deep, and quite rapid...'" [10] Bartlett was describing the river after a rainstorm.

Lt. John Parke described the area north of Tres Alamos in the summer of 1855. He was at that time surveying the San Pedro between the area of Tres Alamos and its mouth at the Gila River: "'In the gorge below [Tres Alamos] and in some of the meadows, the stream [bed] approaches more nearly the surface [of the floodplain], and often spreads itself on a wide area, producing a dense growth of cotton-wood, willows and underbrush, which forced us to ascend and cross the out-jutting terraces. The flow of water, however, is not continuous. One or two localities were observed where it entirely disappeared, but to rise again a few miles distant, clear and limpid...'"[11]

Parke observed the river near the present site of Benson in February 1855. "'The stream is about eighteen inches deep and twelve feet wide, and flows with a rapid current, at about twelve feet below the surface of its banks, which are nearly vertical, and of a treacherous miry soil...The banks are devoid of timber, or any sign indicating the course or even the existence of a stream, to an observer but a short distance removed...'" [12]

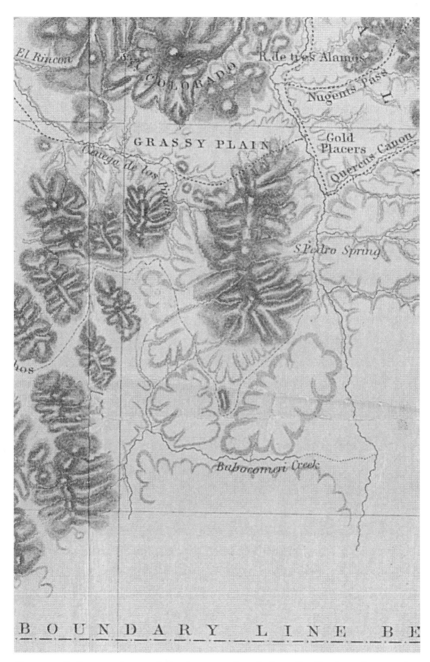

Cropped from the original map by John G. Parke, from the collections of John D. Rose.

Approaching the U.S. Mexican border in 1857, William Emory, now a Major, had this to say about the upper San Pedro: "'At this point [on the International Boundary], approaching from the east, the traveler comes within a mile of the river before any indications of a stream are apparent. Its bed is marked by trees and bushes, but it is some sixty or one hundred feet below the prairie, and the descent is made by a succession of terraces. Though affording no very great quantity of water, this river is backed up into a series of large pools by beaver-dams, and is full of fishes...'" [13]

It is clear, as explorers described this river region moving north to south, that the environments along the river are unique in vegetation and water flow. From Davis' book alone, there is substantial evidence that water flow in the river was inconsistent and limited, and that cottonwood trees appeared in particular areas but not completely lining the river.

With the history of lawsuits against Fort Huachuca and also the enjoyment many in Sierra Vista derive from visits to the river, an article was recently published in the Sierra Vista Herald Dispatch about the San Pedro and efforts to further its study.

The article echoed what has now become an accepted refrain. Local writer Shar Porier offered the following summary of the river. "What it boils down to is what was said to me over and over again-everyone living in the San Pedro River Basin has to care about this narrow, sliver-green band of life that astoundingly flows almost continuously in a high desert environment providing life to creatures that crawl, hop, trot and fly-and us as well."

She continues, "Where would we be without this river that draws people from around the world to seek the feathered avians that find their ways here every year on migrations to every corner of North America?" These are valid points, as many in the area, including myself, are proud of the San Pedro River and what it offers as a natural resource not only to our area but others as well, since various species use it as a corridor. Such nature enhances all of our lives. At the same time, the other point that many Sierra Vista residents would raise is, "Where would we be without Fort Huachuca?"

The missions of the fort are of strategic significance. Many in the area are also proud of the ample contributions of the men and women who wear their nation's uniform here, and are ready to sacrifice all if their country requires it of them. Both of these views should be able to coexist in harmony. All who live in the San Pedro River valley must surely understand that our national security, of which Fort Huachuca plays its own part so importantly, allows all of us to enjoy the natural beauty of our area without concern for the safety of our families.

Part of gaining harmony in the area is the establishment of a baseline of facts about the river. That baseline, which for far too long has been woefully neglected, is the historical record that has been waiting to be told. The truth of this record is harmed when Porier asks "Or maybe the more valid question is where would they be [the migrating species that frequent the San Pedro] without this feisty river born from a gentle wetlands hundreds of years ago? How that must have looked," she continued. "A vast marsh, a cienega, spread out miles and miles and ringed with hardwoods. It's hard to even conceive that picture now. The San Pedro River valley cienega is gone for the most part." [14]

From the perspective of recorded history, what the river area was like hundreds of years ago is hard to say, as it precedes the written historical record. It is clear though, that by the 19th century, the area had evolved to the conditions of travelers' and ranchers' descriptions in those times. The testimony from the Hill vs. Herrick case makes it clear that small cienegas existed in pockets here and there along the river, but not as a vast swampland. The substantial stands of hardwoods speculated upon that once ringed the San Pedro were no longer present, either. So that vast cienega and forest of hardwood trees no longer existed by the time pioneers began coming into and through the area. If they had ever existed, they were lost for reasons other than human intervention, such as wood cutting and settlement. It would be inaccurate, therefore, to blame early settlement along the river for that loss.

To be clear, author Hanson and writer Porier are by no means alone in publishing such statements. This is why the larger issue has to be a desire to follow the history of the river, its facts, its record, its truth. At some point between 1880 and the present a change has occurred within the river environment which encouraged the proliferation of the cottonwood trees. Some in the environmental movement believe that preserving this relatively new phenomenon is as import as keeping alive an entire community that owes its existence to the substantial payrolls of Fort Huachuca.

At the opposite end of the spectrum, there are those who would wish to see substantial development. This unbalanced approach to land use would only grade into oblivion much of the wide open spaces that give the area its appeal. It may also diminish the water from aquifers which have been supplying this area, upon which Sierra Vista now sits, with water for over 100 years. (Sierra Vista was officially established in 1956, but settlement of the area long preceded the founding of this mid-20th Century city.)

On February 15th, 2013, the Wall Street Journal reported, "A Water Dispute Nears a Boil in Arizona." Castle and Cooke Inc., a Los Angeles based real estate company, has proposed a 7,000 home development (in Sierra Vista) which would "pump roughly 3,000 acre-feet of water a year from state land near the San Pedro…to service its new residents. (One acre-foot is generally taken to represent annual water usage of a suburban household.)" The Bureau of Land Management, some landowners, and environmental groups are fighting the proposal. In between these extremes are those who enjoy the river, enjoy their homes and the quality of life that the Sierra Vista area provides, and believe that the San Pedro River, Sierra Vista, and Fort Huachuca can all exist together and without continual strife.

Having resided in this area since 1966, I have been struck by the substantial population growth of my hometown. And while Sierra Vista has grown, so I have seen the cottonwoods grow and mature along the San Pedro. Such parallel growth argues against the assertion that Sierra Vista is harming the stands of trees along the river. If the cottonwoods had declined as the population of Sierra Vista grew, one could argue that the groundwater pumping of a growing city adversely affected the numbers and health of the cottonwood stands. But this has not been the case. On the other hand, wise management must dictate how much more development the watersheds in this area can support.

Caring about the San Pedro River and being accurate about its history should not be mutually exclusive pursuits. In fact, a key part of caring for the San Pedro is unlocking its hidden truths, so the historical record has to become part of this discussion, and this book offers just that. It may also help to remind the reader that the San Pedro River flows from south to north. When testimony refers to "above" and "below," this is in reference to the flow of the river. "Above" indicates upstream, or south. "Below," therefore, indicates downstream, or north.

CHAPTER 2

DREW'S STATION AND ITS AFTERMATH
"I have seen Mrs. Drew living on that place...I think she left there the summer of 1882..." -John Hill

John and Aubrey Rose stand inside Drew's Station. Photo by Stephanie Rose.

William Drew's now very famous station was a humble enterprise, beginning on April 10th, 1878. A small adobe building would play host to visitors journeying along wearisome stage routes, and provide revenue as well as their shelter. A crude structure that utilized canvas for window coverings, it was located just north of the second wash to the north of Contention City, approximately one mile from the Sunset Mill, which bordered Contention on its northern boundary. Drew would die the following year, succumbing to typhoid before the end of 1879. It was a fateful event for the family; his widow, Anne Drew, and their children were now facing an uncertain future.

Before his death Drew had won his court battle with Robert Mason, his cantankerous and at times dangerous neighbor to his south, over an irrigation ditch that ran parallel to the river and kept his seven acres of crops alive. [15] Not surprisingly, issues related to water use and this ditch would resurface just over a decade later, as a new group of settlers attempted to make a living on the very lands that Drew and his neighbors had toiled and fought over. The ensuing lawsuit was Hill vs. Herrick, 1889. Through this case we learn the succession of owners of many of the ranches along the river from Drew's south to the original site of Hereford.

H.M. Christianson had arrived to the north of where Contention City would later be built, in September of 1877. He labored on the Mason ditch not long after arriving. "They were building it in December. They started building it and I found them about the first of December building the ditch and dam there, or they were working on the dam then…I used to go down there from my place every Sunday, as there was no other settlement nearer by than that…"

Christianson offered intricate details of the ditch's construction phase that only an onsite witness would know. "They aimed to take the water about a foot, I reckon…some places in [the ditch] was made with a plow and what they call an A scraper—an A or a V, all the same…Of course it was various widths, but the cuts were made with a pick and shovel and were about four feet…The first dam was made in 1877, in the last month of that year, and in 1878 it was made at the mouth of the slough. It first comes into that slough and comes a little ways and then they had a big dirt dam in the slough and in that slough was a big body of water ten or twelve feet deep and fifteen or twenty feet wide, and then they started right from that slough.

"The dam being over there (illustrating with a chair) and the dam in the river where Mr. Noyes is over there…They dammed the water up in the slough and took the water from the slough and then…a cut for two or three hundred yards and then it comes out on top of the ground again—kind of low ground—and then it goes into another cut and then it comes out on top of the ground again and runs for a distance of probably a half mile or three quarters of a mile on the ground along side of the hill. They made that cut along side of the hill with a pick and shovel and there was where I worked for Robt. Mason for a dollar a day—Me and Mason and Bruener…Bruener and Claflin."

Christianson partnered with Bruener on a farming project. "I went in with Bruener and put in a little wheat and barley—[it] wasn't very much. I don't recollect just how much, but it was a little patch, and then afterwards I plowed some ground on my own place–and then I went partners with [Daniel] Cable and put in a crop of corn." According to testimony in 1889, Christianson's ranch was in the vicinity of one to one and one half miles above, or south of, Fairbank. Of course, Fairbank did not exist when Christianson first arrived.

He recalled that the initial labor on the dam was quickly reduced to nothing, as "the dam washed out entirely that year [1878], and as I understand it…they didn't build any dam there any more. They built it higher up." This would mean they rebuilt the dam at a point further up the river, higher in elevation, to the south. "The first dam was built in 1877 and 1878 and the other one was built in 1879."[16]

Richard Parks had also worked on that ditch and accompanying system for the Contention Mill, and he testified on Herrick's behalf. "I was told by Mr. Hardy—I don't know that date exactly, but in 1879 or 1880, I think—but he told me to go--that they didn't have water enough--" Parks added that Hardy was "superintending or running the Mill for the Contention Company." Parks was further told that "…the ranches didn't have water enough. It seemed that they had given the Contention Company some water and it was then getting short and they wanted the gate improved and to raise the dam…They sent me up there to put in a flume and gate…Mason and Cable told me not to build it less than four feet…It was near as I could possibly build it from the lumber. It might have been a quarter or half an inch short, but not much more than that." [17]

Peter Rufly arrived in Contention in the fall of 1880, later working for the Contention Company in the very dangerous position of amalgamator. This means that Rufly handled the mercury in the stamp mill, likely making about $7.00 per day, three dollars more than a Tombstone miner during the heyday. It also meant that his chance of one day dying from "smelter sickness" had now been increased by such a promotion. But first he had to work his way up the ladder, starting on outside duties working for Mr. Harvey. As he told attorney Colonel William Herring, "I have no trade; I am a mill man—some people call it a good trade…I am an amalgamator by trade."

Rufly would also tend to the headgate of the Mason/Cable ditch, also referred to as the Contention ditch and the Upper San Pedro ditch, and later known as the Union ditch. This headgate was a source of much discussion during the hearing. "…the gate went down into the box and there was another piece on top to keep all the water in the dam. When we wanted to get all the water in the ditch, we put that headpiece on top. Generally the gate, when the big floods would come, floated away and then I took a stick and measured it and got another one made…I took the measure lots of times myself when the gate washed away, to the carpenter so he could saw off planks, and I hauled them up there." [18] Rufly named Mr. Spatz as the carpenter who sawed the replacement boards to rebuild the headgate.

Another early settler, S.B. Curtis, witnessed first-hand the changes that would occur in an otherwise peaceful, meandering stream, just after substantial rains had fallen. "When I come down this side of the river, [the eastern side given he's testifying in Tombstone] in the neighborhood of eight or nine years ago, the bottom [of the river] that I spoke of was over-flowed with water, at that time there had been a heavy rain and…we were bothered about crossing the river." [19]

John Hill would arrive after William Drew had passed, but he became very familiar with the home Drew had left behind. Hill, in partnership with friend D.P. (David) Kimble, initially bought out Robert Mason, which placed him just south of the old Drew's Station site, though he would acquire other properties in the area later. "I bought that place in the last month of 1881 or the first month of 1882," as he recalled. The purchase of the Mason Ranch included 160 acres and access to this all important manmade irrigation ditch. "It is what we call the Union ditch, it was called then the Mason and Cable ditch…I bought a fourth interest of that ditch," which was sufficient to irrigate his crops, as it had been for his predecessor on the property, Robert Mason.

Hill's purchase was almost a turnkey operation. "It was fenced with wire fence clean around…when I bought the place we went over the alfalfa and he [Mason] told me there was forty acres on the side next to the house and five acres that the railroad [The New Mexico and Arizona Railroad, commonly referred to as the N.M. & A.] cut off on the other side; the railroad run through it at the time I bought it." [20] Regarding the fencing that Hill noted when he purchased the ranch from Robert Mason, the Tombstone Daily Epitaph reported on March 17th, 1881, that "Mr. D.N. Cabie [Cable] and Mr. Robert Mason have fenced their ranches with a wire fence. If the grant men don't take it from them they have complied with the fence law; others will go and do likewise if they can get an undisputed title…" This article may imply that many ranchers on the Boquillas grant had not obtained a secure title to their properties.

Hill's testimony continued to offer insights into the Drew's Station area, long after its usefulness as a stage stop had ceased and the Drew family had moved on. William Drew had drawn a map illustrating the area from his ranch and south, to include the other five ranch owners between him and the dam and irrigation ditch: Mason, Davis, Cable, Griffith, and Jennings. This map establishes the owners of the ranches in this locale in 1879 and will prove useful in understanding how these ranches changed hands over the years up to the Hill vs. Herrick lawsuit. Hill elaborated on A.B. Wild's purchase of the Cable Ranch when he was asked "Did Cable turn possession over to him?" (Wild) Hill replied, "I wasn't there when he done it, but I have seen the papers that he got for the land." But further questioning of John Hill would bring Drew's Station into focus.

The Mason Cable Ditch, aka, the Upper San Pedro Ditch, later known as the Union Ditch. This manmade waterway was once labored on by Robert Mason, William Drew and further played a key role in the Drew vs. Mason case in 1879, and the Hill vs. Herrick case in 1889. These all important cases combined offer a wealth of historical data and breakthroughs. Note the wooden supports still visible in this early 1990's photo. This is all that remains of the bridge that allowed wagons, horses and stagecoaches to travel from downtown area of Contention City, and onto other destinations. On the evening of March 15th 1881, Bud Philpot, with Bob Paul at his side, drove the Kinnear and Company Stage across this very bridge, before his murder just south of Drew's Station. Photo by John D. Rose.

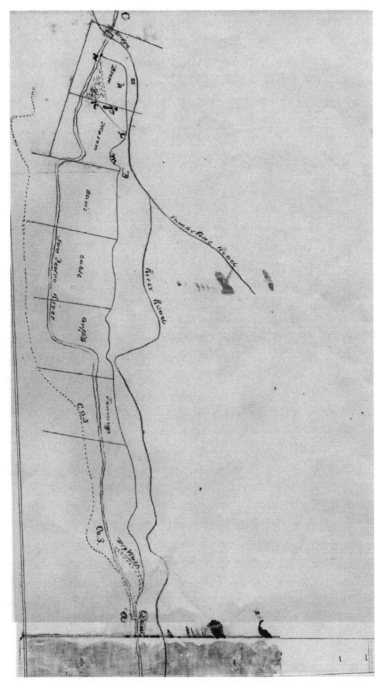

Drew's original hand-drawn map of 1879. Courtesy AHS.

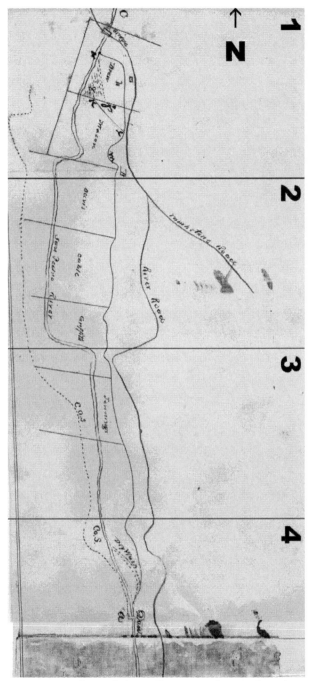

William Drew map, altered into four sections. On the pages that follow each of the four sections has been magnified for improved reader viewing.

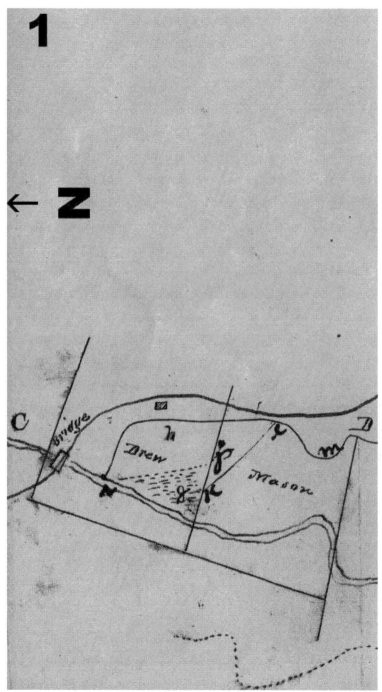

Drew and Mason are the original owners of these plots of land.

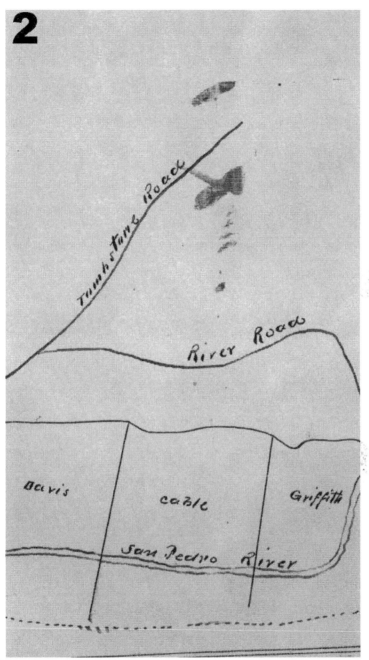

2

Tombstone Road

River Road

Davis

cable

Griffith

San Pedro River

Davis' ranch was first owned by Fred Bruener. Cable is the original owner of his ranch. Griffith's ranch was first owned by C. Claflin.

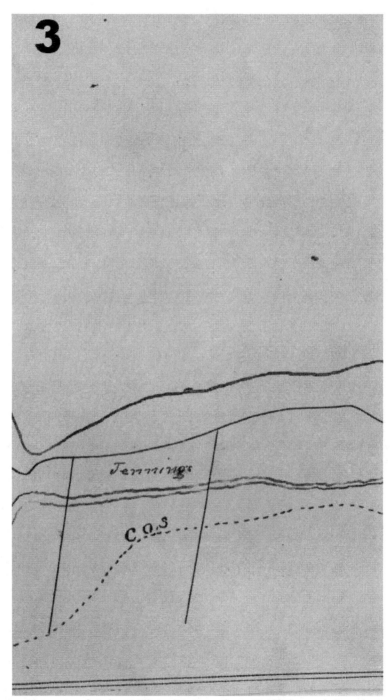

The testimony of John Hill indicates that Griffith and Jennings had left their ranches by the spring of 1882.

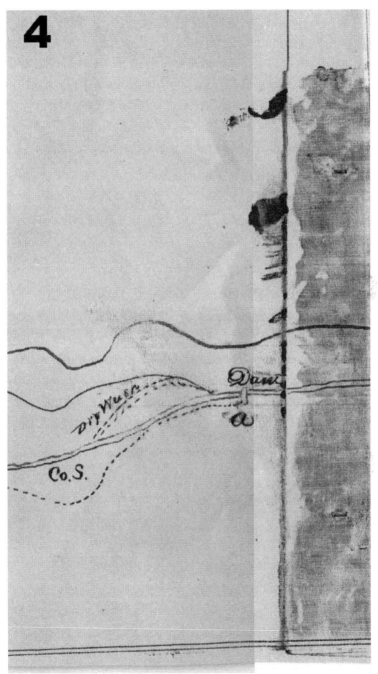

Drew notes the Dam that created a small reservoir. It was this water supply that fed the Mason Cable ditch.

Hill was able to clarify the succession of ownership on the old Drew Ranch and farm. He was asked "How many acres of land did Mr. Clifford have under cultivation in 1882; he lived on the old Drew place?" Hill answered that "He didn't live there then." He added that when he arrived in the area and purchased land, Mrs. Drew still lived there, and noted to whom she sold. "She sold out before the crops were put in to H.J. Horn...I should think from the appearance of the land that I know Mr. Horn bought there, that there was in the neighborhood of fifteen acres [cultivated]...the termination of the Union ditch goes right to his land; it joins right on to my north line."

As the new owner of what once was Drew's Station, Henry James Horne was 43 years old when he acquired the Drew Ranch and farm in 1882, and would have fast need for irrigable crop fields to feed his substantial family. Horne and another arrival, D.P. Kimball, made a visit to an area newspaper office and gained a bit of notice for the labors which were about to begin. "Messrs. D.P. Kimball and H.J. Horn, two energetic and enterprising Mormons, passed through Tucson today with their families and stock, en route to the San Pedro, where Mr. Kimball has purchased the Mason ranch, which he proposes to make his future home. Both gentlemen are well-to-do, as their seven wagons and seventy-four head of fine-looking stock, and twenty-two children at once denote. Mr. Kimball has nine children, several of them are young men grown, and Mr. Horn, with his thirteen children, is like favored. The good people of the San Pedro may congratulate themselves on so valuable an addition to their numbers."[21]

In 1888, H.J. Horne paid taxes on what was Drew's Station. For decades researchers have looked for traces of this famous location in tax roll records, but the Hill vs. Herrick case proves Horne was the second owner. Duplicate Tax Roll Book 1, pg. 137. Courtesy of Cochise County Archives.

It appears from records that William Drew's widow, Anne Drew, may have been taken advantage of in disposing of property left to her by her late husband. She received a much smaller payment from the N.M. & A. when she sold an easement to them, compared to the payout that Robert Mason received just to her south. And such was the case when she sold the land and building that had once been that memorable little stage stop known as "Drew's Station." Whereas Robert Mason would sell his place and share of his dam and ditch for $2,000.00, Anne Drew sold for a scant $200.00. The details of this key transaction had remained elusive until the discovery of the Hill vs. Herrick case, and they have yet to surface outside of this suit. John Hill's testimony provides the details that only an insider would know. This is because although he did not purchase the Drew Ranch, he loaned its buyer the funds to do so.

The use of the old Drew Ranch would now be in the hands of the successive owners, first H.J. Horne, and later Elijah Clifford, although related testimony does not identify when Clifford bought from Horne. Both owners would continue to increase the amount of crop fields on Drew's former ranch and farm. "The biggest part of his land was broke up when he come on it…It was after H.J. Horne went away from there, and I don't know how long Clifford has been living there--I think this year is his second crop." Hill added that at the time of the hearing Clifford had an estimated 25 acres under cultivation. This marked a significant expansion from the seven acres of mostly corn that William Drew had testified to having a decade before.

Col. Herring then asked Hill, "Who claims now the right of taking water from that ditch under the Drew interest?" Hill testified that Elijah Clifford was now using the water, and he was now living in the old Drew home, as he had followed H.J. Horne in ownership of the property. "Do you know whether Drew ever conveyed to him [Clifford] any such right?" Hill answered that he didn't know. William Drew died in 1879, his wife didn't sell out until 1882, and she did not sell to Clifford, but to H.J. Horne, who later sold to Clifford.

As if to put a finer point on it, Col. Herring further pressed Hill on the Drew location. Do you know the lands that were formerly the old Drew place?" Hill replied "Well, I know what I understand to be the old Drew place." "Is it there where Clifford is living?" "Yes sir," Hill answered. "Have you seen Drew living on that place at any time since 1882?" Hill reminded Herring that "I never saw Drew in my life. He was dead, or said to be, when I came to the country. I have seen Mrs. Drew living on that place…I think she left there the summer of 1882, the next summer after I come to the country."

"From the summer of 1882…up to the time Clifford moved there on that place, did anybody live there?" Hill again attempted to explain to Herring, noting that "I didn't say Clifford moved in 1882." Herring asked "No, I didn't suppose you did say so, but I said from the summer of 1882 till Clifford moved there did anybody live on it [the Drew place]?" It was not for lack of knowledge that Herring badgered his witness; this appears to be his personal style of questioning, and Hill wouldn't be the only one to be favored with it during this case.

An exasperated Hill responded saying, "All I know [is] my son---Horne is father-in-law to my son, and I heard John [John Hill, Jr.] say that he sold it to Clifford for Horne…I loaned Horne the money to buy it" from Mrs. Drew. "Two hundred dollars he gave for it." [22] (The court reporter spelled "Horne" both with and without an "e".) This very famous location on the high Arizona desert, with a history remembered for over a century, was sold for just $200.00. In today's collector market a letterhead of J.D. Kinnear, Philpot's employer, is valued in the thousands, simply because of Kinnear's connection with Philpot and his shooting death just south of Drew's Station.

COL HERRING TESTIFIES

As attorney for H.C. Herrick, Col. Herring offered his own testimony. He wanted to clarify the succession of ownership of related properties along and in the area of the San Pedro. Some of the testimony had been vague and contradictory, owing perhaps to the fact that not all the ranchers up and down the river knew each other well or the precise time when their neighbors had come and gone. So Herring would take the stand sharing his research on the matter. "I found the original locators to be Robert Mason, W.H. Drew, W.T. Griffith and D.N. Cable. The first conveyance by them is to the Western Milling Company, now the Contention Consolidated Milling Company, conveying an undivided interest of one thirty-fourth in each undivided share of, in and to a certain dam and water ditch, known as the Upper San Pedro ditch. W.T. Griffith conveys to Josiah H. White [owner of the Contention Mine and Mill] a one quarter interest in the same dam and water ditch and White conveys that to the Contention Milling Company. Robert Mason conveys his interest to David P. Kemble and Kemble conveys to John Hill Hoops. Then D.N. Cable conveys his interest in the dam and ditch to A.B. Wild and S.B. Curtis…I find no conveyance of record from Drew."

Herring continued, "I will offer in evidence record of conveyance, dated [the] 15th of September, 1879, between Robert Mason, W.H. Drew, W.T. Griffith and D.N. Cable to the Western Milling Company, for the consideration of one dollar, and the further consideration that the party of the second part shall or does enlarge the ditch hereinafter described from the head thereof to the mill-site of the said party of the second part: conveyance of an undivided interest of one thirty-fourth of each undivided share of, in and to that certain dam and water ditch...constructed...for the purpose of taking water from the San Pedro river at a point below or near the place known as the old Ruins and about one half mile above the Mill-site of the said party of the second part. It is in Book 2, Deeds Cochise County Transcribed records, Pages 58, 59 and 60 and recorded September 17, 1879." [23]

William Herring, courtesy of Roy B. Young.

Hill was asked "Does the land of Mr. [Elijah] Clifford embrace part of the 140 acres which you claim in this suit that you have a right to irrigate?" He replied, "Yes sir, I understand it so—the Drew place." [24] Ever in the middle of issues in his area, Hill also served as water master, meaning that he was in charge of turning open check gates so that all got their normal allotment, when the water was flowing.

CHAPTER 3

EDWARD DREW REVEALS NEW INFORMATION

"Mason got after me with a shot-gun, and run me off. I recollect that pretty well."-Edward Drew.

Edward Landers Drew, courtesy of the Drew Family Archive.

Ed Drew came with his family from Montana and settled first in Signal Arizona, and later in the Tombstone District where his father and older brother Harrison built their home and stage stop. Young Ed, or Eddie as some called him as a teenager, heard shots ring out on the night of March 15th, 1881, and he raced toward the gunfire. This instinct to ascertain quickly the nature of danger nearby may have led him to become a lawman later in life. And the graphic example of what lawlessness can do that he witnessed that evening may have further fueled his desire to protect the innocent, a calling that would one day tragically end his life.

Image of Ed Drew on the right, and the badge pictured was his when he died in the line of duty. Courtesy of the Drew Family Archive.

Ed Drew heard the shots that claimed the lives of driver Bud Philpot and passenger Peter Roerig, and outside of the murderers, was the first to see Bud's remains as they laid in the wash just south of his home. Ed noticed that Bud still had his whip in his hand. He quickly raced to Contention City to get the word out, a courageous act given that murderers were on the loose and in the area. That night Ed would visit a Contention City cattle dealer suffering from chronic theft, T.W. Ayles, who had chosen that evening to write to the law and order desk at the Tombstone Epitaph. This was indeed ironic timing. Ed knocked on his door with news that startled even Ayles, who had seen much of the lawlessness and suffered from it as well.

"Right here I am stopped by the entrance of a messenger who reports that the down coach from Tombstone to-night, and which passed here at 8p.m., had been shot into, and 'Budd,' the driver, is now lying on the road-side, dead, with his whip alongside of him. And just now Eddie Drew, a young son of the Station keeper at Drew's station, informs me that he saw the dead man and recognized him as 'Budd,' the driver of the coach. If this proves true, 'Budd' ha[s] been shot, and falling from his seat must have carried the lines with him, and the probabilities are the six horse team has run away and we can only conjecture what may happen to the passengers, coach, and horses.... [25]

Ed Drew, twenty-four years old in 1889, was drawn into the Hill vs. Herrick case. His testimony offered little that would alter the proceedings of the case or its eventual outcome, but he did reveal information that was not stated by his late father in the Drew vs. Mason case a decade before, in 1879. He was asked "Whose place did you first come to going up the river on that ditch?" Drew answered, "Mason's...I recollect the day we got there, very well...I was there in April, along sometime in 1878." Drew noted that no one at that time lived below, meaning downstream or north of Mason's, and that above Mason's (to the south) was Fred Bruener, then the Cable Ranch, and then a place owned by "Claflin." (Two of these ranches changed ownership by the time of Drew's hand-drawn map in 1879. Bruener sold to Drew, who sold to Davis; Claflin was the owner before Griffith who appears on the Drew map.) He noted that Mason was raising some barley and a small garden. When asked if he was familiar with what was once known as the "Mason ditch" Drew said "Yes sir, I am a little acquainted with it...The third day of April was the first I saw it...In 1878." He added that his late father, William H. Drew, was not one of the original locators of the ditch once again in litigation, and that he purchased a right to one square foot of water from Fred Bruener. "The land that he [Drew] bought from Fred Bruener, he rented it to--He sold it to a man named Johnny Davis."

Charles Noyes, a rancher further south, confirms this with his own testimony: "Drew owned some land down there, but Drew's land was below the original location, and in the spring of 1879, him and Johnny Davis bought one of the upper ranches out and Davis, he went onto the upper ranch and Drew undertook to take his water across Mason's land and they had trouble about it." [26]

Drew was asked, "Where did the family go then? [after Bruener's]" He continued, "We had located that place right below Mason's now known as the Horne place," further verifying the testimony of John Hill that H.J. Horne followed Anne Drew and family in ownership, although, by the time of this suit, E. Clifford was on the old Drew place. (It may seem curious that Ed did not acknowledge Clifford as being the contemporary owner of that land; however, Ed Drew was in and out of that area after his mother sold their property.) He continued, "It was 1878 when we came there and it was late and we worked that winter clearing off the land…it was the spring of 1879 the first crop we put in there." It would appear then, that the Drews originally stayed at Fred Bruener's location, even though William Drew also owned the ranch site below Robert Mason. William Drew purchased Bruener's place, sold it to Johnny Davis, and moved down the river, or north of Mason's ranch to the site that became home to Drew's Station. Ed Drew seems to indicate that it was late in 1878 when the family finally moved onto that land.

They may not have lived on it right away, but work at the second Drew location began almost as soon as Drew had purchased it. From his sworn testimony in the Drew vs. Mason case we learn, "That the plaintiff on, to wit, the 10th day of April AD 1878 settled upon and improved as a homestead a certain tract of public land…in the San Pedro valley…about three miles North of the old San Pedro ruins…along the North line of Masons ranch…containing 160 acres."

It may have been a tactical move on Drew's part to purchase the Bruener place before selling to Davis, in order to obtain a water right to irrigate his lower property. This would be necessary if he understood that Mason would be difficult about granting him a right to the ditch. Drew had not been one of the four original owners on the ditch. The original four - Mason, Bruener, D. N. Cable and C. Claflin - had each a one quarter interest in it, and would have had to split it again for Drew, for his new ranch site.

Drew also needed to dig an extension of the Mason Cable ditch to reach his property to feed the crops he would plant on the southwestern corner of his ranch. In exchange for this extension, which would run to the north line of Mason's ranch, Drew agreed to do maintenance on the ditch from the dam to Mason's southern line. "…and in consideration of said extension plaintiff worked upon said ditch from "a" to "d" during the summer of 1878 as much as one month which work was worth not less than $50.00 and plaintiff and defendant extended said ditch from the North line of defendants ranch through the plaintiffs land to the river as shown in said diagram…" [27]

Ed Drew recalled the troubles he and his father had with Robert Mason. "…he took the ditch out and wanted to run the water through Mason's field and Mason would not let him. He wanted to extend the ditch down to that place, and Mason let the water run for awhile and they had a law-suit [Drew vs. Mason] and stopped it. Mason served an injunction on us and wouldn't let the water [flow] and we couldn't get the water down there…I went up one day to turn the water on and Mason got after me with a shot-gun, and run me off. I recollect that pretty well."

THE DREW FAMILY AND D.T. SMITH'S RANCH

As Ed's younger sister Cora would later recollect in her writings in the 20th century, her mother moved to D.T. Smith's old place after selling off their home and land. Referring to Smith's ranch, Ed Drew stated, "I have been on it several times but I never lived on it. My mother lived there for a couple or three months." Ed was asked what year she lived there. "1880, I think." Ed's account differs from Cora's in the year they stayed at Smith's, but testimony of John Hill would clarify that issue, as he arrived on the Mason place early in 1882, and Ann Drew was still on her ranch. Smith's ranch was located approximately two miles south of Fairbank. When Ed Drew was asked whether or not Smith was cultivating land at that time, he answered, "I have no recollection about it. In fact I wasn't there but very little; I was off...I was teeming on the road then." Smith's ranch was subsequently owned by Walk Williams, and then the Crane brothers in 1884. The Crane ranch is named on the Rockfellow map. D.T. Smith became a shooting victim at the Bisbee Massacre, December 8th, 1883.

Cora Drew, courtesy of the Drew Family Archive.

Cora Drew elaborated on their move. "When the railroad came through to Contention...we sold our home and we moved near Charleston on D.T. Smith's old place (he had been killed in the Bisbee Massacre.)" [28] The New Mexico and Arizona arrived in Contention City in the spring of 1882, and John Hill testified that he believed Mrs. Drew left her home in the summer of 1882, corroborating Cora's statement.

Anne Drew, widow of William Drew, founder of Drew's Station. Courtesy of the Drew Family Archive.

The critical issue of what happened to William Drew's share of the disputed water as well as the ditch which carried it was now raised by attorney Goodrich. "Do you know what became of that water right?" Drew stated, "I couldn't say. I think she [his mother Anne] sold it to [Josiah] White the Contention man…I am pretty positive she didn't have any water right to sell to Horne; she sold it to [the] Contention." [29]

John Hale Martin also testified in the Hill vs. Herrick case and noted his closeness to the Drew family. When asked who got the Drew right to the water, he answered, "Mr. Sturrit. He was Supt. of the Head Centre mill…The Sunset Company bought it out…I am telling what Mrs. Drew told me. I was very familiar with the family and lived there a good deal." Actually the Head Centre bought out the Sunset Mill, and not the other way around. [30] Martin offered additional details about the movements of Mrs. Drew after leaving the Drew Ranch. His account differs somewhat from that of Ed Drew. "You say Mrs. Drew moved to the Smith place in 1882, what time?" Martin replied, "She moved there that time on the place where Patrick Gale lived, and stayed there awhile during the fore part of that summer of 1882 or the spring of 1883, and from there she went to Smith's." [31] (John Hale Martin was listed as an American born 27 year old farmer at Contention in the 1882 Cochise County Great Register.)

There may be validity to Martin's statement, even though it differs with the account of Ed Drew. V. Kimble, who owned a ranch at the confluence of the San Pedro and Babacomari, testified that Walk Williams went onto Smith's place in 1880, but was not able to honor his purchase agreement, so Smith took the place back before his death. So even though there is still some discrepancy about when Ann Drew stayed on the Smith ranch, this scenario put forth by Martin does offer a viable timeline, and places her briefly back onto the site of her original home on the San Pedro, first owned by Fred Bruener. Bruener sold to Drew, who sold to Davis. Recorded testimony in this case does not conclude whether the Gale brothers were owners or renters of Davis' property. A T.C. Merrill owned it and sold to John Summers in the spring of 1882. So Summers actually owned Bruener's place by the time Ann Drew stayed there.

A FORMER DEPUTY FROM CHARLESTON TESTIFIES

"Oh, no, she couldn't jump, she was much too fat to jump." - William Bell, re his wife crossing the ditch in question.

When William Bell was brought in to testify on behalf of Robert T. Swan, trustee of the Boston Mill and Mining Company, it was self-evident that this was a witness of a different cut. Just his response to "What is your business?" offered a clue. "Selling whisky…Well, Deputy Sheriff." Arriving in December of 1878, he first came to Tombstone, traveling along the river, and noticed "a couple of Irish boys camped at the mouth of the canyon." By June first he had "landed at Contention." He saw a small farming operation near Mason's, and was asked how many acres he had under cultivation in 1879. "…ten or fifteen acres or something like that." Bell recalled that although Mason had his ranch north of Contention, he lived in Contention. Aside from Mason, "A couple of boys had a little land in, named Jennings, I believe—two brothres [sic]." When asked how much land they were cultivating, Bell used terminology suited for a worker who is paid on what they pick--"…I couldn't say I took a contract to take their beans off the ground on shares."

William Drew, from the Drew Family Archive.

When asked if anyone else had crops along the same ditch that flowed past Mason and Jennings in 1879 he recalled one woman in particular. "I believe the widow there had a little crop." Judge Stillwell asked "The widow who?" "I don't remember her name. A widow…Her husband had died and was buried there at Contention."

Judge Stillwell pressed for a more precise answer. "Would you know the name if you heard it? Drew?" "That is the widow," Bell testified to the Judge. He pursued by asking how many acres she had in cultivation in 1879. "I was never on her place much, only just riding along, and I couldn't say for certain how many acres, but she didn't have very much in cultivation."

Contention City Cemetery, the final resting place of William Drew. Grave robbers have left portions of coffin boards atop the surface. Photo courtesy of Richard Bauer.

Though he told the court more than once he was not a mill man, he was able to note that in a typical stamp mill operation a one inch pipe has to remain full of water to feed each battery of five stamps, adding that mills would have to pump the water from their ditches on the final leg of the journey inside of the mill, and such pumping had to lift the water 20 or 30 feet in some cases.

Given that Josiah White of the Contention Mill and Mine had acquired a one thirty-fourth share in the Upper San Pedro River ditch Company's ditch, "I was sent up two or three times by the foreman on the Contention grade there to help clean it out…I was working there, shoveling and blasting on the grade for White…I was working as a laborer…I used to go and shovel out a few shovels where it was low, or high, and let the water down. That was about all I attempted to do." He had also visited the gate to the ditch, adding that he could easily step across it, "that is, just make kind of a little jump, without any exertion…take a little spring and jump clear across…it was about four feet."

He further was able to briefly comment on the old ditch verses the newer one, and the construction that was required. "A couple of furrows plowed out or something like that, and the dirt thrown out on the lower side to make a bank…That was the old ditch. The new ditch I don't know anything about…it is a new ditch to me…Only down close to Contention this ditch run into the old one…it run through a flat before and now runs [along] the side of the hill." While living at Contention Bell took in hunting when time permitted. Col Herring asked "When you were at Contention or in that vicinity in 1879, did you have occasion to go around that country any?"

Bell stated that "Sundays we used to go round hunting…My wife would go with me." Herring really wanted to know if they encountered the ditch which was such a part of the case. "During your hunting did you come across Mason's ditch, and if so how did you cross it at that time?" "Step across it anywhere," Bell replied. "And how about your wife?" "Stepped across."

Herring continued asking "Did you have to jump any to get across?" Bell showed signs of the kind of courage that anyone who accepted the role of Deputy Sheriff at a place like Charleston was born with. "Oh, no, she couldn't jump, she was much too fat to jump." Bell was asked if he knew any of the Drew boys. "I know one of them by sight." Bell also observed another of Robert Mason's enterprises that involved piece work for the Contention Mill. "I know Mr. Mason had a contract there to make adobes…You might say right in the town of Contention he made them there…they took water out of the ditch to make adobes." Judge Berry was now questioning Bell, and asked

"Do you know whether or not there was sufficient water flowed down that ditch to allow them to make adobes during the day time?" Bell told the Judge "No, they had to make the mortar at night." Judge Berry followed by asking "Was that on account of the scarcity of water in that ditch?" "Yes sir," Bell replied, adding that this was due to the fact that the ditch at that time was not large enough to carry any volume of water.

Even though Bell had seen the area in detail north of Contention City in the late 1870's, he would continue to visit the area working for a new boss in an old avocation. "…I am over there nearly every year. I have got business for [Sheriff] Slaughter over at Contention. I am now a deputy sheriff under Slaughter and have business over there."

Bell stayed in that part of the Tombstone District but later moved on to Charleston, living there until 1882. He would take notice of N. W. Storer and his crew working on the ditch at the Boston Mill, as he visited that area leaving from Charleston "Three times on Sundays" for an unstated reason. He added, "I believe the Chinaman had a garden down there, the Chinaman that had a boarding house at the [Boston] mill: I wouldn't be positive but I think they had a garden down there."

Col. Herring asked Bell if he had held any official position while living at Charleston. "Yes sir, Deputy Sheriff…till the spring of 1882…I commenced along in 1880, I don't remember when. The first work I done I caught Tom Harper. You remember, you were there; and Charley Shibell afterwards deputised [sic] me in place of McDowell." [32] Herrick had reported to Bell that a Chinaman who was farming nearby had stolen from him, so Bell went there to arrest the Chinaman. "He was farming and a Chinaman stole hoes from him and one thing and another, that he was…farming, or that is what he told me." [33] The only Chinaman who repeatedly shows up in the evidence presented as having farmed near Herrick is his co-defendant, Hop Kee. (William Bell was listed as a Scottish born 43 year old Charleston laborer in the 1882 Cochise County Great Register.

Henry P. Schultz arrived in Tombstone early on, in 1878, possibly May 28th. He was asked what he was doing in the Boston Mill area in 1879. In differing areas of his testimony he replied "Following some cattle for Mr. Bowers" and coming back to the same issue in latter testimony had added that he was "…working some cattle there for Mr. Bauers." (Both spellings of this name, Bowers and Bauers, are used in the court records.) It is possible that the Bauer that Schultz worked for running cattle is Appolinar Bauer, a Tombstone butcher who had supplied some of the needed provisions to Richard Gird at Signal A.T. for the expedition that led in part to the creation of the Tombstone District. Bauer would be among the many who would later follow Gird to Tombstone, running a butcher shop, as well as testifying at the Spicer Hearing, which was held in the wake of the Gunfight near the O.K. Corral. [34]

Meats Retailed over the Block at Reduced Rates.

I do my own killing, and raise and fatten my own cattle, sheep and hogs, and in consequence can furnish Meats Cheaper and better than any other market in the city.

A. BAUER, Proprietor.

Henry Schultz worked cattle for "Bauer," who may be the Appolinar Bauer noted above. Tombstone Epitaph, December 17, 1887.

Schultz remembered as did many others the D.T. Smith Ranch, and that he was a freighter during his lifetime. He recalled that in 1878, "I was working a short time in the mines here and one thing and another; after that I was butchering a little while…different occupations…no particular thing. There wasn't a great deal going on in the country at that time and I did whatever I could get to do." While working cattle for Bauers, Schultz took note of the location of ranch sites up and down the river. He explained the proximity between a rancher involved in the suit and the Boston Mill. "…where I was stopping is right at the point of the hill and the road goes over to the Noyes place. The mill was right close by…or, I was stopping right close to where the mill is now…I worked for Bauer's with the cattle for three months; I held them right down here for a month and then held them there for about two months…At Watervale." "Up this side [east side] of the river on the road?" "Yes sir," Schultz replied.

Schultz recalled Daniel Cable, and was asked if he knew a man named Drew. "Yes sir, Drew was living there when I came." He also remembered Fred Bruener (Court records show Bruener and also Breuner as spellings), and that he lived near the Cable ranch. He added that since his early arrival in the area, "The river has been settled up since." When asked how far John Hill lived in 1889 from the other settlers mentioned he told the court "Not a great ways…Right in that vicinity." [35]

ROBERT MASON'S TRAVELING COMPANION

Another witness not only knew the locations of Mason and Drew, but he also knew Mason and Drew personally. Robert H. Upton arrived in the fall of 1878. William Drew had already settled on the Drew's Station site, beginning his improvements immediately after arriving on April 10th, 1878. "I came down by the way of Prescott and Tucson and from Tucson here…Bob Mason and me came here. When I got to Tucson, Parcels and White were there and they introduced me to Bob Mason and so I came out with Mason." He added that Mason settled on the location "Where Mr. John Hill lives now." (Mason was already settled on his ranch in 1877, and was likely in Tucson on business when Robert Upton met him, and then journeyed with him to the San Pedro.)

His testimony named the ranches that were visited when coming south from the area where Benson was later built, although he mistakenly recalled Benson as having been there in 1878, a common mistake made by many who had gotten used to a location that was once new, but by now routine. "The first party after we left old Man Merrill's I think was Drew." He stated that the next place was Mason's, and further south of that was "Cable or Breuner or some such name as that…I think there were four" places in the area at that time. Early on he would also venture further south along the river, where he noticed that "Gird was preparing to build a mill there at the time."

He was asked how much land did each settler claim that he had just mentioned. "I don't know how much either one of them claimed excepting Drew. I was acquainted with Drew in the northern part of the Territory [possibly Signal A.T.] and I think he said he had a hundred and sixty acres, and Mason I think he told me, he had a hundred and sixty…they had a ditch started out. I think one of the parties was up the river…I think his name was Cable or some such name as that and he had come down, and I think Mr. Noyes was working for Mason, and I think he went up with one of the parties to fix the ditch…I think they were [adjoining], they all appeared to be connected right along."

A CONVERSATION WITH WILLIAM DREW AND ROBERT MASON

Seeing that he had a witness who had firsthand knowledge of the early owners of the ditch that led to the current suit, attorney Goodrich asked if Drew was the lowest down the river. "Yes sir," Upton answered. Reflecting on earlier conversations with Robert

Mason and William Drew, Upton questioned the two pioneers at the time as to the viability of their locations. It was a remote area as far as population goes, even though traffic had already started coming through the area. "I asked them if they were going to be able to make a living there, and they said Yes, they were going to irrigate the ground and raise everything they wanted, and I told them that it was so far away from [the] market, that they could not do anything, but they thought they could and they were going to irrigate and put in truck and corn and one thing [or] another…The only ones that I talked to were Mason and Drew, because they were the only ones I was acquainted with at all." Upton didn't know Daniel Cable, who was further to the south, but did see a worker of his in the area. "…one of the parties came down to get somebody to help about the ditch, and I think it was Cable or a man that was working for him, or something of the kind."

Not long after his conversation with William Drew and Robert Mason, Upton was out on errands and saw the inception of the ditch. "Two days afterwards I came down the river with a little pair of Mules that Parsons had and a small skeleton wagon, and went back up the river, and it was maybe two weeks afterwards…The ditch at that time I should judge to be four or five feet wide and probably eighteen inches deep…I haven't seen the ditch for a good while."

He was asked about the condition of the roadway between Fairbank heading south to Charleston. "Not much of a road. We had a little bit of a skeleton wagon and a little pair of mules and got along as best we could, might say there was no road. We followed along the river as best we could among the brush…" Attorneys Goodrich and Herring were trying to ascertain the existence of ditches and improvements on the river between Fairbank and Charleston in 1878. Upton was familiar with the area. "Well, there was I think a little house where the Boston Mill is now or somewhere near…and a little patch of corn…At that time I don't think there was a ditch out at all, or if there was I didn't see it."

Herring wanted to know how far Upton went on the river and what things looked like. "To this...narrow place in the river where the banks come pretty middling close together, you know, a little ways above Charleston." "Do you remember when you first came up through there...whether there were patches or distances along the bank of the river where the willows stood pretty high in places?" Upton replied, "Yes sir." Herring asked whether ditches or farms could be seen through the willows. "You might not of course. There is a good deal of those heavy willows there...and it was narrow and there was places in there you could not see anything at all." [36] What is interesting about this testimony is the identification of the flora along the river. T. S. Harris also made use of willow poles from the trees on Mason's place for his brake blocks, as later testimony shows. So there appears to be intermittent thickets of willows along the river. Conspicuous by their absence are comments about cottonwood trees. (Robert Harrington Upton was listed as an American born Tombstone Miner, 48 years old in the 1882 Great Register.)

Charles Noyes would testify on behalf of John Hill and the other plaintiffs. Living two miles above Fairbank on the San Pedro, he had arrived in the area in 1879 and had personal knowledge of the sites key to the Hill vs. Herrick case. "Well, there wasn't any Tombstone" when he arrived "...I came with my two brothers and Mr. Randolph...I first landed at Mr. Drew's...it was on the San Pedro river below Contention below the Hill ranch...Mr. Hill is in possession of the ranch...that was owned by Mason and outside of that I don't know anything about it." This is noteworthy as it verifies John Hill's statement that at the time of the suit, he was living on the old Mason place, which is south of where he would later locate as documented on the Rockfellow map. He also mentioned, "At the time I went there Davis was working for Mr. Drew...He and Mr. Drew bought a place after that." [37] He also added that Drew had an interest in the ditch in 1879 that was the source of the current lawsuit, but he was not one of the original locators of it.

THE THIRD OWNER OF THE OLD DREW'S STATION ARRIVES

As the third owner of Drew's Station, Elijah Clifford pays taxes on the old Drew place. 1889 Duplicate Assessment Roll, Book 1, page 56. Courtesy of the Cochise County Archives.

Elijah Clifford saw his fortunes cast with his neighbors, John Hill, Andrew Wild and Samuel Summers, all new owners of the first four ranches on the Mason Cable ditch. When asked where he lived, he told the court "Down on the San Pedro river." Attorney Goodrich asked specifically, "Whereabouts?" Clifford replied, "Down on the old Drew farm…what is known as the old Drew farm." He spoke to the issue at the heart of the litigation, the loss of crops on his and neighboring ranches. "Well, all the places but Wild's…I wasn't up there…but Summers and Hills and mine I was on and they were in a suffering condition from want of water…to such an extent that parts of the fields were entirely dried up, bur[n]t right up."

Clifford had an estimated twenty to twenty five acres on the old Drew place under cultivation at the time of his testimony, adding that "I have had it under cultivation for the last two years." Goodrich asked "Who was cultivating it before you was?" Clifford told the court that it was "H.J. Horne." This confirms the succession of ownership as outlined in John Hill's testimony, as well as others, and gives us a general time frame as to when Clifford moved onto the ranch – sometime in 1887. Clifford had lived along the river since 1880, offering insights to the rainfall that the area counted on. "There is some showers around the hills earlier than that [referring to September], maybe as early as June, July and August...We need the water for irrigating purposes from about the first of February to the last of November" adding that the water is the most scarce "About the first of July...sometimes we get a shower or two that will raise the river...a little on the mountains which will make a little more than there has been during the dry season."

Col Herring's questioning was aggressive, referencing the summer of the previous year. "Don't you know that on the 30th. Day of June, 1888, there was a copious rain along that river and that the water fell in such quantities as to flood the river and send more water down the river than anybody there could use or know what to do with?...Don't you know that again before the tenth of July there was another copious rain all over the part of the county of Cochise which flooded the river again...Have you any recollection of the copious rains during the month of July..." Clifford told Herring, "...the only time I recollect of the water raising last year was when the earthquake shook the dams loose and let the water down." [38]

A TEAMSTER TESTIFIES

T.S. Harris arrived in the Tombstone District in 1879, first arriving at Millville with equipment for the Gird mill on February 28th. Harris was a teamster hauling elaborate milling equipment for the mills that would soon drive the local economies of Millville, Charleston, Emery City and Contention City. It was an occupation that would make him well versed in area transportation networks, as well as giving him an early view of areas that were just at the inception of a substantial economic boom. "I crossed the San Pedro river at this old station where Billy Ohn[e]sorgan lived. I think it, was the old Butterfield station...Then I came up this side of the river [The Tombstone side] all the way till I came to Fairbanks. There was an old smelter there at that time, and there I crossed the river [to] the other side and I went up that side [the western side of the San Pedro] of the river and passed through the ranch that [D.T.] Smith owned and occupied to the right of those hills, and then come down to what is now the Ochoaville road and then came back to Charleston down the river again and crossed the river at Charleston." He noted that he had between 175 and 180 mules, forming 16 to 18 mule teams. "It took me from Benson, to deliver the mill, nine days." On yet another journey he chose a camp site of historical significance. "After I delivered this mill and hauled this timber that I spoke of I went back to Gila bend for the other mill and on the way back I camped at Drew's station and I had left some extra stock I had there, and it was at that time that I noticed this cultivation."

Harris elaborated on his hauling runs. "I came up the San Pedro river all the way from just below where Benson now is, at the old stage station. That is where Bill Ohrnersorgen [sic] lived...I camped the teams at Charleston in 1879 and I never brought the teams here to Tombstone till the latter part of 1879...I believe after I unloaded that mill I went up to the Huachucas and hauled the timbers to build the mill, and then I went back to Gila Bend for what is called the Corbin mill...I took the teams and went back there after it. And that was the time my attention was called to this ditch. I stopped there over night and left some stock there, extra mules and horses...I believe I left Charleston on the sixth day of April 1879 and I went

In addition to living at the old stage station on the San Pedro River at Tres Alamos, Billy Ohnesorgan also partnered in a stage line. His Contention City office is shown above. Copy photo from the collections of John D. Rose.

back to Gila Bend and got the mill and came back to Charleston immediately. In the meantime they had got the first mill up and in running order, and immediately after I commenced hauling quartz for that mill, and it was during that summer…I was six weeks or two months making the trip…" [39]

Of the area near Mason's and Drew's Station, Harris added that "I was frequently there. The stage came that far and then branched off for Tombstone, and I used to frequently go down there on business from Charleston to meet the stage or to take somebody down…I would be there about an hour maybe." This was in the early days before Contention City would make Drew's Station obsolete.

Harris recalled meeting Robert Mason, noting that "he was farming a little…commencing to farm…had some stock there…he wasn't farming but very little, raising a little garden stuff there." When Harris was asked about the size of Mason's ditch, he replied, "it was a very small affair…I made the remark to Mason…a man could irrigate as much pretty near with a pump and well bucket…I believe he [Mason] said the ditch would carry more water than I thought it would." He added, "There was quite a number of families living at St. Davids" at the time. He also recalled a neighbor of Mason's, "a man named Drew, I think." This testimony verifies that to many of this time, the area just north of Contention City was referred to as St. Davids, among other names.

ONE WHO REMEMBERED WILLIAM DREW

Harris had cause to visit Mason regularly. "I bought a lot of willow poles to shoe brake blocks, from him, on these big wagons, and I got the willows off of Mason's ranch; he cut them for me." When asked for further details about Mason, he noted that "He was keeping a restaurant at Contention." Harris thought that by the fall of 1881, Mason had 75 – 80 acres under cultivation. He also recalled "The old gentleman died there that fall," referring to William Drew, in 1879. When Harris was asked if he saw any ranches other than

Drew's or Mason's when travelling the road from 1879 to 1881, he replied, "Those were all the ranches that were on the road…These parties that you speak about [Cable, Davis, Griffith, Bruener, Jennings], if they cultivated lands at all, they lived down back of the road…there may have been people living down in there that I never saw."

Robert Mason's Contention City Hotel and Restaurant.
Copy photo from the collections of John D. Rose.

In the summer of 1881 Harris paid another visit to Robert Mason, who wanted to show him around his place. It may be that Mason was already thinking of selling out, and showing the property's attributes might aid in finding a buyer. "I went down there and Mr. Mason called my attention to his place, the amount of alfalfa he had in and the amount of land he had in cultivation, and I should judge he had about 75 or 80 acres under cultivation at that time…I should judge it was close to half a mile" when walking across it. When asked if the alfalfa extended from his house to the river, Harris stated "No sir, not entirely."

Harris was then asked, "Don't you know, from experience, that a man teaming in Arizona in 1879 with 175 head of mules and horses on his hands has his attention pretty well attracted in his occupation…And it keeps him pretty busy…Is not an alfalfa field a pretty attractive spot to a man with 175 head of horses, in 1879?" "Yes sir," was Harris' reply.

Given he earned his living transporting across the wagon roads of the area, Harris was asked if the road from Benson to Contention had seen many changes. "Well, if I recollect, there was one road run around the hill to the right as you come up, and the other road runs over the hill to about where it runs now…after you pass by and after you pass around the hill you can see down on Wild's place…that is on his furthest place…After you get around the hill pretty near Contention you can see in there and see those particular fields…When you get…to where the road comes down to the river again…The road leaves the river entirely just below Contention…Just below where the Head Centre Mill is." Harris was asked "Don't it leave before that?" He answered "No, not half a mile below then." He was then asked "Do you say you can see the cultivated lands on Wild's place from that point there?" Yes, sir," he replied, "It is a plain view. You can see it plain right through there." (After rediscovering the Tombstone Stage Road, and doing extensive field study of that roadway, this author can confirm that Harris' testimony is proven by evidence on the ground of the roadway, and further confirms his claim that "The road leaves the river entirely just below Contention…Just below where the Head Centre Mill is.")

Harris was asked if he had personal knowledge of D.T. Smith and his ranch, and he did. "Smith got hold of a mule that belonged to me and we had some little trouble and I went there and took the mule away from him, and I went up to the garden to see him about the mule, and there was a water melon patch there and when we got through the row he invited me to have a water melon with him." [40]

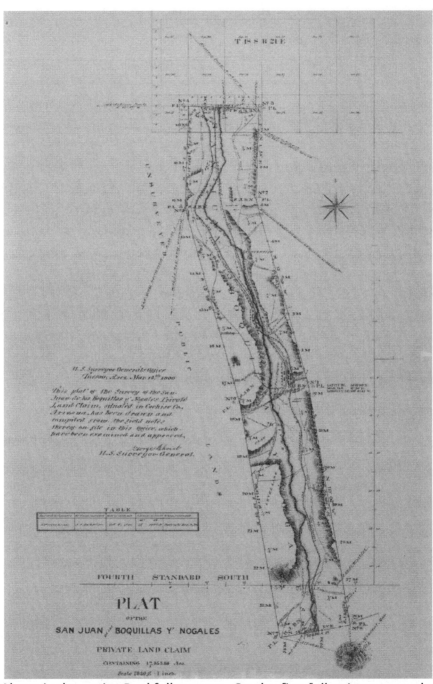

Above is the entire Rockfellow map. On the five following pages, the map has been divided for better viewing. From the collections of John D. Rose.

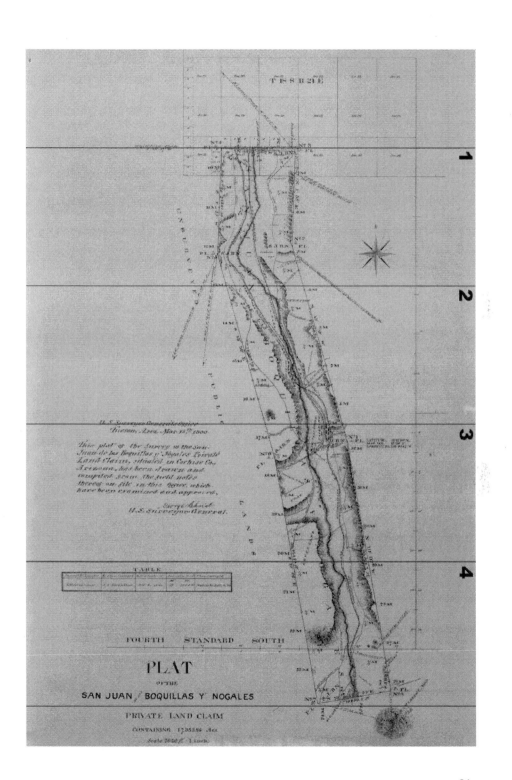

PLAT

OF THE

SAN JUAN / BOQUILLAS Y NOGALES

PRIVATE LAND CLAIM

CONTAINING 17.355.84 Ac.

Scale 2640 ft - 1 inch.

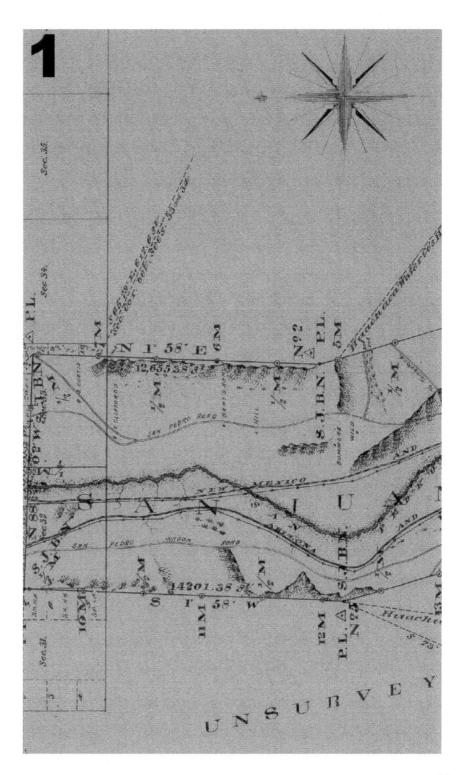

2

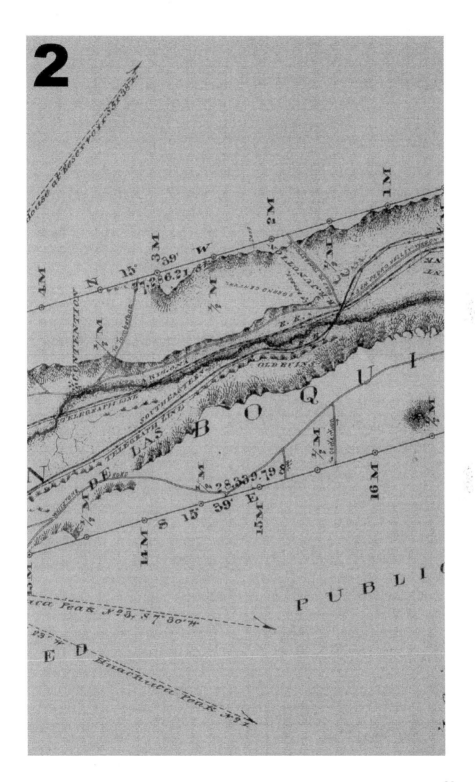

3

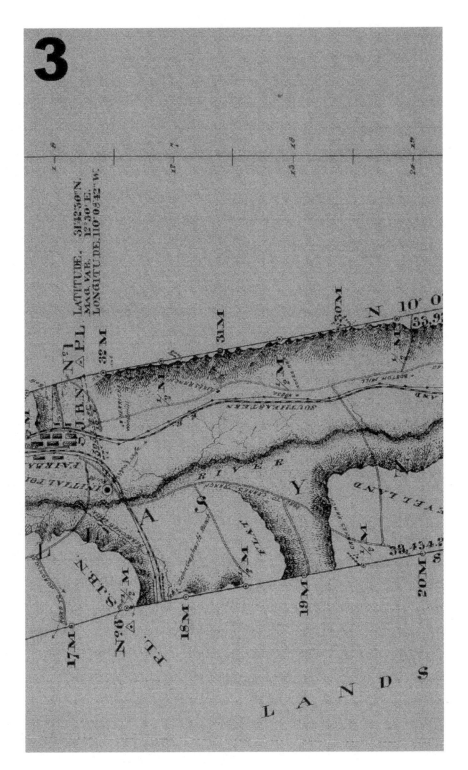

4

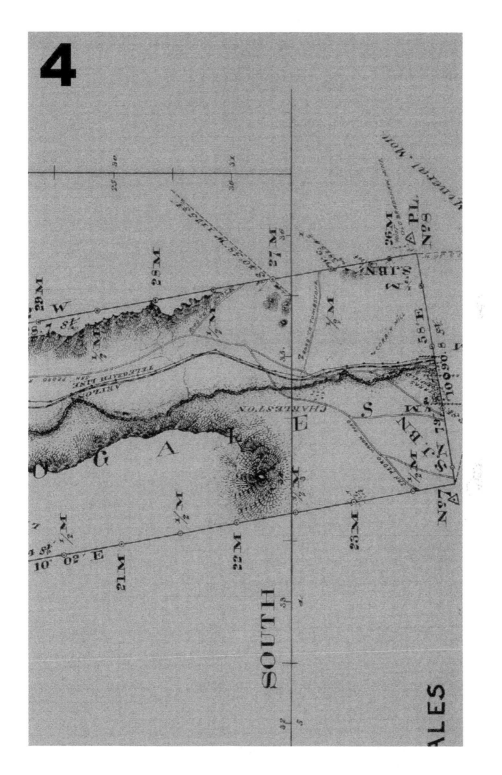

65

CHAPTER 4

THE PRIMARY PLAINTIFF TESTIFIES

"We didn't have water enough there to water the ga[r]den and I had trees die on account of no water." –John Hill

John Rose stands at the foundation of John Hill's northern Ranch site as designated on the Rockfellow map. Photo by Aubrey Rose.

When John Hill arrived in the winter of 1881/1882, the irrigation system was briefly not in use. "At that time it was in the winter and they were not irrigating, when I went there. I was on the river in December and I came there in 1881. When I bought the Mason place I would not state—I can tell from the deed—whether the first month of 1882 or the last of 1881." Hill added that neighbor "...Summers took possession that spring after I bought." Hill stated that the Summers Ranch was not occupied at John Hill's arrival, in late 1881/early 1882. Summers took it over in the spring of 1882.

When Hill was asked "And who had possession before Summers went in?" he replied that "Nobody had it until Summers went in." [41]

According to the testimony of John Martin, it had been abandoned by the Gale brothers who went to work in the mills, and the next owner was Summers. [42] This site, originally owned by Fred Bruener, may have been purchased but not worked or inhabited by himself or Davis who shows up on the Drew map. Hill may not have been aware that anyone owned that land prior to its purchase by Summers. After Davis, according to Hill's testimony, Summers bought that ranch from a man named T.C. Merrill.

Hill would also do his share of maintenance on the irrigation ditch. The dam that corralled the San Pedro River water that flowed to these ranches was once saved by Robert Mason during a massive flood that broke through Dick Gird's dam south of Charleston. Now Hill was asked "When did you first see that old dam?" "I saw it the same time I bought. In the spring I was cleaning out the ditch...Spring of 1882."

Other ranchers had problems with their head gates and dams, as well. Nearby rancher Crane, farming on the old D.T. Smith ranch, also had physical damage to his irrigation system, noting that his water control gate was "lying out on the bank on a side of the ditch and all the water that could get in it went in; it was full to the top of the high bank, a good flow of water running through." But for Herrick, things looked much better. Also located on the east side of the San Pedro, his irrigation was "Running full and onto the grass and mesquite brush some three or four rods, [a rod is sixteen and a half feet] running over the side of the banks...there was a big pond of water there and the stock were drinking there, on the east side of the railroad." [43] This would be the N.M. &A. Hill had gone up the river to check out the problem. His efforts at minor repair were of no avail. "I could not see the hole, it was so filled with water. I tried to push the head gate down further and it was down as far as it would go and the water was running under it."

Hill believed given his purchases that he had an undisputed right to one fourth of the water from this key artery. When that amount became restricted, and he saw a great deal of this water at the ranches of H.C. Herrick and nearby Chinese rancher Hop Kee who were higher in elevation and closer to the Fairbank area, he chose to sue. He contended that both were using more water than Hill believed to be justified, and he testified that such water use was taking its toll.[44]

THE CROPS ARE BURNING

"Do you know what the condition of Summers' crop was last summer?" Hill answered, "It was burning, the same as mine. We didn't have water enough there to water the ga[r]den and I had trees die on account of no water." Hill agreed that the amount of water that flowed through the old head gate which was five feet wide by eighteen inches deep was necessary for the cultivation of his and other farms in the area. According to John Hill, his crops were dying and H.C. Herrick and Hop Kee were to blame. "They were getting very dry when I come up here and tried to enforce the injunction about the tenth of this month…Then they were commencing to get dry…There was a hole under the head gate and I stood and saw Noyes measure it. He measured fifteen inches deep and four feet two inches wide."

The injunction referred to was for many, public notice that a water war had broken out on the San Pedro. The Arizona Weekly Citizen told its readers on April 27th, 1889 that "An injunction has been issued by Judge Barnes, and will be served to-day, restraining Wm. F. Banning, Levy Scranton, Peter Moore, W.C. Green, Joseph Hoefler, Peter W. Roberts and C.B. Kelton, all of this county, from using the water of the San Pedro river until N.W. Stori [Storer] and John Hill et. Al., the plaintiffs in the water case now before the commissioner, have sufficient water to irrigate the growing crops." It was but one salvo in what would become a substantial case, drawing in ranchers and farmers up and down the San Pedro, with a great deal at stake.

"The [Hill vs. Herrick] suit was instituted by John Hill, Samuel Summers, S.B. Curtis and H.B. Hill, who claim that by an appropriation of the water by them years ago they are entitled to it, and they have enjoined all other ranchers from using any water out of the river until they have been fully supplied. The injunctions have been issued and the people are now and will be restrained from using any water until the case comes up for trial, greatly to the loss and damage of a large number of farmers who are now without its use. These people, many of them, have their crops planted and one company [Boston Mill ranch] has over 640 acres that is now suffering for the water which is in the river but which they dare not use." [45]

Hill was asked about the condition of his crop at the time the suit commenced. "Well, burning up...the alfalfa, for acres, it just looked dry and burnt yellow—burning up for water." Hill had contacted Herrick, Storer, and Crane before the injunction demanding that they increase the amount of water for his ailing crops, but to no avail. As for Herrick, "he told me that he had twelve hundred inches of water...recorded, in the river, and that was more water than there was in the river....if you think you can get any turn yourself loose." Herrick never helped himself with such statements.

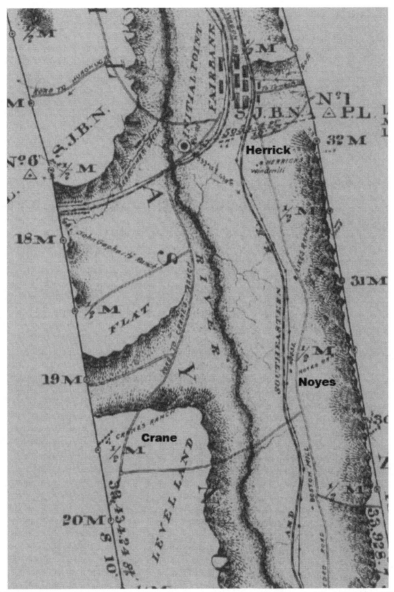

Fairbank, Crane's Ranch, the Noyes Bros. and Herrick's Windmill are visible on this cropping of John Rockfellow's 1899 map. From the collections of John D. Rose.

When asked about cultivation by his neighbor Samuel Summers, Hill stated, "He didn't have any in...the spring, when I bought. In the summer he put some under cultivation. In 1882, along in May sometime, he farmed a little patch...He now has in the neighborhood of 140 [acres], about the same as I have got."

CHANGES IN MR. DREW'S FORMER NEIGHBORHOOD

Properties north and south of the old Drew's Station site continued to change hands. The testimony revealed the actual size of Hill's ranch and neighbors Samuel Summers, A.B. Wild, and the old Drew place. Hill replied that they all were 160 acres. When asked whose premises A.B. Wild bought, Hill said, "Mr. Cable...I think Mr. Wild went there in 1882; I wouldn't be positive whether he went the same spring or the next one, but I think the same spring that I did, in 1882, and commenced farming there...It was away from the road and I didn't go to look. The biggest part of it [the Wild place] was across the railroad..." Wild too was industrious in his crop raising as Hill noted. "I think from sixty to seventy five acres altogether" were under cultivation which also relied on the Mason and Cable ditch. By 1884, Wild had an estimated forty to fifty acres under cultivation, and had an estimated 60 to 75 acres by 1888. "It is an out-of-the way place," Hill added, "away in below the railroad, and I haven't any business in there and don't go there very often. I have been through there with Mr. Wild." [46]

He added, "...Mr. Wild, Hubbard and Curtis bought out the Cable right, 160 acres of land there. Wild owned one third of that and they divided up... Mr. Curtis takes his water from this Mason place and takes it to the distributing ditch down to his place. There is the whole of it—Moves it from the Cable place and takes it there. But the terminus of our ditch is on our north line." "Where is the Curtis place?" Hill was asked, responding that "It is below the Drew place." [47] Curtis had moved north to the location noted on the Rockfellow map.

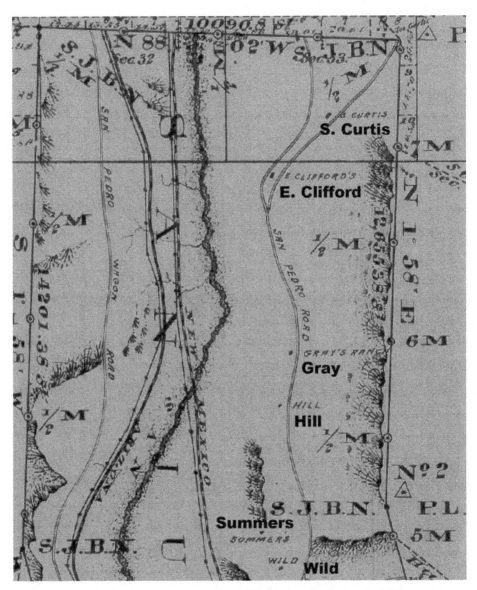

A cropping of the Rockfellow map with names added in bold for easier viewing. Contention City is south of Andrew Wild's location and will be seen on the map to follow. Map annotated by Kevin Pyles.

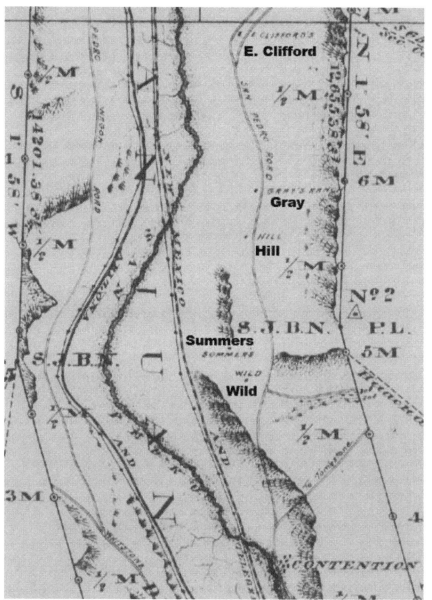

Plaintiffs Andrew Wild, Samuel Summers and John Hill are noted by their last names only on the 1899 Rockfellow map, showing that Elijah Clifford has left the old Drew Ranch and has moved northward. Near the bottom of the map "Contention" City is visible. This spelling of "Sommers" differs from the court's "Summers." From the collections of John D. Rose. Annotated by Kevin Pyles.

For Hill it was a gradual process of developing more and more raw land, or the "commons" as he referred to it, over years of toil. Starting in 1882, he irrigated the alfalfa fields "that I had when I bought of Mr. Mason, what he told me was from forty to forty five acres—I didn't measure it. And this raised quite a lot of corn, I don't know how many acres, I never measured it...I broke up another piece and put in a garden, and the latter part of the season I sowed alfalfa." By 1889, Hill testified, "Yes sir, got fine farms now, lots of grain and alfalfa in—lots of it." When asked, "Have you bought any land since then?" Hill answered, "Yes sir." The questioner did not ask where the new lands were located, but it is likely that these were the lands north of the Drew place that appear on the Rockfellow map.

Hill also offered a description of the area that the current dam was in, as well as the nature of the San Pedro there. "Mr. Hill, how far is the mouth of the Union ditch below the point where the Babacomari empties into the San Pedro river?" Hill replied, "...I should think the present dam is a mile and a half or a mile and three quarters, as near as I can judge it...from our dam a short distance the river bottom—the bed of the river is a heap wider than it is above, and when it gets up above it is not so gravelly and narrows in more, you know...The river don't raise [enough] to do any of us any good till the latter part of July or the first part of August...We irrigate in February, when we commence to put in our crops, to wet our land...when we suffer for water it is in July most." [48]

Hill's claim to this critical water supply began in concert with D.P. Kimble; Hill would later call the ranch formerly owned by Robert Mason home. "In the first place I purchased it in partners with D.P. Kemble [Kimble] and then bought him out afterwards. The deeds were made out in D.P. Kemble's name and I was partners with him, and I afterwards bought him out and he deeded it back to me and I have got both deeds...I think when D.P. Kemble deeded me that place [Mason Ranch] back after I bought him out that I made out some writing to him that if there was any waste water that he could have the waste water from that place, but there has never been any."

(David Patten Kimball was 42 and listed as a St. David farmer in 1882.) [49]

Of these land transactions, Hill further stated that "I have got the two deeds—the one that Mason gave him [Kimble] when we bought in as partners, and then I have got the one that he gave me when I bought out his interest. I have got both of them. That is, I did have them, and I think I have got them yet." Hill's trust in Kimble was based on a long-time relationship. "I have known him for forty years." Before investing in San Pedro River Valley real estate, Hill believed that "he lived in Mesa City, on [the] Salt river...He was up there before that and afterwards moved out..." [50] Mesa was an early Mormon community in the Arizona Territory. Kimble remained along the San Pedro, moving north, after leaving the Mason ranch.

Hill was pressed by council, who pointed out that he was not on this deed, as he had claimed to be a partner. Details of this kind may have been of secondary importance to a man like Hill. "Don't you know that your name does not appear in that conveyance by Mason?" Hill responded saying, "I told you, he bought it and it was deeded in his name, the whole business." "Did Kemble afterwards live at St. Davids?" "Yes sir...He was living there at the time I bought him out... living below where the old Carlisle bridge is, a mile or a mile and a half." After that Hill stated that Kimble moved "Below to the old McMiniman place..." Hill knew the area well. When he purchased the Mason Ranch, he didn't move on it at that time; instead "I put a man down there hauling hay." At the same time he was living "At the bridge on the San Pedro river—the old Carlisle [Carlyle] bridge." [51] (In November, 1880, William Carlyle had proposed a toll road and bridge near Drew's ranch, noting that location on his hand drawn map at the time he submitted his proposal to Pima County authorities. See Carlyle's map below, copy from the collections of John D. Rose.)

Differing spellings such as McMiniman and McMenomy were common for the owner of this site, who was murdered. One newspaper account referred to him as "Patrick McMenomen." When the Cochise County Board of Supervisors voted a reward for the capture of his killer, they spelled his name "McMiniman."

The Cochise County Board of Supervisors directs Sheriff Behan to offer a $500.00 reward for the murderer of Patrick McMiniman. Minutes Board of Supervisors Vol. 1 1881-1885 Meeting noted on pages 177-179. Courtesy of Kevin Pyles, Cochise County Archives.

Of the tragedy diarist George Hand, who was visiting Contention City at the time, recorded the following hearsay. "Report of a dead man [McMenomy] at a sheep ranch 8 miles below here caused the J.P. to summon a coroner's jury to investigate. They brought the body here late in the evening and adjourned until morning." The account of George Hand gives a distance from Contention City to the McMenomy place as eight miles. This, coupled with the testimony of John Hill that D.P. Kimble had moved "Below to the old McMiniman place," provides key information as to where this site actually was.

Billy Ohnesorgen stated that Mormon ownership of the McMenomy homestead followed his tragic death. He said that McMenomy had "located a lot of land and herded sheep. He used to carry a sack around with him and gather mesquite beans. Had a whole shack full. One day he was found dead-was found in the back of the room with a bullet hole through him. The Mormons brought suit for title to his land and got it." Ohnesorgan does not state that the subsequent ownership of the property was a motive for his brutal murder; he simply offers this succession of ownership. [52]

A SUCCESSION OF OWNERSHIP AS ONE GROUP OF SETTLERS PASSES THE TORCH TO ANOTHER

Robert Mason, who had shot at William Drew, only to miss and be clocked by a shovel, finally decided to move on. It was good news for all the settlers north of Contention, as Mason's temperament and presence had to be a continuing source of uncertainty. He would sell his memorable ranch to David Kimball, also spelled as Kemble in the Hill vs. Herrick transcripts. John Hill would state that although he had interests in the purchase, he did not show up on the deed.

"Robert Mason to David P. Kimball Jan. 21, 1882 This indenture made the twenty first day of January in the year of our Lord one thousand eight hundred and eighty two between Robert Mason, county of Cochise, Arizona the party of the first part and David P.

Kimball, of Maricopa County, Arizona the party of the second part. Witnesseth that the said party of the first part [Robert Mason] for and in consideration of the sum of two thousand dollars lawful money of the United States of America to him in hand paid the receipt whereof is hereby acknowledged has granted bargained sold remised released conveyed and quit claim and by these presents does grant bargain sell remise release convey and quit claim unto the said party of the second part [David P. Kimble] and to his heirs and assigns forever all the right title and interest estate claim and demand both in law and equity as well in possession as in expectancy of the said party of the first part [Robert Mason] of in or to that certain lot piece or parcel of land situate lying and being in Cochise County of the Territory of Arizona and more particularly described as follows, to wit:

"All his right title and interest in the water ditch and dam located 200 yards north of the old ruins [Today correctly known as Santa Cruz de Terranate, often referred to in the 19th Century as the "old ruins," or the "old San Pedro ruins"] known as the Mason Dam and Ditch located November 17th 1877 A.D. with his ranch situated and now occupied by him about one and one half miles from Contention on the San Pedro River and mostly under fence, containing about one hundred and sixty acres more or less with all the buildings and improvements thereon.

"Together with all and singular the tenements hereditaments and appurtenances thereto belonging or in anywise appertaining and to rents issues and profits thereof and also all the estate right title interest property possession claim and demand whatsoever as well in law as in equity of the said party of the first part of in or to the said premises and every part and parcel thereof with the appurtenances.

"To have and to hold and all singular the premises together with the appurtenances and privileges thereunto thereunto incident unto said party of the second part [David P. Kimble] his heirs and assigns forever." [53]

Eight months later, this deed was written:

"D.P. Kimball to John Hill Hoops Sept. 15 1882 This indenture made the fifteenth day of September in the year of our Lord one thousand eight hundred and eighty two. Between David P. Kimball the party of the first part and John Hill Hoops the party of the second part both residents-county of Cochise Arizona Territory. Witnesseth that the said party of the first part[David P. Kimble] for and in consideration of the sum of Two Thousand dollars lawful money of the United States of America to him in hand paid the receipt whereof is hereby acknowledged has granted bargained sold remised released conveyed and quit claimed and by these presents does grant bargain sell remise release and convey and quit claim unto the said party of the second part [John Hill Hoops] and to his heirs and assigns forever all the right title and interest estate claim and demand both in law and equity, as well in possession as in the expectancy of the said party of the first part of in or to certain lot piece or parcel of land situated lying and being in Cochise County of the Territory of Arizona and more particularly described as follows to wit: All of his right title and interest in the water ditch and dam located 200 yards north of the old ruins known as the Mason dam and ditch located November 17th 1877 A.D. with his Ranch situated and now owned by the said party of the first part [D.P. Kimball] about one and one half miles from Contention [City] on the San Pedro River and mostly under fence containing about one hundred and sixty acres more or less with all the buildings and improvements thereon.

"Together with all and singular the [sic] tenements hereditaments and appurtenances as thereto belonging or in any wise appertaining and the rents issues and profits thereof and also all the estate right title interest property possession claim and demand whatsoever as well in law as in equity of the said party of the first part of in or to the said and every part and parcel thereof with the appurtenances. To have and to hold all and singular the said premises together with the appurtenance, and privileges thereunto incident unto the said party of the second part his heirs and assigns forever." [54] This deed was not recorded at the time of its execution, but rather, four months later on January 17th, 1883.

This next deed made provision to Kimble for the waste water running in the Mason/Cable ditch:

"John Hill Hoops To D.P. Kimball Sept 15 1882 This indenture made the fifteenth day of September in the year of [our] Lord one thousand and eight hundred and eighty two: Between John Hill Hoops the party of the first part and David P. Kimball the party of the second part both residents in [the] County of Cochise Arizona Territory. Witnesseth that the said party of the first part for and in consideration of the sum of Five hundred Dollars lawful money of the United States of America to him in hand paid the receipt whereof is hereby acknowledged has granted bargained sold remised and conveyed and quit claimed and by these presents does grant bargain sell remise release convey and quit claim unto the said party of the second part and to his heirs and assigns forever all the right title and interest [and] estate claim and demand both in law and equity…As well [as] in possession as in expectancy of the said party of the first part of in or to that certain water right and interest in the dam and ditch known as the Mason ditch lying and being in Cochise County of the Territory of Arizona and more particularly described as follows to wit:

"All the surplus water in said Mason ditch and canal after the necessary supply is given for the cultivation of about one hundred and twenty five acres of land now occupied by the the [sic] party of the first part [John Hill] and under fence and known as the Mason farm or that portion thereof lying [on the] East Side of the San Pedro River with the right in common to an enlargement of said ditch to the dam on the San Pedro River and located 200 yards north of the old Ruins and all other rights thereto pertaining." [55]

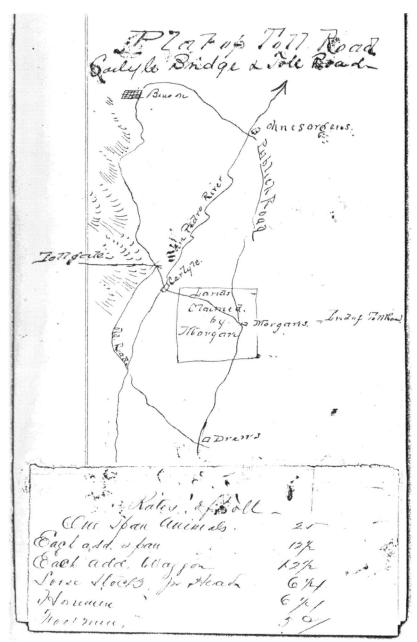

In November, 1880, William Carlyle proposes a toll road and bridge near Drew's Ranch. The site north of Drew's known as "Lands claimed by Morgan" may be in the area where Solon Allis misidentified Drew's Station. Copy from the collections of John D. Rose.

Hill was caught by surprise when proof of a precedent to his water claim was presented to him. "Were you not informed at the time of transfer by Mason to Kemble that each of the parties—Robert Mason, W.H. Drew, Griffith and [Daniel] Cable—that each conveyed a one thirty fourth interest in that ditch to the Contention consolidated Mining Company?" He answered "I never understood any amount at all…it wasn't set out in the light, no sir." Hill was again pressed, "You never had the fractional by Mason, Drew and Griffith to the Contention Consolidated Mining Company, stated to you?" "No," Hill replied, "not to my recollection." As if to save face and not appear that he was taken advantage of in his deal with Mason, Hill countered saying "Of course I may have been informed but if I was I don't recollect it to-day. It is a long time ago. I may have heard it talked over, I don't remember…" [56]

And this may well have been true. John Hill's testimony illustrates an ambitious man who had big dreams for the land on which he settled, but one whose attention to minor details was less than complete. He was repeatedly asked for the amount of acreage under cultivation, not only of his ranch but of others in the area who chose to join him in this suit, and time and time again he simply had little detailed knowledge of his own operations, and those around him. Wily Robert Mason may have sensed this about Hill when he sold to him and Kimble, and Hill likely never thought to look into such things. He appears in the record to be a man who could be taken at his word, and may have been taken advantage of by those of lesser character like the sometimes shifty and violent Robert Mason.

Hill may have indicated as much in the following exchange. "What proportion of the water in the Mason and Union ditch does the sixteen inches—miners inches, which you referred to in your testimony just now, form?" He replied "I don't know. I am not a mathematician, and I could not figure it up if I should try." [57]

Below is the deed that Hill was not sure he had heard of, and of which Mason may not have made him aware.

"This indenture made the 15th day of September A.D 1879...Between Robert Mason W.H Drew W.T.[?] Griffith and D.N. Cable of the County of Pima Territory of Arizona of the first part and the Western Mining Company, a Corporation duly organized and existing under the laws of the state of California the party of the second part, Witnesseth that the said parties of the first part for and in consideration of the sum of One Dollar lawful money of the United States of America to thence in hand paid by the said party of the second part the receipt whereof is hereby acknowledged and for the further consideration that the said party of the second part shall and does enlarge the ditch herein after described from the Head thereof to the Mill Site of the said party of the Second part [Western Mining Company] here granted, bargained, Sold, and conveyed and by these presents, do grant, bargain, sell, and convey unto the said party of the Second and to its successors and assigns forever an undivided interest of one thirty fourth (1/34) of each undivided share of in and to that certain dam and water ditch situate in the County of Pima and [the] Territory of Arizona heretofore, Constructed by the said parties of the first part for the purposes of taking water from the San Pedro at a point below and hear the place known as the Old Ruins; And about one half mile above the Mill Site of the said party of the second part and conveying the same past said Mill Site on the lands of the said parties of the first part. The said undivided interest of one thirty fourth 1/34 of each undivided share of water to be taken by the said party of the second part from the ditch at or near its said Mill Site and the said party of the second part to perform and contribute its proportion of labor and expenses in keeping the said dam and ditch in future repair...The said party of the second part to have and to hold the same together with all and singular the tenements hereditaments and appurtenances thereunto belonging or anywise appertaining and the reversion and reversions remainder and remainders, rents issues and profits thereof...To have and to Hold all and singular the said premises together with the appurtenances to the said party of the second part and to its successor and assigns..." [58] The document lists

R. Mason, W.H. Drew, Wm. Griffith and Daniel Cable as having signed the original, which was in Pima County, the transcribed version owned by Cochise County is the one that I have cited and published in this book.

The San Pedro River was a key area for settling, ranching and farming. And yet, it was common knowledge in the 19th Century that illness could spread across settlements along the river. Sometimes referred to as "Guaymas Fever," or "River Fever," such issues at times ran homesteaders out of the area. Early Charleston newlyweds Alexander and Carrie Miles moved closer to Fairbank as Charleston's economy declined and later crashed, but one of Alexander's teamsters died from fever, and his own wife contracted the same. Daniel Cable, an early pioneer of the area who was on the ground when William Drew and his family arrived, would suffer it also. "It was sickly down in there where Cable lived and they wanted to get out and get on the mesa, and how much they had I don't know. They were pretending to farm or trying to do some thing," as Hill recalled. …" [59]

NO IRRIGATION MEANS THE LAND IS WORTHLESS

Hill also testified that a diversion ditch installed at the Boston Mill also diminished the water for his crops, adding that without the water his home and fields "would be worth nothing." "Can you raise a crop on your land without water?" Hill was resolute. "No sir." "Can anybody?" "My experience says no, they can't." Other ranchers along the river echoed this same sentiment. Judge Lovell questioned Charles Noyes about water needs in his area. "State whether or not your land or your brother's land…will produce any agricultural crop without irrigation?" "Well," Noyes replied, "there is no land on our ranch that would…" Without water to irrigate your lands are they of any value whatever?" Noyes answered in the same vein, "Well, I would not stay there if I couldn't irrigate. I shouldn't consider them of any value, no sir." [60]

> An injunction has been issued by Judge Barnes, and will be served to-day, restraining Wm. F. Banning, Levy Scranton, Peter Moore, W. C. Green, Joseph Hoefler, Peter W. Roberts and C. B. Kelton, all of this county, from using the waters of the San Pedro river until N. W. Stori and John Hill et. al., the plaintiffs in the water case now before the commissioner, have sufficient water to irrigate the growing crops.

The public learns of the inception of the Hill vs. Herrick case. Arizona Weekly Citizen, April 27, 1889.

Hill would also arrive in time to have dealings with D.T. Smith, who would later be gunned down during the horrific event now known as the Bisbee Massacre, which took place on December 8, 1883. Hill recalled that back in 1882 D.T. "Smith sent word to come up there and cut hay and take a contract, and I went up and looked at the land and saw it was the big sacaton and I wouldn't cut it because it would injure the machine, and then he wanted me to take a contract to put in a ditch there." Hill was asked if he knew when D.T. Smith was killed. "No sir, only from hearsay; I didn't see him killed." [61]

Also at issue for Hill was that when he arrived in the area, H.C. Herrick's place was not irrigated. He made the point that Herrick's water use was more recent than many others in the area, which he hoped would undermine Herrick's claim to the disputed and scarce flow. Referring to Herrick's recent land development upstream, Hill stated, "…when I came to the country there was no fields there, it was all commons." But Herrick would argue that point and testify that he was cultivating portions of his land by 1880.

Herrick's own testimony revealed that he had broken an estimated 19 acres of land on the west side of the river, but chose to irrigate 65 acres on the east side of the San Pedro, even though he had no crops planted there, and no ground broken to even receive any seeds. It seemed like a remarkable waste of water with no justification, making it a challenge to understand why he hadn't been sued much sooner.   However, there is testimony of ranchers watering unplowed land to prepare it for cultivation. [62]

CHAPTER 5

OTHER CHARACTERS EMERGE
"…Mr. Herrick said he had first right to the water…" –I. Nicholson

John H. Martin testified on behalf of H. C. Herrick and the other defendants. He arrived in the San Pedro River valley in early summer of 1880, at Contention City. "The first work I did was working for Robert Mason in a restaurant in the town of Contention…After I quit [w]ork for Mason I went to work there making brick…I worked about twenty days right below the ditch, making brick…For Maulton & Lynn [Malter & Lind]…Mill builders and contractors…" He described himself as a "laborer. I worked in the mill, at [the] carpenter trade and do anything to make a good living at. I worked in the Grand Central and Head Centre Mill and Contention Mill off and on and I have ranched it here in this country, and I have farmed and carpentered."

Remaining bricks on the grounds of the Sunset/Head Centre Mill. Photo by John D. Rose.

Of his time with Robert Mason, Martin added that "…I worked a great deal for him that summer [1880]; that is, I drove hi[s] teams in grading there on the mill-site…when we were making brick there the ditch used to break between there and the dam and on several occasions we had to stop making brick and go fix up the levee to keep the water back…to the best of my knowledge the ditch might have been a foot and a half or two feet wide at the bottom. You could step across it most anywhere without any trouble…with the exception of places—there were low places, a good many, in the levee on the lower side and places where the water backed up and made quite a wide ditch, and in going around curves. They would throw the earth on the lower side and no attention was paid to the upper side at all and it would back up there."

SWIMMING AT THE CONTENTION DAM

Like the more substantial Gird dam to the south, a pool of water on the Arizona desert proved an attractive spot for recreation. "We used to go there swimming in the dam—a lot of boys would go up there bathing in the dam maybe twice a week, and I had occasion to go up and shut the headgate down by order of the parties that I was working for…I should judge the headgate in 1880 was three feet wide…maybe a foot or a foot and a half high…The water in 1880 run in the headgate there without any pressure at all, just a natural flow of water. That was the trouble, the ditch at that time would not carry near all the water that run into the headgate."

Repairs to the dam were also a continuing issue. "I helped fix it on several occasions, built the levee up again on the lower side—piled in dirt—filled sacks and put them there on the lower side of it…We hauled rocks both sides of the river and dirt and brush and hay and manure and built the dam up again—everything that we could get from the ranches, and throwed it in and hauled in rock all that four mules could haul with a chain around them."

Between July and August of 1881, the ditch and head gate washed out. When asked who made the new ditch, he replied, "Mr. Mason was there himself, Cable and a lot of the boys working at the Head Centre mill at that time and a lot of men from the Contention."

"I helped take out the new ditch and put in the headgate again, and helped put in the new dam…To the best of my knowledge the new headgate that we put in the dam was made by a Mr. Spatz, a carpenter at the Contention Mill at that time…Mr. Bosfield came around and he says to us to make the headgate large enough so we shan't [b]e bothered any more…I think we put in an extra board in the bottom, I think a board a foot wide. That made it a foot wider, to the best of my knowledge…" [63] John Henry Spatz was a German born carpenter living at Contention City.

Martin was also asked a number of questions about the D.T. Smith place. He had been up there in August and September of 1879 and saw that the ground was broken up, "and rotten water melons and musk melons laying there," but no new cultivation. "Do you know who broke it up?" "Mr. Smith told me that [Walk] Williams and George Hearst broke it up…Yes sir, they were living there the year before." Given his wealth and stature at the time, it is unlikely that George Hearst was living along the San Pedro and active in plowing fields in preparation for the planting of crops.

Martin recalled Patrick Gale and his brothers, Edmund and Courson, and noted that they lived on two places: "first place below the Head Centre which I understood to be the Bruener farm and was the Bruener ranch before he sold to the Head Centre Company. And another place down below, where the Summers place was." The reader might question just how much Martin really knew of the area, since Summers bought the Bruener place, so they are one and the same ranch. He further stated that Bruener's ranch was primitive. "There was never any house on Mr. Bruener's place; there was an old adobe chimney there where there had been an adobe house some years before." He also notes that the Gale brothers farmed on it; it remains an open question as to whether they rented it or not.

Patrick Henry Gale was a Contention City based teamster who also worked on the dam that offered the critical flow to the ditch over which so much fighting took place. About him John Martin stated, "I come along there---I was going to get some horses down river—it was in the spring of 1882 or 1883, and Patrick Gale had a crowd of Mexicans, I should judge from eight to twelve of them, digging the ditch, taking the bank down, making the ditch larger as he went, straightening the crooked places and throwing the dirt on the lower hillside…I stopped and talked with him an hour; I was very well acquainted with him. At that time they were working very nearly half way between the dam and Contention, and the next time I saw them, a week or so after that, they were down in Contention—the lower edge of it, cleaning out and building up, taking the upper side of the ditch away and putting it on the lower side, making it wider." Gale and his brothers had already left the Bruener ranch to work for the mills, which also required water from the critical irrigation ditches to feed stamping operations. [64]

Frank C. Perley arrived in Contention City in May of 1880. A brick maker by trade, he found employment working for Malter & Lind, "just below Contention on the site of the Head Centre mill." Testifying on behalf of H.C. Herrick, he had reason to be grateful to Herrick. "I had been ill with fever and ague and I met and formed the acquaintance of Mr. Herrick at Contention, coming to Tombstone, and he invited me to go to his ranch instead. He said that he had plenty of vegetables and I could get milk and the like of that, and it probably would do me more good than to come to Tombstone, and it would be a benefit to him to have someone there because he was away a great deal of the time…most of the time. Well, I was down there on this land and I wasn't very strong at the time and I confined myself to that point principally when I left the house." [65]

Frank Perley worked here during the construction of the Head Centre Mill, shown in the background. Photo of John Rose at the Sunset/Head Centre Mill by Stephanie Rose.

A CONTENTION CITY STORE WORKER HUNTS QUAIL

Samuel Sweetman was by Contention City standards a long-term resident. Arriving in 1882, he left for a year only to return and stay. He was, as were so many, asked about the head gate and the system to which it connected. "In September 1882 I went there and in October I went up hunting there and saw it," adding that "It was washed out the last big rain we had here." In October 1882, Sweetman was working for Simon Marks in his Contention City store, and in his free time, hunting. "...I would go along the river hunting for quail...I used to go up the river almost every day." He added that a portion of the newer ditch was found "From the crossing of the road to Moleno's house, about [a] quarter of a mile." As to the functioning of the system, the shop worker may have offered a far more succinct explanation than many who were working on the irrigation system professionally. "The river is there and the headgate is put a little below it, a few feet, and when the water is low they throw up a dam and that throws the water into the ditch." The changing nature of the San Pedro, with its seasonal flooding, took its toll on the entire system. "They had a dam and now they haven't any dam…that is, they have a dam but not a big dam, and the other one is up in the river, and they only have a small dam there to throw the water into the ditch. The other [dam] was big enough to ride across horse-back—the old one was." [66]

Thomas Gribble was an English born engineer who arrived in Contention City on January 30th, 1883. He would find opportunities to get paid while shooting ducks which lived on the large pond that gathered at the Contention dam. "…my capacity at the Contention Company required me to look out for the water and passing up and down with nothing to do, we would walk up to the dam to shoot ducks and I had a gun and I would walk up there occasionally to shoot, and of course walking right by the gate and walking over it on the dam." [67]

INCONSISTENT WATER SUPPLY AT THE GRAND CENTRAL MILL

S.W. Wood played a key role in the early development of the Tombstone District. His wife, Mary, would later write a brief but important account of her impressions of Charleston. In the latter 1880's, the Woods would move to the Grand Central Mill, living there while S.W. operated the mill, an operation which was drawn into the Hill vs. Herrick case. "I am Superintendent of the mill," he told the proceedings, "I live at the Grand Central Mill." (The mill was located between Contention City and Fairbank.) Wood was asked about the state of water flow in the ditch prior to the injunction that led to the lawsuit. "Before that the water was very low in the ditch," and the Grand Central had actually been shut down due to lack of water. Following the injunction the situation improved, slightly. "We haven't had to stop this year but there was times this spring when there was barely enough water to run the mill…Last March and the first part of April…The first part of April, about the first week— possibly the eighth or ninth."

Wood saw firsthand the injunction that forced a reduction in the water used upstream by Herrick and Hop Kee. "I saw in the paper that an injunction had been served on parties up above to prevent them [from] taking the water and the day before that there was but very little water in the river, barely enough to run our mill and that day or the day after that there was water enough running in our ditch. I should say it was about the first of the month, but I couldn't tell you without looking at the newspaper to get the exact date, but I took particular notice of the fact that the injunction had been served…There has been an abundance of water for our purposes there and some going by that don't flow in our ditch—that is, a greater portion of the time." [68] Wood also added that following the injunction his water flow had doubled.

It was brief but strong testimony by one of the few employers of any significance left on the San Pedro River. Charleston was gone and Contention City had declined dramatically. Millville still sputtered along with a small smelting milling operation, and so putting at risk the few

S.W. Wood was in charge of the Grand Central mill during the Hill vs. Herrick case. From collections of John D. Rose.

good mill jobs left because of the farming of Herrick and Hop Kee made little sense in many circles. This was an inherent advantage for those who initiated the suit as John Hill and other plaintiffs continued to garner key support from mill operators and management, a factor that they hoped would carry weight in any legal determination to come. Hill and his neighbors may have also been seen in a differing light than Herrick by the Contention area mills who were also downstream from the Chinese-punching potato-stealing farmer.

Edward W. Perkins worked and lived at the Grand Central Mill as well, and was there the year before his testimony took place, 1887. He told the court that he had taken notice of the suit, and considering conditions at the Grand Central, it wasn't much of a surprise. He told that the amount of water reaching the mill "was barely enough for our purposes at the mill...Since then there had been a larger flow of water..." adding that things had improved about a week prior. [69]

The timing of the improved water flow paralleled the issuance of the injunction and would make the argument that increased ranching and farming to the south (upstream) of the Grand Central was at fault after all, and further support the claim of Hill and his fellow plaintiffs. It should be noted as well that Perkins was called to testify on behalf of Hill and the other plaintiffs, making his testimony that of a friendly witness, not at all a hostile one. (Edward W. Perkins was listed as an American born 31 year old Tombstone mill man in the 1882 Cochise County Great Register.)

ORGANIZED CATTLE BUSINESS ON THE BABACOMARI

C.M. Bruce was part of a partnership that controlled the San Ignacio del Babacomari Land Grant. Others in this partnership included W.C. Land, Robert Perrin, and Thornton and Hugh Tevis, known as the "Tevis, Perrin, Land & Co." When asked if his company had any interest in the waters of the San Pedro, he answered that they did not, but then he corrected himself. "I beg your pardon...I take that back. We have a camp down there off below the Babacomari just opposite to St. Davids…for cattle and horses."

The partnership had been in control of the grant since October 27th, 1883, adding that "…in 1883 there was no water in the river [referring to the Babacomari] at all from Huachuca down to the crossing…down to where the road crosses about five miles below. In fact the water didn't run there till we put in cattle." When asked if he had ever known water from the Babacomari during the dry season to flow into the San Pedro, he said, "…I haven't witnessed it, but it is generally understood that the water don't go into the San Pedro during the very dry season."

He offered his own observations as to how the water in the Babacomari interacted with the soil conditions. "The nature of the soil there is a hard gravelly soil full of stones and you stop up the river and the water runs right on top of the stoney earth, and below there is a kind of a tank caused by the railroad [the N.M. & A.] and the water would run right out of the river and into those tanks, I suppose, two or three feet deep and be a very large pond of water there and would then run out of the tanks on down to the ditch, but one point, owing to the inequalities of the soil it would be about three feet deep and then again it would run along the surface of the earth and by the time it gets to the pasture it is on the surface of the earth and there is no ditch at all." [70]

I. Nicholson testified on behalf of Hill and the other plaintiffs, living at Fairbank back in 1884. He had worked for Herrick making dams and ditches, and in their conversations he related a dialog that was damaging to Herrick's case. "I made some remarks, I can't remember just how it was now, and Mr. Herrick said he had first right to the water and was going to have all he wanted…he said we have the first right to the river or the ditch and was going to have all the water he wanted whether anybody else got any or not…What I was thinking about was the scarcity of the water in the river…below the dam." [71]

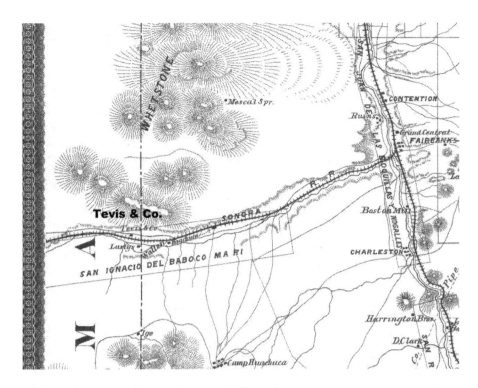

Tevis & Co. were drawn into the Hill vs. Herrick case, as they ranched on the Babacomari river, which drains into the San Pedro River near Fairbank. Where the map notes "Tevis & Co." a second notation of the same has been added for the reader. From the collections of John D. Rose. Map annotated by Kevin Pyles.

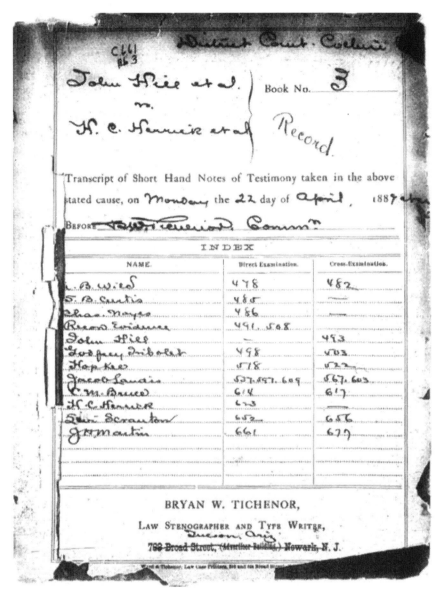

Although the original testimony from Hill vs. Herrick was typed by Bryan Tichenor in 1889, the following three pages show documents from the case in longhand. Courtesy AHS.

District Court Gehrie Co.

John Kiel et al } Book No. 4

vs.

N. C. Herrick et al. } Record

Transcript of Short Hand Notes of Testimony taken in the above, stated cause, on Monday the 22 day of April, 1889, etc.

BEFORE B. W. Tichenor. Comm.

INDEX

NAME.	Direct Examination.	Cross-Examination.
S. Harris	697. 714	706. 714
Chas. Noyes	722	—
C. Herrick	724	730. 778.
H. Martin	776.	765
Wm Beel	802 839	817.
W. B. Crane	852	859
Robert Dodd	860	864
Wm C. Green	868	871
Edward Drew	884. 892	889

MAY 30 1889

FILED

BRYAN W. TICHENOR,

LAW STENOGRAPHER AND TYPE WRITER,

Tucson, Ariz.

799 Broad Street, (Market Building,) Newark, N. J.

Ward & Tichenor, Law Case Printers, 813 and 815 Broad Street, Newark, N. J.

District Court - Cochise Co

John Hill, et al.
v.
H. C. Herrick, et al.

Book No. 2

Record

Transcript of Short Hand Notes of Testimony taken in the above stated cause, on Monday the 22' day of April, 1889 a

Before B. W. Tichenor, Comm'r

INDEX

NAME.	Direct Examination.	Cross Examination.
Watson Avanenio	286	265
Robert H. Upton	246, 294	284
Chas. Noyes	296, 283, 286	341, 349
A. N. Noyes	352	—
Henry C. Schultz	354, 364, 365	366
I. Nicholson	267	—
John Hill	377, 444	394, 418, 451
I. Clifton	463	455
J. B. Curtis	463	469, 471

BRYAN W. TICHENOR,

LAW STENOGRAPHER AND TYPE WRITER

Tucson, Ariz.
788 Broad Street, Newark, N. J.

THE UNITED STATES OF AMERICA,

CERTIFICATE No. 8765

To all to whom these Presents shall come, Greeting:

WHEREAS *William Henry Harrison Drew, of Dane County, Wisconsin,*

ha*s* deposited in the GENERAL LAND OFFICE of the United States, a Certificate of the REGISTER OF THE LAND OFFICE at *Mineral Point,* whereby it appears that full payment has been made by the said

William Henry Harrison Drew, according to the provisions of the Act of Congress of the 24th of April, 1820, entitled "An act making further provision for the sale of the Public Lands," for *the North West quarter of the South East quarter of Section six, in Township five North, of Range eight East, in the District of Lands subject to sale at Mineral Point, Wisconsin, containing forty acres,*

according to the official plat of the survey of the said Lands, returned to the General Land Office by the SURVEYOR GENERAL, which said tract ha*s* been purchased by the said *William Henry Harrison Drew,*

NOW KNOW YE, That the United States of America, in consideration of the Premises, and in conformity with the several acts of Congress, in such case made and provided, HAVE GIVEN AND GRANTED, and by these presents DO GIVE AND GRANT, unto the said *William Henry Harrison Drew,* and to *his* heirs, the said tract above described: TO HAVE AND TO HOLD the same, together with all the rights, privileges, immunities, and appurtenances of whatsoever nature, thereunto belonging, unto the said *William Henry Harrison Drew,* and to *his* heirs and assigns forever.

In Testimony Whereof, I, *James K. Polk* PRESIDENT OF THE UNITED STATES OF AMERICA, have caused these Letters to be made PATENT, and the SEAL of the GENERAL LAND OFFICE to be hereunto affixed.

GIVEN under my hand, at the CITY OF WASHINGTON, the *first* day of *September* in the Year of our Lord one thousand eight hundred and *forty eight* and of the INDEPENDENCE OF THE UNITED STATES the Seventy *third*

BY THE PRESIDENT: *James K. Polk* By *J.K. Stephens*, *Sec'y.*

S.H. Laughlin, RECORDER of the General Land Office.

William Drew is noted on this and the following page filing land claims in Wisconsin thirty years before settling along the San Pedro River and founding Drew's Station. Courtesy of the Drew Family Archive.

THE UNITED STATES OF AMERICA,

CERTIFICATE
No. 8,934.

To all to whom these Presents shall come, Greeting:

WHEREAS, *William Henry Harrison Drew, of Dane County, Wisconsin,*

ha*s* deposited in the GENERAL LAND OFFICE of the United States, a Certificate of the REGISTER OF THE LAND OFFICE at *Mineral Point,* whereby it appears that full payment has been made by the said

William Henry Harrison Drew,   according to the provisions of the Act of Congress of the 24th of April, 1820, entitled "An act making further provision for the sale of the Public Lands," for *the South West quarter of the North West quarter, of Section Seventeen, in Township Five North, of Range Eight East; in the District of Lands subject to sale at Mineral Point, Wisconsin, containing Forty Acres;*

according to the official plat of the survey of the said Lands, returned to the General Land Office by the SURVEYOR GENERAL, which said tract ha*s* been purchased by the said *William Henry Harrison Drew,*

NOW KNOW YE, That the UNITED STATES OF AMERICA, in consideration of the Premises, and in conformity with the several acts of Congress, in such case made and provided, HAVE GIVEN AND GRANTED, and by these presents DO GIVE AND GRANT, unto the said *William Henry Harrison Drew,*

and to *his* heirs, the said tract above described: TO HAVE AND TO HOLD the same, together with all the rights, privileges, immunities, and appurtenances of whatsoever nature, thereunto belonging, unto the said _____ _____

William Henry Harrison Drew, and to *his* heirs and assigns forever.

In Testimony Whereof, I, *James K. Polk,*

PRESIDENT OF THE UNITED STATES OF AMERICA, have caused these Letters to be made PATENT, and the SEAL of the GENERAL LAND OFFICE to be hereunto affixed.

GIVEN under my hand, at the CITY OF WASHINGTON, the *First* day of *September,* in the Year of our Lord one thousand eight hundred and *Forty Eight,* and of the INDEPENDENCE OF THE UNITED STATES the Seventy *Third.*

BY THE PRESIDENT: *James K. Polk,*

By *F. K. Stephens* Asst. Sec'y.

S. H. Laughlin RECORDER of the General Land Office.

Just over two years after her husband's death, Mrs. Drew sells an easement to the N.M. & A. railroad to cross her ranch, for a scant $70.00. The following two pages are part of the same legal instrument. A portion of the above page is missing. Courtesy of the Drew Family Archive.

Cochise Territory of Arizona and bounded and
particularly described as follows to wit:

Commencing at a point 50
feet distant and opposite to and east
wardly from a point in the center line of
the New Mexico and Arizona Railroad
91 feet southerly from Station 630 of the line
of said railroad thence southwardly
and parallel with the center line of said
Railroad 2909 feet to a point opposite
Station 660 of said Railroad thence at
a right angles westwardly across said
Railroad 100 feet thence northwardly and
parallel with the said center line of said
Railroad 2909 feet to a point 50 feet
distant and opposite to and west
wardly from said point in the center
line of said New Mexico and Arizona
Railroad 91 feet southerly from said
station 630 thence at a right angle
Eastwardly 100 feet to the place of begin
ning containing six $\frac{65}{100}$ ($6\frac{65}{100}$) acres

Together with all and singular the
tenements hereditaments and appurten
ances thereunto belonging or in any
wise appertaining and the reversion
and reversions remainder and
remainders rents issues and profits
thereof.

To have and to hold all and singular
the said premises together with the appurte
nances unto the said party of the
second part and to its successors and
assigns forever.

In witness whereof the said party of the first
part has hereunto set her hand and seal
the day and year first above written.
                        Ann Drew. (seal)
Territory of Arizona) ss.
County of Cochise)   On this 20th day of Feb.
A.D. 1882, before me A. J. Jones County Recorder
for the County of Cochise personally appeared
Ann Drew a widow woman whose
name is subscribed to the annexed instru
-ment as a party thereto known to me to
be the person described in and who executed
the said annexed instrument as party
thereto and who duly acknowledged to
me that she executed the same freely
and voluntarily and for the uses
and purposes therein mentioned
In witness whereof I have hereunto set
my hand and affixed my official
seal this 20th day of Feb. A.D. 1882.
(seal) A. J. Jones. County Recorder,
Filed and recorded at request of
W. M. Johnson Feb. 21- 1882 at 9 am
                    A J Jones
                    County Recorder.

In the District Court of the
First Judicial District of the
Territory of Arizona in and for
the County of Pima

W^m H Drew }
    Plaintiff }
      vs }
Robert Mason }
    Defendant }

This action came on regularly
for trial, The said parties appeared
by their attorneys, A Jury of three
persons was regularly impaneled
by consent of both parties, and
sworn to try the issues of fact in
said action, Witnesses on the part
of the plaintiff and defendant
were sworn and examined, After
hearing the evidence, the argument
of counsel, and instructions of the
court, the jury retired to consider of their verdict, and subsequently returned into court, and
being called answered to their
names and say "we the jury
find for the plaintiff and assess
the damages Twenty Dollars", Where
fore by virtue of the law and

The page above and the three that follow are the decision of Judge
C.G.W. French in the Drew vs. Mason case. Courtesy AHS.

by reason of the premises aforesaid it is ordered and adjudged that said plaintiff have and recover from said defendant the sum of Twenty Dollars damages together with the said plaintiffs costs and disbursements incurred in this action amounting to the sum of $_____

And it is further ordered adjudged and decreed that the plaintiff has a one fourth undivided interest in the ditch described in the complaint as the "Upper San Pedro irrigating ditch" and one fourth undivided interest in the dam of the same and the use of one fourth of all the water running in said ditch and has the right to have his said one fourth of said water flow without obstruction through said ditch across the land and ranch of the defendant to the land and ranch of the plaintiff on the San Pedro River described in the complaint in this case,

And it is further ordered adjudged and decreed that the injunction heretofore issued in this case, and on motion of the defendant dissolved on a previous day of this term of the court, be and the same hereby is revived in the following modified form reinstated and made perpetual as follows "It is therefore ordered by the Judge of said District Court of the First Judicial District, that the said defendant Robert Kenson and all his counsellors, attorneys, solicitors and agents, and all others acting in aid or assistance of him do absolutely desist and refrain from using, interfering with, or in any way place or manner impeding, diverting from said Upper San Pedro ditch, or obstructing in any way, place, or manner the water running in said ditch belonging to the plaintiff, consisting of the use of one fourth of all the water running in said ditch, and that they absolutely

way place or manner interfering
with the plaintiff in repairing said Upr San Pedro Ditch
or in running his said one
fourth of all the water in
said ditch or any part thereof the plaintiff may desire,
in said ditch through the
defendants land and ranch
to the plaintiffs land and
ranch on the San Pedro
River described in the com-
plaint,   C. G. W. French
June 5th 1879   Dist. Judge

Territory of Arizona
County of Pima
District Court
First Judicial Dist

Wm Zeckendorf Drew
vs
Robert Wearn

Final Decree

Filed June 5th 1879
Geo Tyng P Clerk
by Atchison Dep

Hon. C. G. W. French, ⎫
Hon. D. H. Pinney, ⎬ Justices.
Hon. A. W. Sheldon, ⎭

William Wilkerson,
Clerk.

SUPREME COURT OF ARIZONA.

Prescott, Arizona, April 21ˢᵗ 1885.

Dear Sister & Niece

Your kind letter of April 14ᵗʰ came this morning I had been anxiously awaiting it I hope you will keep me advised of Brother Israel's condition My health is good I am 65 years old I expect to visit your locality some time next Winter I expect to go to Washington & [...] [...] will go north I am all alone in the world now Israel is the last of our family If he departs there will be none of my Fathers family left except myself My wife died years ago and her boys are now men in business one Virgil at Deadwood Dakota lately the other George at Kansas City Missouri I thank you very much Miss Adelia for writing to me All my other relatives have failed to write except Sister Sarah once

Affectionately your Uncle
C G W French

Judge C.G.W. French, who wrote the final decision in the Drew vs. Mason case, writes his sister and niece in the letter above, telling them "I am 65 years of age...I am all alone in the world now..." Original letter written and signed by Judge French from the collections of John D. Rose.

John and Aubrey Rose conduct a non-scientific measurement of the foundation of Drew's Station. Photo by Stephanie Rose.

A member of the Drew family who lived at Drew's Station wrote an account of those times. It would be a challenge for any of us, late in life, to recall with accuracy the days of our youth. And, of course, personal bias will normally play a role, and the account does contain errors. But such accounts offer at least a glimpse of a time and place that otherwise we would know very little about. Cora Drew Reynolds wrote of her family's move to Arizona, and the little adobe building known as Drew's Station which would become a memorable part of the Tombstone and Earp story. The four pages that follow are Cora Drew's account, written almost a lifetime after her days as a young girl living at Drew's. Copy of her account from the collections of John D. Rose.

My Life in the Early West

CORA DREW REYNOLDS

IT has occurred to some that reminiscences of my early life in the old west would be of interest. My memories now go back nearly eighty years. Although I was born into a famous theatrical family I knew none of the sophistication of urban civilization until I was a grown lady. The only remembrance I have of my uncle, the late great John Drew, was his visit to our farm in Montana when I was a very small girl; we were in the carriage together and we disagreed over the whip. After a struggle I bit him as hard as I could and ran for the house. Though many members of my family, such as John, Ethel, and Lionel Barrymore, have gained international fame, none have had a more interesting life than I!

I was born fifteen miles from Bozeman, Montana, on August 9, 1872. My mother was a graduate of the University of Edinburgh (Scotland) and married my father in New York City where I believe he was born. At the time of my birth my father raised blooded cattle and Arabian horses; prior to our leaving Montana my father's assessment on this property was a hundred and eighty thousand dollars, which was a considerable amount for those days. At about this time father's brother, John, got in some serious trouble in the East and he was forced to go to New York. Having mortgaged the farm to help out in this family crisis, we soon found ourselves in financial difficulties, brought on in part by a very severe winter in which most of our cattle froze to death.

That spring my father decided to sell out, and with two covered wagons, four horses and a span of mules (Jane and Lyde) we started a small herd of cattle toward California. Our first stop of any duration was Signal, Arizona, where we remained all that summer and winter. We were not far from an Indian encampment and could see their fires and hear their war dances and chants. We children laid awake many a night, terrified with fear. From Signal we moved to a spot on the San Pedro River about eighty miles north of Tucson which was our closest trading post. Father and my oldest brother, Harrison — who was around eighteen — with the help of two Mexicans, built a three-room adobe house. It had dirt floors and doors made of logs with thick canvas covering the window

openings. That year we had a nice garden and a good crop of corn.

During this period the Contention Mine was opened up about ten miles north of what was to become the town of Tombstone. A smelter was built and material was brought in by mule teams. Before the smelter was completed my father passed away in November of 1880. I was then eight years old. Soon afterwards, my brother Ed was able to secure the contract to deliver wood for the smelter. He hired Mexicans to cut the wood from the Chiricahua Mountains.

I am not sure but I think at this time we were very poor people. For Christmas of 1880 the only thing that Santa left me was a plain dark blue bottle. To me it was the most beautiful thing a child could have and I kept it for many months. Using it as a doll, and it being my only plaything I was heartbroken when I accidently broke it on a rock one day.

That spring a man came to our ranch on foot. He begged his supper and breakfast and we bedded him down for the night in our stables. That man was Ed Schiefflin, and he went from our house and discovered the fabulous tombstone lode around which grew the fabled mining town. We saw him many times afterwards both at our ranch and in Tombstone but in time he forgot those who had been a friend to him.

We were able to secure the stage stop between Benson and Contention. The four horses were changed at our place and Mama would give the passengers breakfast for a dollar apiece. We also had the Tombstone stages to change. Tombstone ran two stages daily, one second class four-horse stage and one first class six-horse stage. Bud Philpot was the driver of the first class stage, and we children always got up and waved goodby when he left late at night.

My brother Ed bought a large herd of burros and my youngest brother David and I each had our favorite which we rode constantly. When we heard that they had all been sold, David and I left home as fast as we could which is not very fast on a burro. We were finally overtaken and forced to walk home, our hearts heavy, knowing that our own personal burros had been sold with the herd. Burros carried most of the freight in Arizona at this time. A pack of about fifty used to stop over at our house regularly loaded with burlap sacks. Sacks of oranges sold for fifty cents so we usually had all the fresh fruit we wanted.

Early in the eighteen eighties we again became more financially independent and I am sure that we put all the money that was not needed into expanding our cattle herd. I don't know where we got the grain for the horses but the hay was wild grama grass which is good feed and was plentiful.

I don't think that there has ever been a town anywhere that grew as fast as Tombstone. Most of the men that the movies and books have immortalized were intimate friends of my childhood. I knew "Curly Bill" well; he was tall, blonde and heavy set and wore his hair like a girl in long curls and ringlets. The Earps, Harry Head, Doc Halliday, Jim Crane, Frank and Ed Lowery, and Billie and Ike Clanton were frequent visitors to our ranch. They gave my mother their word and they kept it that she need never worry about our cattle being rustled. Desperados frequently came to our place; one day we heard the familiar sound of gunplay across the river and shortly thereafter four or five wild-eyed men arrived and demanded a horse of Mama saying, "Any horse will do as we shall soon get a good one." Of course Mama had to let them have a horse and they gave her a hundred dollars.

Once the stage was robbed but a short distance from us. The nine o'clock left our place, with Bud Philpot driving, loaded with silver bullion from Tombstone. Hardly had we said goodnight to Bud and he had reached the narrow wash to the north when we heard a shot ring out, and then the shooting sounded as if a bunch of firecrackers were going off. The bright Arizona moonlight made it possible for Mama and us children to see the whole thing and we saw the holdup men ride around the hill and off into the distance. My brother Ed went down to the stage and found Bud dead on top. Ed saddled a horse and went to Contention to tell of the holdup and murder, and shortly men came from Tombstone and took Bud away in a spring-wagon. Early the next morning the Earp brothers arrived with the sheriff and Mama gave them breakfast. We told them what we knew and they left in pursuit of the robbers, only they went in the opposite direction from what we told them. There is not a doubt in the world but what they were the holdup men! A week or so later we three children went to a small cluster of trees west of the wash where the holdup had been and we found a black horse tied to a tree, all but dead from thirst and hunger. We had to take his feed to him for days before he could be brought to the stable. We told the sheriff but the horse was never claimed. We later found out that on the night of Bud's murder, Hollydan — an Earp henchman — brought his horse to the livery stable covered with sweat and he himself staggering from hard riding. The Earps were also out of Tombstone that night!

Shortly thereafter Ike Clanton came to our house and wanted to give me a diamond ring that had belonged to his mother; Mama would not let me have it. Ike said "Let Cora have it as it is only a matter of time until the Earps and Hollydan get me." Soon thereafter they did!

Not long after this my brother Ed and I were walking down the main street of Tombstone when we saw Tom and Frank McLowery with Ike Clanton's brother Billy coming toward us. Suddenly from a side street came the Earp boys and they opened fire killing the three men instantly. The three murdered men had been at a distinct disadvantage as they had put their guns up along with their horses when they came into town. So far as I know I am the only person now living who saw this famous western murder. It is the absolute truth when I say the Earps committed it in this cold-blooded way and then went unpunished. When such tragedy is stamped upon a child's brain she will carry the scene to her grave. A little later one of my own brothers was murdered by an outlaw in Pima. The murderer was caught and sentenced to life in the Arizona State Penitentiary.

The last I knew of William "Billie the Kid" Claibourne was that he was killed while leading a band of Indians on the warpath. I'm not sure whether these were Apache or Yaqui Indians. He put a notch in his gun everytime he killed a man and when they found him there were 21 notches.

When the railroad came through to Contention (and I think Tombstone), we sold our home and we moved near Charlestown on D. T. Smith's old place (he had been killed in the Bisbee Massacre). In going to Charlestown we stayed all night at a friend's house near Contention, and the next morning Mama put me on Molly, a large blue-roan mare, and sent me back to our old ranch as we had discovered that Molly's colt had been left behind. Molly ran away with me and it was no easy feat riding a racing horse bareback down steep hills; I remember of thinking of trying to jump off, but we made the ranch and the return trip. This was my first really wild ride.

Next day we went on to the Smith ranch, Mama driving one team and me the other with my brothers following along with the cattle and horses. I rushed out to greet the boys when they arrived and ran into a bull coming around an adobe wall. He picked me up and carried me off into a field but did not hurt me. While we were on the Smith place, which was only a few months, David, Charley and I had to ride the range and try to take care of the horses and cattle.

From Russeville, just east of the Dragoon Mountains, at Dragoon Circuit, Ed got the contract to haul coke to the mining town of Johnson. He had two twenty-mule teams and four wagons; each wagon held a carload of coke. The wagons were loaded at night and one trip a day was made. A twenty-mule team is driven with one line called a jerk line which fastens to the bridle bit of the first left hand mule. When you wanted the team to turn to the right you would jerk the line and call "gee-gee"; to turn to the left you would just pull the line. The first two mules are the leaders, and they are fastened together with a light-weight iron bar. The two mules hitched closest to the wagon are known as pointers. If you wanted to turn the wagon to the right you would call "gee Pet" and he would jump over the chain and turn the wagons; the wagons would be going to the right and the rest of the team would be going straight ahead. To turn left you would call "haw Maggie." These two pointers are very valuable to a team and we were very attached to our own "Pet" and "Maggie." When they were later sold I put my arms around their necks and told them goodby and of course I cried.

From a neighbor who had race-horses, Ed bought Tempest, a fast black bald-faced horse. I would sit astride him, strapped on, with my legs drawn up. I could not fall off, but when I straightened my legs out I was free.

When the Johnson mine closed down, Ed sold the teams and wagons and we all left with a man named Melvin Jones who had located a ranch in the Galluro Mountains. It had a good range with running water and hot springs. With two Mexicans they gathered a herd of cattle together and left for the ranch. To reach it they had to take down bars and pass through Dr. King's place. King came down and ordered us back. Ed told him we were going through; King then shot both bridle reins from Ed's hand. Melvin pulled his Winchester and shot at King as one would shoot a revolver; he killed King instantly. We stayed with the cattle and they went on into Tombstone to tell what had happened.

King had two adobe houses, one with a large store-room filled with sacks of grain. Under these were sacks of sand, and when they were removed we came to a room in back which held two skeletons and one body with flesh on its bones. This latter person was later identified by his mother through his horse and saddle. There were a great many cats on the place and it was said that King kept them to eat the flesh from the bodies of his victims. When I visited here in 1942 I found King's two adobe houses still standing but not a trace of our ranch.

After King's demise, Colonel Hooker of the Serria Bonita bought his ranch and became the cattle baron of Arizona. It was his daughter-in-law, Forrestine, who did so much to popularize the old west and its history through her books earlier in this century.

Our ranch, which adjoined the Hooker's, had a one room house with a bunkhouse for the men. We started to build on to the house and had one room all finished when Ed left for Mexico to buy horses. After about three months he returned with about 1000 head, but as Melvin had done little during Ed's absence to improve the ranch, they dissolved their partnership.

This section of Arizona was constantly being terrorized by roving Apache Indians under the leadership of the infamous Geronimo. We had two vicious bulldogs who would come into the house and refuse to move if Indians were about. When they were in the neighborhood we could not light a lamp or start a fire. The Indians were the very worst kind of sneaks and never showed themselves if they could help it. They used to signal each other with owl hoots and coyote howls. We saw Indians break our water troughs and slaughter yearling cows within sight of our house. Many times we were up all night, all of us armed, prepared for the worst.

As for myself I don't know when I first learned to ride, but when we came from Montana I was riding Topsy and I couldn't have been more than three. The only place we children were not allowed to ride was across the San Pedro River as Topsy would always get in midstream and roll us off. I have no idea how many times I have been thrown from a horse but the only time I was ever hurt was once when exercising King, a race horse, and he ran away with me, headed for an embankment and proceeded to get his foot caught in a barbed wire fence. I jumped and was badly bruised but I raced and exercised him many times afterwards.

I sat side-way in races and could easily take a

three-foot jump. I went into my first riding contest when I was sixteen and shortly held the championship of Arizona and New Mexico. (I was still riding at 70.) My show horse was a magnificent bay with a black mane and tail by the name of Quirty (Spanish for whip). He was the only horse I have ever ridden that I was afraid of. He had a tendency to throw people and then severely paw them; however he was always gentle with me. Besides it was always my practice to ride any horse that offered a real challenge or that had been expressly forbidden to me.

My first schooling was in a three-wall brush shed with a neighbor-woman as the teacher. School was only held when the weather was pleasant and warm.

Next I attended a school made of bear grass. This is a fine blade palm which will turn wind and water away. It grows in patches all over Arizona. You separate it as one would celery and tie it to poles, roots up. Both Indians and Mexicans make their homes from this.

Early in 1892 Buffalo Bill urged me to join his Wild West Show which he was taking to Chicago for the World's Columbian Exposition. Mama wouldn't let me go but to compensate for my disappointment she allowed me to go to the Fair with friends. I saw Buffalo Bill many times that next year in Chicago. It was while in Chicago that I met and married R. J. Reynolds. After that time, except for vacation periods, the Old West became but a memory as new and different horizons opened up for me in the East.

Ben and Joe Gibson, who have been swinging 'round the circle for a month, returned home a few days ago. They visited Salt Lake, Denver, San Francisco, Los Angeles and other places of interest in the circuit, and of course had a good time. They were in Salt Lake during the celebration and Ben Gibson and Ed Drew, of Aravaipa, entered the steer tying contest and captured the prizes, Drew winning first and Gibson second. Ben tied his steer in 30 seconds, but the pesky critter struggled so that Ben, fearing he might get loose, went back and tied the steer the second time, which cost him the first prize. In cowboy contests Arizona takes the lead.

Years after leaving Drew's Station and testifying in Hill vs. Herrick, Ed Drew takes his considerable rodeo skills on tour. Arizona Silver Belt, September 2, 1897.

A Story of Ed. Drew's Skill and Prowess.

Patsey McQuilken who has lived in the territory for years, speaking yesterday of the steer-tying contest said:

"Why, I knew that Doc Goodin would have to get a hump on himself if he beat Ed. Drew. That Ed. Drew is without doubt the greatest expert in the world--I saw him get away with a fellow about twelve years ago at the Hooker ranch in the Sulphur Springs valley who pulled a Winchester and threw it down on him intending to kill him.

"Ed was on horse back and didn't have a gun, but he got down his rope and whiz it went around the neck of the fellow with the Winchester, at the same time put spurs to his horse and went the fellow over the limb of a tree and there would have been a coroner's inquest and all that sort of thing if it hadn't been for Billy Whalen or Dan Ming I don't know which."—Republican

As a teenager, Ed Drew had an early view of violent death being the first to discover the remains of Bud Philpot after his murderers had fled. Drew's renowned steer-tying skills are credited as having saved his life in the above account. Arizona Weekly Journal Miner, April 18, 1894.

The Steer Tying Contest.

A large crowd witnessed the cowboy contest between Doc Goodin, the local expert, and Ed. Drew, the famous Sulphur Springs valley vaquero, last Sunday. A unique street parade, headed by a band of music, stimulated the attendance. Each man tied four steers, Goodin entering the arena first. His time was 1:29½, 1:45 and 1:17; average, 1:23⅔. Drew's time was 1:16, 1:04, and 0.46; average, 1:02. Drew's time in the last trial was materially lessened by the wonderful training and intelligence of his horse. Drew is now the champion of the territory, though his time was beaten last year by Goodin, who made a record of thirty-eight seconds.

In the bronco riding contest Goodin won, though the horses were too slow to arouse a great deal of interest.—Republican.

Ed Drew is referred to as the "Sulphur Springs Vaquero" and also the "Champion of the Territory." Arizona Weekly Citizen, April 14, 1894.

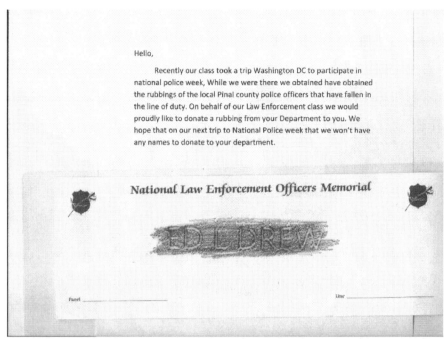

Hello,

Recently our class took a trip Washington DC to participate in national police week, While we were there we obtained have obtained the rubbings of the local Pinal county police officers that have fallen in the line of duty. On behalf of our Law Enforcement class we would proudly like to donate a rubbing from your Department to you. We hope that on our next trip to National Police week that we won't have any names to donate to your department.

National Law Enforcement Officers Memorial

ED L DREW

The above rubbing in the name of Ed L. [Landers] Drew is from the National Law Enforcement Officers Memorial located in Washington D.C. It was presented to the Drew family, who graciously sent me a copy of it. The Drew family of today has done much to preserve the remarkable history of their family's predecessors, and they are to be commended for this. Courtesy of the Drew Family Archive.

The final resting place of Edward Landers Drew, courtesy of the Drew Family Archive.

Last night, between 7 and 8 o'clock, the house of Mrs. Drew, widow of Edward Drew, on Ninth street between Bruce and Fulton, caught fire in the kitchen and was rapidly in flames, illuminating the whole of the northern portion of the town. The Rescue Hose Co. was quickly on the spot, although too late to save the building, which is a total loss. Considerable furniture was saved. David McFawn and family were also inhabiting the house, having moved in only four days ago.

A source of confusion for some is that there was another Drew family in the Tombstone area in the 1880's. Making matters more complicated, this family had an "Ed," aka, "Edwin" as one of their number. The Ed Drew who resided in Tombstone is clearly not from the family of Drew's Station fame, and he died in 1885, years before the tragic shooting death of Ed Landers Drew, who had once lived as a teenager at Drew's Station. Daily Tombstone Epitaph, February 5, 1886.

WEEKLY CHAMPION.

SATURDAY, DECEMBER 1.

M. Abernethy has returned to Hackberry.

John M. Miller left for the Needles to-day on a business trip.

D. P. Kimball, Mormon bishop, died on the San Pedro, A. T., on the 20th ult.

The last entry above notes that D.P. Kimball, Mormon bishop, has died. Kimball had once partnered with John Hill on the old Mason Ranch. Kimball was one of a number of Mormons who came to settle north of Contention City as the first wave of pioneering settlers moved on. Arizona Weekly Champion, December 1, 1883.

BENSON, Nov. 21.—D. P. Kimball, Mormon bishop of St. Davids on the San Pedro, Cachise county, died last night of typhoid pneumonia.

Arizona Weekly Citizen, November 24, 1883.

As will be seen in our news column, D. P. Kimball, Mormon bishop of St. Davids, Cochise county died at the Mormon settlement on the San Pedro, on the 20th, of pneumonia. Bishop Kimball was not only spiritual adviser of the Mormon settlement at St. Davids, but he was their business manager as well. While the strong young men were at home, working on ranches, the bishop, was often away looking after the interests of the Mormon settlement. He attended to having homestead and pre-emption papers properly made out, to paying the taxes or any other business of the community that required his attention. This we believe is a part of the duties of a Mormon bishop; at least Bishop Kimball made himself useful in this way.

Showing the prominence of early Mormon settlers in the Arizona Territory, D.P. Kimball is remembered at his passing. Arizona Weekly Citizen, November 24, 1883.

Stray Mule.

THERE HAS BEEN TAKEN UP BY undersigned, living on the San Pedro, five miles below Charleston, one brown mule about twelve years old branded with L on left side of the neck and 2 Spanish brands on the left thigh. Apply to

D. T. SMITH.

When the testimony of T.S. Harris turned to a missing mule, he stated that D.T. "Smith got hold of a mule that belonged to me and we had some little trouble and I went there and took the mule away from him...he invited me to have a water melon with him." The astray notice above shows Smith as willing to return lost stock to its owner. Arizona Citizen, August 15, 1879.

C. E. Alvord, justice fees.....	117 00
W. D. Shearer, folio work...	33 30
S. Hills, cartage............	3 50
Huachuca Water Company, water	78 35
Macneil & Moore, county hospital supplies...........	262 32
E. Clifford, road mending...	56 00

The last entry above notes a $56.00 payment to E. [Elijah] Clifford, who was to become the third owner of Drew's Station. Daily Tombstone, October 7, 1886.

Precinct No. 8, McDonald's—E. Clifford, inspector; Marion Somers, A. B. Wild, judges. Polling place, John Hill's house.

Drew's Station owner Elijah Clifford acts as election judge in the McDonalds precinct, one of the names that became popular in the late 1880's to describe the area just north of Contention City that William Drew had called home prior to his death. Note that neighbors Andrew Wild and John Hill are also noted. Tombstone Daily Prospector, October 11, 1890.

Republican County Central Committee.

Pursuant to call, the Republican County Central Committee will meet at the Court House to-night at 8 p. m. A full attendance is almost assured, as most of the delegates had arrived at noon to-day. The following is a list of the members:

Tombstone—First ward, A. Walker, T. McCafferty; second ward, G. J. Myers, George Meek; third ward, T. Allison, G. W. Nichols; fourth ward, W. Constable, John Prenderville.

Bisbee—L. Williams, R. P. Stewart. Wilcox—J. A. Bright, Max Mayer. Benson—W. Shilliam, H. Gerwein. Clarksburg—R. J. Trezona. Dos Cabezas—T. C. Bain. Fairbanks—E. W. Perkins. Huachuca—A. H. Emanuel, Ch'm'n St. David—E. Clifford.

At the final entry above, Elijah Clifford is noted as living at St. David, yet another designation for the old Drew's Station and nearby lands to the north. Tombstone Daily Prospector, July 26, 1890.

AND STILL ANOTHER !

An Old Man Murdered near St. Davids.

After the EPITAPH went to press last evening, word was brought from Contention of the murder of an old man who lived across the San Pedro, opposite St. Davids, the Mormon settlement about six or seven miles below Contention. The name of the man was McMenomy. He owned a sheep ranch, upon which he was living alone at the time of his death. He was shot through the head and must have died instantly. It was supposed that he had money, and robbery was the probable cause of the damnable deed. Justice Smith, of Benson, was notified of the murder and proceeded to the spot to hold an inquest, the result of which has not been learned.

News of the McMenomy murder is reported at a time when the San Pedro River Valley is reeling from the shock of the M.R. Peel assassination at Millville, and other killings related to the Earp Vendetta. Tombstone Epitaph April 3, 1882.

T<small>HE</small> Board of Supervisors of Cochise county have authorized Sheriff Behan to offer a reward of $500 for the capture of the murderer of M. R. Peel and a similar reward for the murderers of old man McMenomy.

The Cochise County Board of Supervisors responds to the murders of M.R. Peel as well as "old man McMenomy." Although these murders took place during the same period of upheaval in the area, they were unrelated tragedies. Arizona Weekly Citizen, April 16, 1892.

The Hill vs. Herrick case was noted for the aggressive questioning by Attorney Goodrich. Though court records do not name whether this was Briggs or Ben Goodrich, one of the two attorneys from Goodrich and Goodrich did participate in the Hill vs. Herrick case. The above original 1884 Goodrich and Goodrich cover from the collections of John D. Rose.

No. 199   Tombstone, A. T., Jan'y 25 1883

I, J. H. BEHAN, *Ex-Sheriff and ex-officio Tax-Collector of the County of Cochise, Territory of Arizona, do hereby certify, that by virtue of an Act entitled "An Act Amendatory to Chapter XXXIII of Compiled Laws of Arizona Territory, to provide revenue for the Territory of Arizona, and the several counties thereof, approved April 12th, 1875," approved March 10th, 1881, I have this day sold for taxes to* Territory of Arizona *for the sum of* 19,91 DOLLARS. *the following described property:* From 40 to 50 Head Cattle 500 2 Horses 30 Ranch and Imps Dragoon Mts.

Said property was assessed to Goodrich & Goodrich *on the Assessment Roll of Cochise County, A. T., for the year 1882, in the sum of* $ 2.30 *, the taxes and costs on which amount to* $ 19,91

And the said property is subject to redemption in six months, pursuant to the Statute in such cases made and provided; and that the said Territory of Arizona *is entitled to a deed for said property on the* 25 *day of* July *, 1883.*

J H Behan

Ex-Sheriff and Ex-officio Tax-Collector Cochise County, A. T.

199

In 1883, Goodrich and Goodrich are assessed $19.91 by John Behan after he left the Sheriff's office. Courtesy of Kevin Pyles, Cochise County Archives.

126

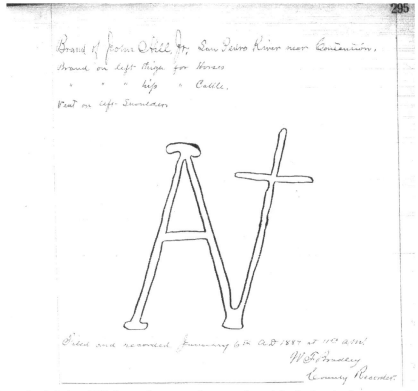

Brand of John Hill Jr., who was integral to his father's farms before leaving the area in 1894. Brand Book 1, page 295. Courtesy of Christine Rhodes, Cochise County Recorder's office.

Miss Rose Hill, daughter of John Hill, of St. David, was Wednesday married to John Haynes of the same place. Justice A. O. Wallace, of Tombstone, officiated. The ceremony was performed at the residence of the bride's parents, a number of guests being present, and a sumptous banquet was a feature of the occasion.

John Hill's daughter, Rose, gets married in the above account. The ceremony took place at Hill's home, which was the former ranch of Robert Mason. Arizona Weekly Citizen, November 5, 1882.

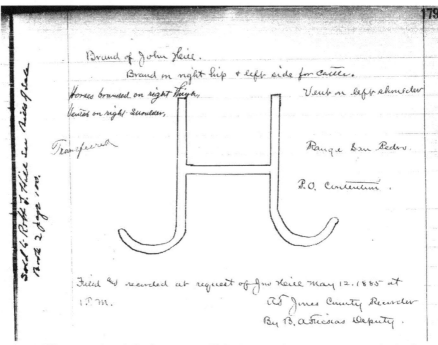

John Hill's Brand, while he was still living at the Mason Ranch, before moving to the north. Brand Book 1, page 179. Courtesy Cochise County Recorder's office.

> The long talked of race between the Parks mare and the John Hill mare from the San Pedro has at last been matched and will be run on the Solomonville race track in the near future. Mr. Parks received a latter from Mr. Hill yesterday stating that he would leave for Solomonville on the 10th, with the mare. The race is matched for $500 a side and will be run for blood.

John Hill's race horse and a $500.00 prize at stake are noted in the account above. Arizona Weekly Citizen, March 22, 1890.

GRAND JURY.

John Montgomery, Thos. Dunbar, Paul Bahn, T. F. Hudson, F. Herrera, T. S. Harris, John Hill, Sr., Chas. Overlock, F. C. Ealy, N. Noble, H. Gerwin, T. K Anderson, Calvin Reed, John Sullivan, F. W. Frame.

John Hill serves on a Grand Jury that includes John Montgomery of the O.K Corral, Fred Herrera of Charleston, among others. Tombstone Epitaph, October 29, 1887.

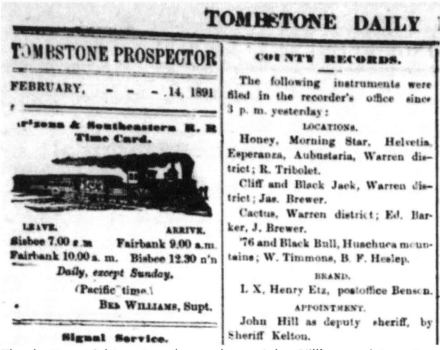

The bottom right entry above shows John Hill's appointment as Deputy Sheriff. Tombstone Daily Prospector, February 14, 1891.

> Mr. C. Lind is in town again from Contention City, and informs us that his firm (Malter & Lind) have commenced grading for the new Sunset mill, which will be erected about a quarter of a mile below the Contention. It is to have 10 stamps, with a capacity for 15, and the reputation of the builders is a guarantee that it will be a good one. It will probably be finished sometime in October. The Boston mill is somewhat delayed by the scarcity of lumber, but Mr. Lind thinks that by September it will be ready for business. Malter & Lind have also taken a contract to build a 10-stamp dry crushing mill in New Mexico, not far from Silver City.

Malter & Lind have begun grading for the construction of the Sunset Mill which will later be sold to the Head Centre Mining Co. Weekly Arizona Citizen, July 10, 1880.

> Frank C. Perley and Joe McCabe, who have been prospecting for several weeks in the Dragoons, returned to Bisbee yesterday.

Frank C. Perley testified in Hill vs. Herrick and was active in prospecting as well. Tombstone Epitaph, June 21, 1896.

130

George Hearst gained control of the the San Juan de Boquillas y Nogales Land Grant, on which Drew's Station, Contention City and many other sites were located. From the collections of John D. Rose.

CHAPTER 6

BEAVERS AND FISTIFCUFFS.
"No, I knocked him down with my fist."-H.C. Herrick

Tombstone O.K. Corral owner John Montgomery had witnessed the water situation at Herrick's, but was called to testify on behalf of John Hill. "At the time we were there I think there was no water running in Herrick's ditch there on the ranch, but there had been a short time before that. They flooded down there to the Chinaman's [Hop Kee]...at one place where there had been a large quantity...quite a quantity of water had been over it [the headgate] and it was muddy and wet." Montgomery added that Herrick claimed the flooding was "caused by the Chinaman running...water over..." Col. Herring pressed Montgomery, asking him if he recalled a conversation that had taken place involving both Herring and Montgomery, as well as Bob Hatch and E.B. Gage. The point of the conversation was whether or not Herrick had indeed begun to develop his place in 1880, in order to prove that his claim to water use predated that of John Hill. Montgomery would only note that he had such an impression that this had been discussed. [72]

H.C. Herrick found himself in the middle of a storm. He and several of his neighbors were at the center of a substantial disagreement over water use, and this dispute would spread to his north and far to his south, involving many whom he likely had never met or heard of, and the same was likely true for them as well. It can be argued that he may not have helped himself in many areas prior to the suit, and being unpopular with so many around him was not an asset, even if lack of personal popularity wasn't considered actionable grounds. Both Hill and Herrick had many friends and acquaintances who testified on their behalf, but several who had worked for Herrick were more than happy to testify against him and on behalf of Hill.

Herrick testified that he first met Jacob Landis on his ranch in November of 1879 about a mile above where the Babacomari drains into the San Pedro, near where Fairbank was later to be built. "He proposed to sell out to me as administrator certain land and a certain water right of his for a certain consideration...He represented to me that he was the owner of a right to 1200 inches of water and which he proposed to sell to me one-half interest in the same...After proper examination I accepted his proposition for sale...We then counseled together as to the proper mode of working together...proceeded and arranged...It was necessary to, have a new flume across the river, the old one having washed out...that I should purchase and bring there the lumber and he would put up the flume and do the work about the ditch, getting the water across the river again...It was necessary because the waters of the main ditch were out on the east side of the river and at that time I deemed it advisable to commence operations on the west side...the land lying on both sides of the river...I went to the Chiricahua mountains and got the lumber and returned with it in January."

A man named Tamblin owned the ranch which Herrick took possession of. Tamblin was staying with Landis and died in his home. Landis "...administered for the estate and got the right from the Probate Court to sell it." So the sale of Tamblin's ranch to Herrick was brokered through Landis. [73]

Herrick's testimony referenced an Italian who had worked for him previously. "An Italian, whose name I could not now speak, and don't now remember, came to me and proposed to rent...after considerable talk we entered into an arrangement by which he was to improve a portion of the ranch...I made a bargain with him based on the fact that I had all I could do and more, that he should go on there and continue a certain ditch which Mr. Landis had already, and which I acquired the right to in my bargain with Mr. Landis..." This Italian may have been a Navoni or a Rossi who both rented land from Herrick on the east side of the river. A short time later, Paul De Martini bought two of the Italians' shares and moved onto the Herrick ranch.

After Herrick bought from Landis, the latter still retained his own 160 acres north of Herrick, and did not sell that to Hop Kee until 1880. This sale would lead Herrick to feel insecure about the verbal agreements he had with Landis about the use of the ditches running across Landis' property. "...Mr. Landis and I agreed that it would be necessary for the proper cultivation of both his ranch and the Italian ranch..." "The ranch which you now occupy?" "Yes sir, that there should be four ditches...two ditches on each side of the river." Herrick was afraid that after Landis left, the Chinaman to whom he sold out (Hop Kee) would not honor that agreement and would cut off water to Herrick's place.

"It was my opinion...that I must secure the rights across his ranch, which he conceded and gave me verbally in the first place...I didn't think I needed [it in] writing with Mr. Landis. Then I went to work and we did these next deeper ditches we made, and he sold out to Hop Kee and talked of going to Mexico, and it occurred to me that sometime I might have trouble about the water and ditches and wrote this little memorandum, but he told me he had already transferred to Hop Kee but had spoken to him about it, and to insure the thing [water access across the land in question] from getting into any difficulty I got them to sign it." Herrick's fears were not unfounded, as he would have trouble with Hop Kee over water flow through these ditches.

AVOID THE SAN PEDRO AT NIGHT

Herrick had a curious habit for one who lived on the river. "I lived on the ranch but kept away from it nights as much as possible all the time through 1881 and 1882, under the theory that I got from the physician, and also got it second hand from other physicians, that a man that had been stricken with biliousness as I had should not be on the river at night, and I stayed away as much as possible at night but conducted the operations during the day time myself with hired men."

In 1884, Herrick raised a crop of oats and alfalfa. "Did you sell any grain or alfalfa that year?" "Yes sir...I sold some to Mr. Blinn; I think I sold him ten tons of oats." Herrick is likely referring to L.W. Blinn who had a lumber yard in Tombstone. Blinn also owned lumber wagons and teams, for which he would have needed the grain. [74]

Herrick was also pressed regarding the roadway that ran through his property which he had fenced off. "That road is there for the purpose it was ever used for at all. It is a private road of mine." When he was asked "Wasn't that road publicly travelled up to 1884," he replied, "That was never a public road." But when he was asked "Was it publicly travelled?" he chose his words more carefully saying, "Not generally travelled." Pressing the point he was asked again, "Was it publicly travelled?" and Herrick responded weakly that "It is travelled as all over the country is travelled...I can simplify this business by saying there was an old road that come along where Fairbanks is now and crossed what would be now pretty nearly the railroad bridge and came down to the river, and had a crossing there."

If Herrick thought his response would end the matter, he was wrong. "Didn't anybody and everybody travel it up to the time that you fenced in the land north of it and up to the railroad?" Now Herrick completely reversed himself saying, "Yes sir, it was free to travel on till it was fenced in....About 1885 or 1886..." Such testimony may have testified to the possibility that at times, Herrick could be his own worst enemy. Many ranchers and farmers had roadways going across their properties, which were accessed by area residents.

William Drew allowed such crossing and saw a way to make money at it as well. Having the right to do something doesn't always constitute the best of ideas, a concept clearly lost on H.C. Herrick. But it appears Herrick blocked off his roadway to prevent damage to his ditches by the cattle of another area rancher, Bertolomeo Avancino, who also used the road to transport vegetables weekly to local towns.

At this point, Colonel Herring informed the court that Herrick was unable to continue his testimony due to a "sick headache and did not feel himself able to continue" so his testimony was temporarily suspended. But he'd soon be back in the witness chair, and dams and ditches would turn to beavers.

THE BEAVER MADE ME DO IT

Reports of the San Pedro having beaver dams in many places are proven, and Herrick also offered an explanation as to why they left the area. It wasn't by choice. "Well, like Smith with the Mexicans I run off the beavers." The subject of San Pedro River beavers came to dog Herrick in the questioning that followed. In attempting to justify his water use, he dismissed a portion of the impact of this use saying "...I took it from the beaver dam which was nearer and much more convenient and would actually require less water because I would not have a half a mile of dry ditch to irrigate before getting the water on my land...To come right to the point there was only a small bit of land irrigated from that beaver dam, compared with the rest...like [D.T.] Smith with the Mexicans I run off the beavers."

Judge Lovell seemed less than impressed. "Well, you ousted the beavers in 1885?" Herrick replied, "I think the high water of last year took them off; I haven't seen them this year. There is no dam now to carry water in the ditches." "Didn't you get brush and make that dam before you ever heard of the beavers?" the Judge continued. "No," said Herrick, "the first work I did was to cut the dam down." "Didn't you get that brush yourself...And make that dam before there was any sign of a beaver?" Herrick denied Judge Lovell's accusation. "No sir, I did not. I swear positively that I did not." "In the winter of 1884...You commenced then cutting brush, didn't you?" Herrick's strategy of "blame the beaver" was clearly not holding sway with the judge, but he showed no signs of dropping the ill-fated approach. "I don't think I ever put a brush there till 1885. During the first season I used that dam at all [,] I had several times during the season to go and tear the top of it off because the bevaers [sic] in a week or maybe in two or three nights, would back it up so it would flow over the banks and into the ditches and do me a damage. That was the first inception of the dam…I am not positive whether 1884 or 1885 I noticed that state of things."

"Of course the beavers had been doing damage?" the Judge asked. "No, I prevented their doing the damage," by stating outright that he was dismantling the beavers' work. Judge Lovell pressed, "When did you first conclude to put a little dam in there yourself in aid of what the beavers had done?…Didn't you in the winter of 1884 put a dam there?" "The [beaver] dam was there in 1884." Lovell continued, "When did you first commence repairing the defective work of the beavers?" "I think [it] quite probable that I put a little hay in there in 1885, but I aint sure of that." Yet, Herrick reiterated that he had torn the beaver dam down to prevent it from doing more harm.

"Now how is it that after that you commenced building it up again?" "Because I thought it was convenient to use it, instead of using the ditch above." The Judge was approaching sarcasm when he asked, "You had changed your opinion about the beavers?" "No," Herrick said.

Now the Judge pursued Herrick who had backed himself into a corner. Taking Herrick's ploy to its logical conclusion, Lovell asked "You found you had made a mistake by destroying the work they had done?" "No," Herrick replied, "I still kept them in subjection and made them useful."

At this point the Judge may have been having fun. "Oh, you supplemented their work?" Herrick's remarkable response implied the powers of an old west version of Doctor Doolittle. "Made some suggestions," was his answer. "And put in an addition?" "Yes sir," he told the court, "To the ditches, yes sir." This line continued on until Judge Lovell asked, "You made the dam a great deal stronger and better than the beavers had, didn't you?" Herrick said, "That is a matter of opinion." "You undertook to make it more perfect…than it was. You hauled brush and straw and supplemented the efforts of your predecessors [the beaver, who apparently were unable to testify]?" Herrick answered "Yes sir, you may have it that way. I repaired it, yes sir." This was a pathetic attempt to disavow ownership of the extra dam he had built, and the water that it blocked from others downstream, especially since he put it into operation at such a late date (1884 or '85).

The back and forth over Herrick and his dam building colleagues continued. Herrick insisted he did not try to block all the water flowing through, only enough to fill one of his ditches. But his credibility must have been shaken by now. That the court didn't believe Herrick is further borne out by the fact that no additional injunctions against dam building were issued by the court against any San Pedro River beavers.

John H. Martin was in demand in the area as a laborer, and was also hired by defendant H.C. Herrick to take care of some dam problems. He was impressed by its builder's skill, noteworthy praise from a man who had worked on the dam at Contention many times. "I was sent there by Mr. Herrick. I had been to work for him in the hay field, and I was sent there to tear down the beaver dam that was being built up in the night time. The beavers would get sticks and build the dam up and get mud from the bottom of the river and pile it up as nice as a man could do it with a trowel, and it would raise the dam and the water would run out through two cuts and flood his crop on each side of the river and he had to watch to keep the water from running out and flooding the crop." "Did you tear it down?" "Yes sir, I did that several times." Perhaps the suit should have been named "Hill and Herrick vs. the Beaver." [75]

THE CASE OF THE STOLEN POTATOES

If the case of the "beaver made me do it" wasn't enough, questions soon arose regarding Herrick taking potatoes from Hop Kee. As Herrick suspected might happen, there were times when Hop Kee, just above Herrick on Landis' old place, would direct all the water into his ditches and not let any down to Herrick's land. So Herrick felt the need to deliver some retribution, in the form of taking Kee's potatoes. Typically, he denied it, only to contradict himself later. He even went so far as to deny that there was previous testimony in that very same case confirming his thefts. "I think counsel overstates the testimony." Goodrich pursued. "I say as I remember. How many times did you take half a sack of potatoes to get even with the Chinamen [Herrick's co-defendant Hop Kee]…" Still working the lie Herrick obfuscated, saying, "I don't think the witness meant to testify that I did take any potatoes…No it is a fact that I never did…I have done it on one occasion…Well, now that potato business was simply y[t]his…Occasionally I was bothered and would have to, go, up there and see about the water and the Chinaman would have all the water in the ditch, and there would be plenty of water in the ditch but he had it all and I went after him with a shovel once but couldn't hardly get…to him. There was plenty of water in the ditch and the river but they unlawfully opened the ditch and took the whole of it out. I told them I should charge them a dollar every time I come up there and found him taking my water…In 1880." Goodrich followed asking, "Wasn't it in 1885 when you went after him with a shovel?"

Herrick corrected him saying "No, I knocked him down with my fist." "For what?" Goodrich asked. "Because he shut my gate down…Four or five or six times, maybe." Goodrich pursued the potato count. "And you absolutely took potatoes every time?" "No," Herrick said. "I went there and told him I would charge him one dollar every time I had to come up there when my gate was shut down…About five or six Chinaman came down and argued with me, and I took out twenty pounds of potatoes…Once, and put them in

139

their sack and carried them home…I took one dollars worth I thought." Herrick not only stole Hop Kee's twenty pounds of potatoes, but the sack in which he carried them home as well.

Goodrich kept following the rich vein that was the testimony of H.C. Herrick. "And on any other occasion?" "On no other occasion," Herrick stated. "They got sick of that, and after that Ho[p] Kee told me 'Boy, damned fool; I tell him to go and open gate.' This was a warning they seemed to understand," Herrick continued, "better than any talk I had had with them."

"How many did you knock down at that time?" asked Goodrich. "Not any that time. My irrigator went up three times to see what was the matter with the water and they had it every time…three times in one day…and I told him if they didn't quit I would stop it and after I got up there I walked up to where the Chinaman was and knocked him down." Goodrich asked "Was that Hop Kee?" "No," said Herrick, "the hired man. He was irrigating, and Hop Kee says, 'Boy damned fool, he send him away.'"

After successfully proving Herrick did steal Hop Kee's potatoes after all, he now pursued motive, a key in understanding any such caper. "This potato business was initiated by you for the purpose of disciplining these Chinamen?" "That was all," Herrick told attorney Goodrich, "yes sir; that was all." Now Mr. Smith took up where Goodrich left off.

"Can you explain why the Chinaman or his boy was just wantonly taking more water than they needed?" With his trademark humility, Herrick responded saying, "Because they lacked the discipline which I afterwards gave them." [76]

Although Herrick's testimony was unique in its incidents of potato theft and fisticuffs, and his close work with his dam building colleagues the beaver, it did bring into focus why the suit began in the first place. It drew a picture of a self-absorbed individual full of arrogance and swagger, a bully who cared little about those around him, or how his actions could adversely affect those who lived nearby whom he could have, if open to the idea, befriended. As with many parts of the American West, Chinese in Tombstone were apt to suffer intermittent waves of racism, but in Herrick's case, the questioning related to his assaulting Hop Kee did not appear to go over well with the court, showing greater contempt for Herrick as the bully he was and perhaps even a bit of sympathy for his victim, who hailed from the land far away.

In this 1886 assessment roll, H.C. Herrick appears at the top of the page. Below Herrick is H.J. Horne, the current owner of Drew's Station. Listed below Horne are John Hill Sr., John Hill Jr. and his brother F.M. Hill. 1886 Assessment Roll, Book 1, page 139. Courtesy of Kevin Pyles, Cochise County Archives, Bisbee, Arizona.

CHAPTER 7

HOP KEE ENTERS THE SAN PEDRO STORY

"That boy, he no sabe; he want more water he go out to the gate..."- Hop Kee.

Hop Kee arrived on the San Pedro "about 1880" as he later recalled, perhaps in the month of March. He and his partner Wong Fung bought a ranch site with a home on it from Mr. Landis, and he later bought out Wong Fung's share, "about 1882" as he noted. When he purchased, it already contained about thirty five acres under cultivation—30 acres on the east side of the river, and about five on the west side–and he quickly set about increasing that number. Landis was raising barley, vegetables and alfalfa, and Hop Kee added fruit trees and some corn. Disputes between Kee and Herrick would soon arise over water from the same ditch, leading Herrick to add another ditch. According to Hop, Herrick said that "He say my boy take all his water...That boy, he no sabe; he want more water he go out to the gate...Mr. Herrick come and make trouble for him."

In 1880 Hop had up to five acres of potatoes in production, and by 1884 he had an estimated 15 to twenty acres, the same potatoes that Herrick enjoyed in payback when he felt Kee had used too much water. The testimony became a bit clouded by lack of communication. "What do you call vegetables; what do you mean by vegetables?" Hop answered, "All the same, some turnip, beet, carrot, corn and water melons." A surprised Col. Herring asked, "You don't call potatoes vegetables?" Puzzled by the line of questioning, Hop simply said "I don't know." Herring pursued, "You saw [say] you have got two or three acres in vegetables, now does that mean potatoes?" "No," Hop replied, "That is beside potatoes."

When Herring asked how many acres he had in vegetables, Hop estimated twenty acres, with some corn and cabbages. "Isn't that a pretty high estimate...a pretty high number of acres?" Hop responded saying "I don't understand." Herring continued to pepper him with questions of little relevance, asking him more than once how many feet were in a rod, and "How many acres have you got in orchard?" Hop's succinct reply was "Don't know orchard."

"How big is an acre?" Herring asked. "About a hundred and sixty rods make an acre," Hop noted. "You are sure of that?" asked Herring. "Yes," Hop answered, "somebody tell me, I don't know that." "Who told you?" demanded Herring. "Well somebody" replied Hop. It wasn't enough for Herring, who kept badgering the witness. "Who?" Perhaps hoping that if the source were not Chinese, Herring might drop that matter, Hop said "A white man." [77] (Hop was correct, 160 square rods are in an acre. Col. Herring as he preferred to be called was known for aggressive pursuit of witnesses at times in questioning, but his treatment of Hop Kee seems unusual, considering transcripts from the rest of the case. He may have had strong emotions toward Chinese. If so, he was not alone in this, and the history of the San Pedro River Valley along with so many other parts of the west is replete with examples of some who demonstrated strong anti-Chinese sentiments.)

John Martin was also acquainted with Herrick's fellow defendant, Hop Kee, noting that his land had "barley in there and corn, vegetables of all kind[s]—quite a nice little patch, when I came there…I should ju[d]ge there was about eight or ten acres on the west side of the river near Hop Kee's house and about, as near as I can remember, twenty acres on the east side of the river…may more or less; it might vary a little one way or the another…" "I should judge from eight to ten acres on the west side, maybe, and from twenty to thirty acres on the east side…They had barley and other crops in of all kinds, corn and potatoes." Martin also seemed to stay busy working for farmers and ranchers along the San Pedro, keeping the irrigation that was the lifeblood of their enterprises flowing. "I was putting in flume ditches for Mr. Kemble when I come up on this case. I have been for over three years making levees and putting in flumes…I irrigated in 1882 at Kembles…I had Kemble's place leased…I helped put in ditches and dam flumes to convey the water all over his ranch."

Judge Barnes' decision in the railroad condemnation suits for right of way for the Bisbee railroad was received by Clerk Daily on Wednesday last. The following are the damages awarded to settlers along the line: H. C. Herrick, $600; Bartellan Avincio, $100; Hop Kee, $25; Noyes Brothers, $800; H. M. Christensen, $260; Gaudalupe Acosta, $95; Peter Haviland, $150; Kirk Brothers, $100; C. Harrington, $100; Stock Gardeon, $750; H. W. Hasselgren, $200.

Hop Kee and others appear in the August 4, 1888, Tombstone Epitaph regarding a decision by Judge Barnes one year before Hill vs. Herrick case.

Mr. Bagg's paper sympathizes with Hop Kee, who receives only $25 for damages to his crop by reason of the railroad passing over his land. As "Poor Hop" only asked for $35, the sympathy seems to be misplaced. And by the way, it is a peculiar attitude for Mr. Bagg to be placed in, that of having a tender feeling for a Chinaman.

Hop Kee is further discussed in the Tombstone Epitaph, August 4, 1888.

LOOAL HAPPENINGS

From Tuesday's Daily.

The old year goes out tomorrow. Good bye, old sun.

Another Skating Carnival is talked of and will be duly announced.

Wang Tie was the gentleman's name who was pulled for smoking opium and not Hop Kee.

Hop Kee was wrongly reported to have been arrested for smoking opium. Tombstone Epitaph, January 4, 1891.

Notice to Creditors.

Public notice is hereby given to all persons having claims against the estate of Hop Kee deceased, to present the same duly verified with the necessary vouchers to the undersigned at the office of Allen R. English 113 Fourth street, in the city of Tombstone, Arizona, within four months after the first publication of this notice.

WONG COK,

Administrator of the estate of Hop Kee, eccased

Dated October 19th 1893.

Notice of Hop Kee's estate being settled appears in the Tombstone Epitaph, October 22, 1893.

Wong Fook has applied for letters of administration on the estate of Hop Kee, deceased.

Arizona Weekly Citizen, November 24, 1893.

Duplicate Assessment Roll, Cochise County

NAMES TAXPAYERS	DESCRIPTION				No. of Acres	3		VALUE OF REAL ESTATE	VALUE IMPROVEMENTS GENERAL ESTATE	TOTAL
Hop Kee 485	*San Pedro River Ranch near Fairbanks* 2 Horses 2 Mules 1 Wagon Harness Tools &c								500	500
Herrick H.C. 486	*San Pedro River Ranch & Imp. Near Fairbank* 12 Horses 6 Grifted Mules 6 Cows 4 Wagons 3 Harness								700	700

In 1889, the year of the Hill vs. Herrick suit, Hop Kee and neighbor H.C. Herrick reside without controversy on this tax roll, but not so along the San Pedro. 1889 Duplicate Assessment Roll. Courtesy of Kevin Pyles, Cochise County Archives.

John Martin's labors would help document key historic sites that are now in ruins along the San Pedro River. He would also gain employment from Mr. Lind, of Malter & Lind, whose construction business advanced the progress of stamp mills along the San Pedro. [78] When recalling Charles Lynn's many projects Martin added, "He was grading and putting up what was then known as the Sunset mill and the Grand Central Mill and putting up the machinery in the Boston Mill." A benefit of working for Lynn was the recreational use of his team. "The boys would go up hunting every once in awhile— the town boys would hitch up Mr. Lynn's mules and drive all over that country hunting ducks and quail."

By June of 1880, Martin paid a visit to H.C. Herrick, and noted an impressive farming operation underway. "...the size of the ground that fall I was over it—he had a patch of water melons, and I would frequently ride along and get melons to eat, and I should judge there was close to twenty acres...On the west side." He also recalled Herrick's hectic travel going from one enterprise to the other. "He was backwards and forwards. I would see him come down in the morning and plow and hitch up at night and come back towards Tombstone. He had a cattle ranch, I understood, near Tombstone…I passed his place often. I would see him driving down, and at that house there, and part of the time living there. He was plowing all that summer, off and on, till July."

Regarding the all-important witness to the irrigation ditches in the area, Martin added that "The only ditch that I knew positively of on the west side of the river leading on to the Herrick place was the ditch running on down through the Chinaman's field and on to Herrick's place. It was a natural zig-zag."

Martin also noted another Herrick employee. "He had an old man working there for him that summer, stayed there all the time, if I aint mistaken—a German by descent—hoeing in the garden, --Smith by name, and Mr. Herrick was up and down to the cattle ranch above here." Martin personally enjoyed helping himself to Herrick's fresh produce. "Several times I went in there to break off a head of cabbage or to get a cucumber to eat as I was going along there, or a water melon or a musk melon."

John Martin's testimony offers a candid view of one man's time in the Tombstone District, an insight to an industrious, hardworking individual of the kind who is much too often overlooked in favor of gunslingers and stock thieves. He helped build and labor in stamp mills which produced the silver lifeblood of the Tombstone District's economy, and worked tending the irrigation systems and dams that gave families an increased chance to thrive in their new environs. Martin is occasionally not careful in his details, maybe due to his enthusiasm to demonstrate knowledge of the area and its inhabitants, without a firm grip on all the facts. But he shows us a view of the San Pedro River bordered by an extensive system of irrigation ditches, and the garden spots along the river which they created for a brief time, before the area reverted back to its natural state. [79]

THE TESTIMONY OF JACOB LANDIS

"There was no St. Davids, nor anybody in the country then…There was nobody but McMiniman and the Butterfield station." Jacob Landis first set eyes upon the San Pedro in May 1877. "I came out from Tucson by way of the Empire ranch and so on to [Camp] Huachuca, right up around there, and from Huachuca down to Tamblin's [next owned by H.C. Herrick] and Hayes place, about nine miles from the river, and I went down there and stayed there all night, and I think I stopped two days there…Me and this man Samson…we camped two days there and then come on down to Petty's and Kemble's place and stopped there…camped there…and in fact I put some beans and some vegetables there, corn and beans and stuff, and then in a few days while we stopped there I went over to this place of mine that is owned by the Chinaman, and looked around to see what I could find…and I found that there had been a ditch taken out…a man named Brown had located it and taken out the water there very readily…it had been taken…so I went to work and put up a dam and run it out to the slough. The mouth of it was seven or eight feet wide or more and I run it into that and run it probably a couple of hundred yards down the slough and then I carried it from the end of that slough–took my ditch out around. Brown had one running down to the lower line between Mr. Herrick and the Chinaman–he had raised some stuff there, and I went on and turned the water in there and run it down the river over the ground, in 1877…Mr. Samson helped me some. He had a claim below, he had the claim of the Frenchman there, this side of the Grand Central Mill." [meaning to the east of where the Grand Central was later built]

"…Mr. Samson stopped with me sometime and finally he concluded that he didn't want to stay there and I bought his interest out and gave him $100…for it…his right in the ditch and what he had done on it, and he left the country…Mr. O'Leary [another neighbor] left here to go to Tucson, and at the time I asked him about this water business, says I 'What are you going to do with your water privilege here?' He says, 'I will just turn that over to you; I am going away and I have no use for it...' I went to California in 1877 and 1878...and went to San Bernardino and got my seed...I went there with my team, a span of mules and a span of horses and a wagon...I built one house in 1877. I had it all completed and I put on the roof when I came back in the spring."

Landis would recall other early pioneers he would see when traveling up and down the river. "...a long in the fall [1877] I went down towards Tres Alamos, going to Tucson, and I met Mr. Mason, Mr. Claflin and Griffith and Bruener all down there working on the ditch...That was the first I met them. They were not working when I met them; it was noon when I met them...they were camped right there near the mouth of their ditch..." In the fall of 1878 Landis realized in a disconcerting way that the ditch he saw in its formative stages had been completed. "I was hauling a load of freight there one time and right down below Contention there was kind of [a] bend in the ditch there and in coming on it the wagon slid in the ditch...The wagon slid in and of course it went down plumb to the hub in the ditch, and the hub just about struck the other side of the ditch from the side that I went in, and I worked there sometime to get my wagon out of there."

He also recalled that Drew had about three or four acres of corn in 1878, and that another area settler, the "old gentleman named Merrill" stopped by Landis' place on a shopping excursion. "He stopped there and bought some melons of me, him and his lady. They had been up to the Huachuca's and stopped there, and they was going right on home from there." It was a T.C. Merrill who, according to John Hill, sold to Samuel Summers in the spring of 1882. Landis later sold out to Hop Kee and his early partner Wong Fung, and also his water and additional land to Herrick, for whom he was testifying.[80]

Paul De Martini was a Fairbank area resident who lived on the Herrick Ranch, having moved there in 1880. Like many others he had moved around pursuing differing opportunities that the booming valley afforded, and at one point, he was looking for a job. "I landed in Tombstone the fifteenth of June, 1880, and stopped at the Cosmopolitan hotel several days…I was a mining man at that time and I went out to Evan's camp and stayed there a few days…Next I came back to Tombstone and I hunted for a job and I didn't find any and Mr. [S.W.] Wood give me a job to work on the mill at Charleston, in place of a sick man…I worked there about twenty five days…Mr. Wood told me to stay there and he would give me a job, but I thought I could make more money on a ranch and I bought two shares of these Italians. They had a ranch on the Babacomari and rented a piece of land on the river [Herrick's] at the same time…two was Navoni and one was Rossi…"

When he arrived, De Martini described Herrick's ranch as having a little house the other side of the river with a small farm there. Martini bought two interests from the other Italians on Herrick's ranch land on the east side of the river that included a primitive shed made out of willow. In 1880 the former owner had "…built up a kind of a shanty, just enough for a man to sleep in, with brush and weeds, or some willows cut right down there on the sloughs, and in the winter of 1881 we brought some lumber and some other wood from the Babacomari and built kind of a log house, of straight posts and in 1882 I built a little adobe house that is torn down now." Martini busied himself hauling produce to the Tombstone market every other day in the fall of 1880, but only for three months, given the limited production his small place could support. John Martin remembered that De Martini had at least twenty acres of land broken up on the southeast corner of Herrick's lot. [81]

De Martini first saw Herrick possibly in the spring of 1881, "building a wire fence connecting with the fence I had there and across the river on the other side. He [Herrick] was there in the water and he had only a pair of overalls on and I told him the water wasn't very good for a man with the fever. That is the first time I ever saw him…I stayed there four years." Martini mentioned that Herrick had rented a portion of his place to a Chinaman, on the western side of the

San Pedro. (Even though Hop Kee testified to buying the Landis place, it is possible that he also leased land from Herrick, or this could be another Chinaman) He also took note of the dam first constructed by Mason, Cable, and the original partners. "...the dam was built in the river about four or five feet high, built with brush, and the ditch was kind of a bank of sand and gravel and I suppose the sand is there yet, and they cut the ditch through, I think it is over five feet, and they come down to where they had this gate," adding that the water flowed "To a little kind of pond where they had a gate."

Paul De Martini described a primitive home located on Herrick's ranch that was "kind of a log house, of straight posts..." The image above shows a similar structure, though not one from the San Pedro River area. Cropped from the original stereoview from the collections of John D. Rose.

He also noted the changing of a roadway along the San Pedro. "...there was a straight road run to the flat...to the end of this canyon to go down the San Pedro river and there was a straight road across the river there, but Herrick claimed that it was in his land...it was moved; it is not the same road now." De Martini was also asked "Were there any fences at all built on any part of that Herrick tract in 1881, except what you built? In a surprising statement he noted that "I built myself in 1881 the first fence, with my own hands. There was no cattle at that time." [82]

FAIRBANK ITEMS

Interesting Items From the Railroad Town

Fairbank Oct 18, 1901.

Mr P A De Martini accompanied by his wife arrived from San Francisco on the 'flyer' Wednesday, 'Paul's many friends will be pleased to know that his visit will not be a short one, and that he is in excellent health. Mr De Martini is the founder of the big mercantile establishment which now bears his name and in which he still holds an interest. He registered at the Montezuma house.

Paul De Martini arrived in the Tombstone District a mining man in 1880. He stayed on the Herrick Ranch for a time, later finding his real success as a long term Fairbank merchant. Tombstone Epitaph, October 20, 1901.

Mrs. Banks Vaughan arrived on the flyer today from Phoenix. Mrs. V. comes to join her husband here, who has accepted a position with the P. A. De Martini Mercantile Co. of this place.

A new employee of De Martini arrives as his success allows him to delegate more of his daily operations to others. Tombstone Epitaph, January 19, 1902.

It is stated that Mr Paul de Martini has sold an interest in his general merchandise business to Mr. Ben Henny of Tucson, who will soon move to Fairbank and reside there.

Paul De Martini sells an interest in his Fairbank mercantile business at the turn of the century. Tombstone Epitaph, May 6, 1900.

ENTER ANOTHER ITALIAN RANCHER

By the time of the Hill vs. Herrick suit, Bertolomeo Avancino was living at Fairbank. He had lived on the Herrick ranch for a month in 1880. He originally came to the area with another witness in the case, Paul De Martini, and worked for him as he planted cabbages and broke the ten to fifteen acres of ground that they had just designated for planting. He recalled that De Martini and defendant Hop Kee both shared the same ditch, which was already there when they arrived.

"At the time I worked there Mr. Herrick didn't do anything on the ranch at all," he told the court. Following his arrival in Tombstone he was fortunate to run into an old acquaintance. "I didn't come on any stage…After I come to Tombstone…I knew Paul Martini in Virginia, and he come up to Tombstone with a vegetable wagon, and I said to him give me a job, because at that time he owned a place on the Babacomari…I worked in the garden…I helped build a house there myself…Some part of it is [there now] but some part fell off….adobe house, and some tule grass tied up together…I stayed there two months and ten days and after that I come down on the river to the place owned by Mr. Herrick."

He began the new year of 1881 by starting work for Herrick and stayed there six months, quitting that following July. "I come up to Tombstone; I had been sick." After recovering in Tombstone for two weeks, he "went down to Charleston and got a job from Mr. [S.W.] Woods in the mill…I worked there about ten or twelve months. After I quit in there, the first time Gerard [the Girard mill at Tombstone] run it, Mr. Wood have it in charge, and he come up and said 'you want to go to Tombstone? I will give you a job,' and I come up." Avancino worked at the Girard mill from its opening, later returning to his original employer in the area, Paul De Martini, who was still farming on a portion of Herrick's ranch.

After leaving De Martini's employ for a second time, he decided to strike out on his own. "I bought the Babacomari ranch in

July, 1883." But hard luck followed him to his new home. "I stayed there till I was washed out. A big flood come up and washed my ranch out…and nobody could live in there any more."

He would end up once again near former boss H.C. Herrick, and things did not remain friendly between the two for very long. The first issue that arose was over an already existing roadway that Avancino had used as it predated his arrival. Herrick had other ideas. "I was down [along the river] twice a week or three times a week, to run the vegetable wagon to Tombstone." When asked how close the road that he took to go to the Herrick ranch was, he noted that the road had been inside of Herrick's fence, before he moved the fence which blocked access to the roadway. "…After he moved his fence in 1884 he changed my road. Before that the road to the Babacomari passed on his ranch…It passed in the middle of the ranch. And after, he changed it to one side…I was passing outside the fence…about half a mile along-side his fence…"

Herrick may have done this in retribution over Bertolomeo's cattle that were in the area. "…he was kicking all the time because he said my cattle would break his ditch…I said to him, if they break it I will fix it." Herrick wasn't satisfied with that, and "wanted to fence in my land and I told him I would burn his posts if he did, that when I wanted my land fenced I would fence it myself…" Colonel Herring then asked Avancino the obvious. "You didn't have a very good feeling towards each other?" "No." "And you haven't now?" "No," he replied, "not so very much."

Avancino also had seen D.T. Smith and his wife pay a visit to Paul De Martini's ranch when he worked there. "I got acquainted with him the last time I worked for Paul in 1883, I guess, because they come there to the ranch to get some vegetables…him and his wife…and Martini told me that was Smith and his wife." He added that Smith was "…sometimes going to Bisbee with his team." Being in Bisbee on December 8th, 1883, during the horrific moments of the Bisbee Massacre, cost D.T. Smith his life.

The questioning then took the following colorful form between Herring and Avancino concerning another of his neighbors. Q. "You have had some trouble with Crane, haven't you?" A. "I think so." Q. "When did you have any trouble with him?" A. "Last year." Q. "And you haven't had very good feelings towards the Cranes since, have you?" A. "No sir, I am just as good friends with them as I was before. After he branded my calf he tried to steal him and I jumped him and he licked me." Q. "Did he lick you or did you lick him?" A. "He licked me." Q. "And you are just as good friends as ever?" A. "Yes sir, just as well." Q. "This was some trouble about a cow?" A. "He branded my calf." Q. "And he said you branded his calf didn't he?" A. "No sir, I say he branded one of mine." Q. "Wasn't there some trouble about accusing you of killing one of Crane's cows?" A. "No sir, and won['］t be either." Q. "Well, your feeling aint very good towards him?" A. "I feel just as good as before." Q. "You are not his friend?" A. "Yes sir, I am as good [a] friend as I was three or four years ago. I say, Good morning, and that's all, and that is all he says to me." Q. "Do you see him often now?" A. "Well, sometimes. Most generally when I go to town on Sunday I see him." Q. "Well, you haven't had a very good feeling towards the Crane's for sometime, have you?" A. "No sir, he aint just the best friend I got after he licked me." Q. "Well, you didn't think a great deal of him before he whipped you?" A. "Before, I never thought he would do such a thing, and when I saw he licked me I am just as good [a] friend, I say 'By God, I got the worst.'"

By the fall of 1888 Avancino had moved away from the area near the Herrick ranch, taking up residence at Fairbank, and taking his cattle with him. The last time he had been at his old place near Herrick "was last winter after a bucket of water because at the time I moved my cattle away I found three or four jack rabbits had fell in my well and I had to go to his [Herrick's] well for a bucket of water. That was the last time I was on the [Herrick's] ranch." Oddly enough, he somehow felt comfortable walking onto Herrick's ranch to get water, even after all the conflict between the two, and he took further liberties, as the owner may not have been there at the time.

"The last time I was on the ranch was last summer." Colonel Herring may not have believed what he was hearing, and asked "On the ranch?" Avancino's resolute response was, "All over." Though perhaps not tangential to the proceedings, Herring's curiosity may have been peaked. "What were you doing there?" he asked. "Going on to the ranch shooting ducks. That is the time I saw that new dam...In 1886 I worked four or five days for him...Pitching hay...me and my partner both together killed ducks...In 1886..." Avancino would continue to move back and forth between occupations which had made others sick, working in a stamp mill and living along the San Pedro. He wasn't immune either, even if he didn't realize the possible connection.

"In July [1882] in the Girard Mill I was sick and I left there and came to Tombstone and Paul [De Martini] came into Tombstone and I told him I was sick and wanted to go to Huachuca; he said, you come to my place and I'll take you to Huachuca and I stayed there two weeks and then came back to [the] San Pedro river and stayed there." [83] (Bertolomeo Avancino was listed as an Italian-born 24 year old Tombstone mill man in the 1882 Cochise County Great Register.)

A TOMBSTONE SALOON KEEPER TELLS OF THE RIVER AND DITCH

Tombstone resident, saloon keeper and Indian war profiteer, Godfrey Tribolet, testified on behalf of Herrick and Hop Kee, the Noyes brothers and Christianson. He had arrived in Tombstone in March of 1879, and quickly set about making himself and his brothers fixtures on the Tombstone business markets. Tribolet had lived in Charleston, and it was there that he met Noyes for the first time, in April, 1879. The disputed Union ditch once proved quite an obstacle for Tribolet and his horse. "I remember I tried to cross it once and my horse would not go and I had to pull him across and I had to jump across…I couldn't step across…I couldn't get through with the horse."

Tribolet recalled the late D.T. Smith as well. "…he was cultivating, I believe, already in the latter part of 1879. I know he brought some stuff up…I believe he brought up some potatoes and vegetables up there…The man is dead now…He always come and got beef there, for the ranch." He noted his route along the San Pedro when tending stock. "I used to come down that way [toward Charleston] from the Babacomari and then go up the river to Charleston with sheep and cattle." [84] (Godfrey Tribolet was listed as a 33 year old Swiss-born Tombstone brewer in the 1882 Cochise County Great Register.)

V. Kimble also offered testimony that gave further insights to the D.T. Smith ranch. "D.T. Smith was on it first…he was teaming mostly. I think Smith was at Contention when Williams bought the place off him…in 1880 is when Walk Williams went there." But apparently, Williams could not fulfill his contract to buy the ranch, so Smith went back on the place. Following Walk Williams, the Crane brothers bought it and had it at least until the time of Rockfellow's map. V. Kimble may or may not have been related to D.P. Kimble who had moved north to the old McMiniman place and died in 1883.[85]

The Rockfellow map shows in 1899 the exact location of the Crane Brothers Ranch. Coupled with the testimony of V. Kimble, this is a key discovery, proving exactly where the ranch of D.T. Smith was located. Given that Smith died before his time in the Bisbee Massacre, such information that traces his life is rare indeed. Considering Kimble's testimony, although Smith is no longer on his ranch as of 1880, he did take it back and reside upon it before his death. The Crane brothers (Peter and Carter) purchased his place in April of 1884. [86]

Charles Noyes, who owned a ranch a little more than one mile above (south of) Herrick, testified to Herrick's cultivation: "In 1880, Mr. Herrick had a garden below which he told me was two acres."

Mr. Goodrich asked, "When did Mr. Herrick put in any more land?" "He put in the greater portion of his land from 1884 up to last year [1888]...He kept on putting in until he got in what he has now, probably 125 or 145 acres in." [87] According to this testimony, Hill and his neighbors were cultivating more than that on each of their ranches prior to Herrick's expansion in 1884.

GOOD HUNTING ALONG THE SAN PEDRO

Noyes found this part of the San Pedro fine hunting grounds and visited the area often. "I stopped there a short...time and used to go around the hills hunting for deer and then moved up to where I am now living" which was closer to Charleston. He added that near the Kimble ranch was the old Landis place, which was later taken over by Hop Kee. He described it as being on a "neck of land between the river and the slough and at the lower end of the slough he constructed a ditch onto his land." Also in the area was the Martini ranch. "...on that side of the river, the Chinaman [Hop Kee] was irrigating two or three acres and Mr. Herrick had a garden below which he told me was two acres...Mr. Martini had a piece of ground there that I should think had ten acres in it, and on the opposite side of the river the Chinaman had a piece of ground, there may have been five or six or may have been ten acres."

Noyes had a disturbing conversation that may have been an indicator of future legal problems for Herrick. Noyes attempted to dissuade Herrick from pursuing what was clearly a provocation to any ranching farmer downstream. "I advised him to put no dam across the slough, in 1888, when the waste [water] ran back in the river....He said he was going to put it in and he didn't care whether Hill got any water or not. He was going to get all he could...I know before the injunction was put on last year a short time, I was down the river and I saw water running from the upper ditches, and when I got down to the lower ditches I saw both running there, and I had a talk with Mr. Bell, who was working on the ranch there...And he said there was four heads of water running there and nobody went to them in days." Noyes on more than one occasion saw Herrick running three ditches at the same time.

Noyes also told of another San Pedro River settler, Walk Williams, who farmed on the Smith ranch. "...in the winter of 1880 a man named Walk Williams and his partner they put in a dam and took out a ditch I should think three or four hundred yards, and turned the water in the slough" and in the "lower end of the slough they had a dam and took the water to the land...He bonded it to a man named Scott in Charleston and had a mill-site location down below there...High water come and washed out the dam, and that was the last till 1885...In 1885 some farming was done there; a new dam was put in and the old ditch was deepened I should think about four feet and the ditch made all the way." The Crane brothers arrived in 1884 and must have been responsible for the new work done. They planted their first crop in 1885. The man named Scott is possibly W.B. Scott, a pioneering Millville and Charleston merchant-for more on Scott see "Charleston & Millville A.T., Hell on the San Pedro," by John D. Rose.

Unlike some in his area, Noyes' holdings were not growing at the rate of John Hill. "...I don't think our acreage has increased since 1884. We plowed a piece of land that has been cut off from the railroad, this fall, to make up for what the railroad took, that we make wild hay on."

Noyes also knew slain Bisbee Massacre victim D. T. Smith. "...I was pretty well acquainted with him," noting that he was largely engaged in teaming and freighting, owning a four horse team, and whose wife lived part time at the ranch. Noyes also had personal knowledge of the Smith ranch house. "I believe my brother done part of that [house] after he came there. I think there had been a house started...He [Smith] come to live upon his ranch sometime in May... up to the time that he went into the store at Contention, then he was away from his ranch for a long time."

Concerning the Boston Mill ranch, Noyes knew of a Lindsey who cultivated 15 acres of that land. He commenced cultivating it the same year the mill was built. William Bell worked for Lindsey for four days helping him clean out the ditch in January of 1880. "…at the time he [Lindsey] left there he said he had forty acres under cultivation…in 1885." When asked who built the ditch for the Boston Mill, Noyes replied, "Mr. Randolph and Mr. Claflin put it in…Sometime in the summer of 1880." "Did you know where he [Claflin] lived, down near Drew's place?" "Yes sir, I knew that because I first became acquainted with him when he used to be going up to the other place." In 1879, after Claflin helped finish the Union Ditch, he began working on his other place, south along the river in the area of Noyes. Charles Noyes and his brother located on the San Pedro River in 1879, and the Noyes Ranch is identified as a location on John Rockfellow's 1899 map. He did not give a specific location of Claflin's new place, but he testified that Christianson's ranch was located right above (south of) his. Christianson and Noyes shared a ditch. V. Kimble's ranch was located at the confluence of the Babacomari and San Pedro Rivers. Landis' ranch was above Kimble and below Noyes, one mile above Fairbank. (Landis sold to Hop Kee.)

Heading south of Kimble were the ranches of Herrick, Landis, Noyes, Christianson, Crane, the Boston Mill, and somewhere in this vicinity, Claflin. Also in the area before 1879 were a Mr. Brown, Mr. Samson, and Mr. O'Leary. Reasoned speculation follows that because Rockfellow did not locate all of these ranches on his map, the owners had probably moved on by late 1899. There were no ranches between the head of the Union Ditch and the Babacomari at the time of testimony in 1889. The reader should also keep in mind when looking at the Rockfellow map, that testimony indicates that most if not all of the 160 acre parcels encompassed land on both sides of the river. The markings he used for the ranches do not show this. It may be that he placed markings on the stage road at the points where these ranches could be accessed, but this is speculative.

Noyes further revealed that co-defendants Herrick and Hop Kee had their own disputes over the limited water provided by the San Pedro. Kee was located just south of Herrick's ranch. A bit of back and forth and payback in the form of stolen potatoes had taken place. "I know that in 1880 when Mr. Herrick was raising a crop of garden stuff, that him and the Chinaman had fre[q]uent disputes about the water. He told me a number of times that the Chinaman had stopped the water on him...he could not get any water and that he went and dug a sack of their [Hop Kee's] potatoes to get even with him every time he stopped the water." Noyes gives us the impression that Herrick's acquisition of potatoes was more than a one-time steal. "I think he said they were pretty good potatoes." Attorney Col. Herring asked again about the case of the stolen potatoes. "Herrick didn't tell you he carried away those potatoes did he?" "Yes sir," answered Noyes. Seeing the humor in the situation Herring followed up asking "Did he ever give you any of them?" Noyes told Herring "No I don't think he ever favored me with any of them."

Noyes added to the historical record of the San Pedro saying, "There was three-quarters of a mile in the San Pedro river above what we call the narrows ...a cienega and three lakes, formed by what we call three beaver dams and covering about twenty acres...about twenty acres of water...I think the last time I was there [,] there was still water on some of it, but nothing like it used to be..." The narrows canyon is but a short distance north of Charleston and Millville as the San Pedro River travels between the hills and rock formations that flank both the Charleston site as well as the Millville site. Ironically, in the 20th Century, under the Central Arizona Project, this same area was slated to receive a dam which would have placed the remains of Charleston under water. Fortunately politics and funding ordained that this part of the canal project would never be constructed.

THE RIVER RUNS DRY AS EARLY AS JUNE 1877

Noyes was further asked about the confluence of the Babacomari and San Pedro Rivers. "I know that in 1877, in June, I had occasion to go to Mr. Kemble's place. I wanted to see a new mowing machine that he got, and I was over [to] his place at that time and there was no water whatever then running in the San Pedro river. It was all dry and he had but very little water to irrigate with." Even before major settlement occurred along the river, the San Pedro was occasionally dry in places. This may indicate that, just as in modern times, the local Sonoran desert suffered then from dry periods when precipitation was intermittent for several years, followed by wetter years, in cyclical patterns. The amount of water ranchers enjoyed was also influenced by where they were located on the river. Peter Moore stated that there was always water at Charleston.

He was then asked "Is there not nearly always a stream of water running out of that cienega below, except in [the] very dry seasons?" Noyes told Judge Lovell that "Sometimes there is, but it seems to sink...very seldom [do] you see it running out of the cienega, but sometimes there is for a short distance. I have seen a considerable quantity of water running out of the cienega down by Pantano, but it sinks very quick." He added, "Below Fairbanks and above Benson, there are three or four different cienegas there and a large quantity of water running out."

Noyes was then asked "When did you ever see at any time a volume of water flowing in a stream from the Babacomari into the San Pedro river?" He told Judge Lovell "Every time we would have a high rain." "A high rain?" he asked. Noyes said, "Yes sir, after what I would call a flood." He offered a further insight. Noyes was asked about the area on the Babacomari three to four miles above its mouth. "...does that stream flow water continuously during the dry season, above the cienega?" and Noyes stated that "I think it does in places, and other places it sinks. I have seen it dry and seen running water both, at the same time." Of the same area he noted that Kimble's ranch located near the confluence of the Babacomari and San Pedro rivers was closer to the San Pedro than to the Babacomari, as the latter never ran with regularity.

Noyes also was asked about the Christianson Farm. "As far as Mr. Christianson is concerned, in 1879 he irrigated what was on the east side of the river to raise hay." But when he disclosed that Christianson also cultivated on the west side of the river, the inevitable question was raised "How does he get his water over there?" Noyes stated that he got it "Through the flume that goes underneath the river…It was constructed by us in 1884. We had about forty acres of land in cultivation on that ranch in 1884, and there was an old flume that went over the river that had been washed out."

Very few ranches could support cultivation without irrigation, but Noyes testified that Christianson had a cienega on his ranch of about ten acres, "…and he cut a ditch from that and run [t]he water into the river. That would produce a crop, I think, without irrigation." His years of farming offered the following insight to the proceedings. "A man can irrigate one hundred acres of land with one hundred inches of water a great deal easier than he can irrigate ten acres of land with ten inches of water." Judge Lovell asked Noyes if his lands had any value without irrigation water. "…I would not stay there if I couldn't irrigate. I shouldn't consider them of any value, no sir. I don't know of any earthly use a man could make of them." [88] (Charles Noyes was listed as an American born Tombstone farmer, 32 years old in the 1882 Cochise County Great Register.)

Robert Todd was called as a witness on behalf of his employer, Robert T. Swan, a trustee of the Boston Mill and Mining Company. Todd was a transient laborer, working in one location for a while, and then moving to another. He's the kind of person whose work is well known when it's completed, but such men are rarely recorded in history given their socioeconomic status. It's commonly known that Richard Gird built his dam south of Charleston, but of the laborers who performed the backbreaking work to make it happen…Robert Todd was such a person.

He worked at the Boston Mill in 1881, arriving in the summer, "about August" as he recalled, but he had arrived in the Tombstone District in the fall of 1880. Of his varying duties at the Boston Mill, he recalled that he was "Sometimes cording wood and sometimes working on the rock breaker." Both are considered entry level positions in a mill, and very hard in their physical demands. He also helped clean the ditch that brought San Pedro River water to the mill. "We started in at the mill and cleaned up to the dam. That was the last job I did, in November." He was asked about the size of the ditch in question, and stated that "I think it was about four or five feet wide at some places...sometimes we tried to jump over it at night when we would come home and couldn't. It was wider in some places, you know." When asked if the width was the same along its length, he added that "there is some big cuts up towards Charleston where it is not so wide." Todd noted that a Chinaman in the area, likely south of the mill, used a great deal of water, and at times it slowed the production of the mill. "...I know they used to send up word to the Chinaman."

When asked about how much land a nearby farmer named Lindsey (on the Boston Mill ranch) had under cultivation, Todd never took notice of how much land he was irrigating, but he did take notice of the results. "I know he had tomatoes because we used to take them at dinner time...I know he had a lot of tomatoes and stuff...vegetables." [89] (Robert Todd was listed as an English born 40 year old Charleston Mill man in the 1882 Cochise County Great Register.)

Charles Noyes was up from the river today fixing up his papers with the government under his hay contract recently awarded.

Tombstone Epitaph, September 30, 1894.

CHAPTER 8

COLONEL GREENE IS BROUGHT INTO THE SUIT

"There is a good deal larger stream running after Old John opened up the springs." –William Greene

William Greene, age thirty five. Copy photo from the collections of John D. Rose.

William C. Greene, also known as Col. Greene, would make his mark on the San Pedro Valley, in the U.S. as well as down into Mexico. He is best remembered for his development of the mines at Cananea, Mexico, and gunning down Jim Burnett at the O.K. Corral.

But the Hill vs. Herrick troubles and the ensuing injunction, though primarily concentrating on the area from Fairbank to ranches north of Contention City, were far-reaching, even past Charleston toward the Mexican border. Even Col. Greene, whose name was misspelled by court reporter Tichenor as "Green," was forced to stop using irrigation waters while the matter was working its way through the legal system. Greene's testimony gives a view of this more southern part of the river, as well as glimpses into day to day life at that time. It was by no means a conclusive part of the testimony, but its real value lies in the illumination of life along the San Pedro, the life of farmers and ranchers alike.

Greene testified that he had already lived along the river for nine years at the time of the suit near the Hoefler place, formerly owned by Smith. (This is John Smith, different from D.T. Smith whose ranch was within the San Juan de las Boquillas land grant. Greene was located near the second Hereford site, on the southern end of the San Rafael de Valle land grant which lay south of the Boquillas grant.) He noted the many springs in the area and along the river, and that they added surface flow to the San Pedro. "I should judge they are 400 yards—Where they start about 7 or 8 hundred yards—a string of them along the bank there…there is a sort of cienega there, and the springs all made into the cienega." In the dry season Greene believed that the springs produced from fifty to one hundred inches of additional water flow to the river, adding that "There was always a good free stream…I guess it run there without any interruption, as far as I know, till about 1885…I think old John [Smith] had a sort of dam or sluice there to turn the water out into a little garden that he had…I think it must have been in 1885 the first to amount to anything, Old John was trying to cultivate a little there from the time I first knew him in 1880."

Following John Smith's efforts at corralling the river, Greene noted that presently "there is a sort of dam built around it [the water flow of the river] and it raised [the water level] about four or five feet, something like that, I should judge, and I think they are cultivating a little land with it—Garden and alfalfa…Last year I think they had under cultivation…somewhere from four to six acres."

Greene was asked if the water could simply be taken from such a ditch in the spring so that the surplus spring water could be allowed to flow into the river bed, as it had before. "It could be done," he told the proceeding, "but it would be a good deal of expense to take a ditch out at the point where they would have to take it to get the water high enough." Greene did note that Smith's tapping of the springs did reduce water flow in the river. "Well, yes, they run directly in it and they were [a] good string of springs...The water now seeps through in all directions instead of running through in one channel." The Smith dam also created a bit of a lake, though not at all a large one, and Greene was asked about water loss due to evaporation. "Yes sir, some [evaporation] but I would not think a great deal though, because the lake is not very large and it was a kind of cienega there originally and the water spread over a good deal of ground, and you might say there was a great deal of evaporation then...I think the evaporation is very slight and hardly noticeable anyhow."

Greene had begun his own ditching project in the area in 1884, and two years later he had enough of a system in to begin irrigating an estimated 140 to 150 acres. He admitted that his dam did divert all the water from the river during the dry season, and his ditch was an estimated two to two and a quarter miles. Old John Smith had developed the springs in question, by digging in and around them in hopes of increasing their output. Greene noted its effect. "It has increased the flow of water a good deal...There is a good deal larger stream running after Old John opened up the springs." Noticing the success of this, Greene did the same thing, and was asked if development of the springs diminished or increased water levels in the San Pedro. "It increased it. Since I opened them [the springs] up there is much more water in my ditch."

W.C. Greene testified that developing springs increased water flow. The photo above is a developed spring that connects to a manmade trough over 100 feet in length on the Greene Ranch. This spring was aided by the use of the culvert, which became popular in the 20th century. Photo by John D. Rose.

Greene was asked, "What is your title to the water you have been using there for irrigating purposes, and from whom did you derive that title?" "Well, I located it." Greene would later give a share to nearby rancher Moore in exchange for labor. "I located it till Mr. Moore came and then I gave him a third interest for keeping the dam and the ditch in repair. In the meantime I bought a quit claim from the San Pedro Grant people in their claim."

Greene noted that it was about five and a half miles from his dam to that of W.F. Banning and Scranton, noting that in the area "...the flow was large above there." The issue of the Boston Mill dam also came into focus, and Greene was asked for the distance from Banning's dam to the Boston Mill dam. "At least thirty five miles by the river, following the variations of the river. It is about seventeen miles by road. The river is very crooked its whole length and it would be at least thirty five miles." Greene also told that between his place and the Sonora line, only C.B. Kelton and E.J. Roberts were diverting any water from the river, and he spoke about the effects of the dam on water levels from Hereford to Charleston. "There is more water in the river in the last three or four years since the dams have been put in than there was before. I know when the Mormons went there to make their colony the stream of water wasn't large enough, I believe, to irrigate twenty acres of land, and they didn't settle there for that reason." "Is there as much water flowing in the San Pedro river at Charleston since the dams were placed in the river above as there was before those dams were placed in the river?" "To the best of my knowledge and belief there is...In fact there was more water than there was higher up the river. Since the dam has been put in we had more water through the summer," Greene replied.

NE, ARIZONA, JANUAR

Gibson & Roberts, San Pedro river, four miles north of Benson—Ranch and imp's, 230 acres, 5 horses, 130 stock cattle, 1 wagon and buggy, harness, tools, etc , total value $2890, total tax and costs................................ 97 23
Green, W C, San Pedro river, Hereford —Ranch and imp's, 160 acres, 2 horses, 1 wagon, tools, etc., total value $500, total tax and costs..................... 16 52

W.C. Greene's Ranch is noted above in the tax rolls. Tombstone Epitaph January 21, 1888.

The ruins of the Greene Ranch. Photo by John D. Rose

In this close up of the ruins at the Greene Ranch, this is but one example of a curious design in the adobe walls. Photo by John D. Rose.

The second location of Hereford, which was advanced compared to its predecessor-a stage stop at another location. W.C. Greene lived nearby and later owned a store at the above location. From the collections of John D. Rose.

Note the circular water tank at the bottom left of the first photo. This close up in the second photo (just above) is all that remains of it. Photo by John D. Rose.

Richard Bauer at the Greene Ranch. Photo by John D. Rose.

W.F. BANNING TESTIFIES AND LATER ENDS UP ON THE MAP

W. F. Banning had what may have been unique soil conditions that inhibited his use of the water that he gathered from the river. Greene testified to his situation. "Banning has a big ditch choch [chock] full of water and by the time it gets to his house he has lost it all, there is nothing but a little bit of a stream to irrigate three acres…The water has run through the sand…It is hard-pan there." Of his own irrigating system Greene added that his first dam was the upper one, and he installed the lower dam the prior year in 1888, adding that "…I have two dams, one is a mile below the other, and I have as big a head [of water] at the lower dam as I have at the others. Mr. Roberts has as full a head as I have, and Mr. Banning below me has the same head I have…I think that whole valley is full of water. I know the earthquake made it spurt up right in front of my house…The water is bound to be close to the surface." It stands to reason that Greene needed two dams; by 1888 he had broken 420 acres, indicating that he owned a minimum of three parcels of 160 acres each. He also stated when questioned that he irrigated his lands both before breaking them and afterwards.

"I would like to know what distance from your place it is to the Sonora line—that part of the river over which the United States has no control?" Greene answered that "…it is about seven miles in an air line" and that the source of the river is closer to sixty-five miles. [The San Pedro begins at Cananea, the very location where Greene would years later gain great wealth before losing it.]

"What is the size of the stream as it trickles along down to where it reaches Hereford or the vicinity of where you are located?" "Well," Greene responded, "there at the Custom House, during the dry season, it would probably flow like Lewis's spring." Mr. Johnson, Greene's questioner, offered at best, a sarcastic follow up. "Well, the court don't know [how Lewis's spring flows]." A patient Greene replied "Well, probably fifty inches, say," adding, "I am below

Hereford…probably from Hereford proper two miles." Greene elaborated on area distances, noting that it was five miles from Hereford to Ochoaville, and that Ochoaville was "About a mile and a quarter in an air line" adding that from "Hereford, you know, to the Mexican line you would not go by way of Ochoaville" and that the distance by the river with its many turns from Hereford to the Mexican line was an estimated twelve to fourteen miles…" [90]

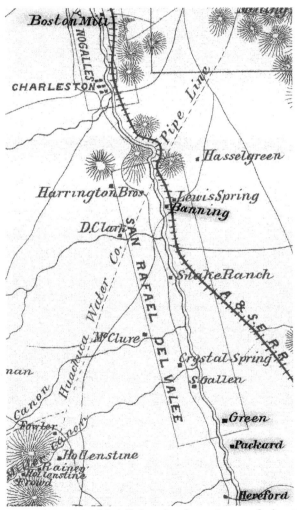

The above map shows in highlight the locations of the Boston Mill, W.F. Banning, W.C. Greene, B.P. Packard and the original Hereford stage stop location. From the collections of John D. Rose.

Greene's neighbor W.F. Banning would have opportunity to testify, stating that he started his San Pedro Ranch in 1885, and began farming there in November of 1888. It was a quarter section of land, 160 acres, with half of it under fence, with a ditch system feeding 65 to 70 acres. Banning added that he was in the area of the Crystal Springs Company, which provided ditches and water flow to some others in the area. His neighbor Levi Scranton also had 160 acres, and both men partnered on the ditch that irrigated their crops, an estimated four miles in length. After irrigating his fields, Banning added that the waste water flows within 100 yards of his home and then back into Mule Pass Creek.

Banning noted that many had begun to move into his area, stating, "I don't know their names—a good many new comers are there now and Mr. Greene and Mr. Moore." He added that there are three large tributaries that flow to the river nearby "on the west side and runs down by Charleston…and horseshoe springs comes in on that side, Mule pass comes in and drains the Mule mountains." But the injunction had an immediate effect on the health of Banning's crops. "…if I don't get water pretty shortly, I shall have to abandon [my] crops." The recent injunction wasn't the only loss that confronted him while living along the San Pedro. "I took up the claim, I think, in 1885 and in 1886 I made my improvements. My stock was stolen and I didn't get permanently established till last year…I completed my ditch last May [1888] and got water through on my place and put in some corn, enough to carry me through the winter…Wheat, corn and various commodities."

Banning was critical of other farmers in the area who used more water than he believed they needed. "I think they can do with a good deal less water than they have been using…I don't want too much of it; it makes the ground too wet and cold and injures the crops… " He added that his farm was on "pretty rough land; sod land most of it and it took a good deal of time to irrigate that." Regarding saving water, Banning stated that "I have tried my best to do it and come might nigh succeeding this year." [91]

A FORMER COWBOY FOR JOHN SLAUGHTER ADDS
TO THE RECORD

Charles Otto was a witness on behalf of Joseph Hoefler, living at the Hoefler Ranch. He was an experienced cowboy, and stated that "A stock-raising country can be turned into a fine agricultural country." Much of his testimony echoed others, with the exception of how he first came to the San Pedro River area. Judge Stillwell asked, "What were you doing when you became acquainted with the springs?" "Driving cattle up the San Pedro river." "Who for?" "John Slaughter," he answered.

Otto's testimony did cross into a subject that would become major local news less than a decade later. He was asked about the dams south of Charleston by attorney Goodrich. "Which is the first ditch above Charleston; I mean [the] ditch that takes water from the river?" He answered, "I guess Mr. Bannings." "Which is the second one or the next one above Banning's taking water from the river" Goodrich continued. "Mr. Burnet[t]'s. I heard he has a dam in there, but I don't know." Otto replied.

"When did he put his in?" asked Goodrich. Otto stated that "He must have put it in recently, if he has one, but I don't know whether he has one or not." Goodrich then asked "Which is above Burnet[t]'s?" Otto told him that it was "Mr. Green's...I couldn't say when he did put his dam in." William Greene would later suffer an unimaginable tragedy, when his daughter and playmate were drowned following the explosion of Greene's San Pedro River dam. Greene came to believe that Jim Burnett, the former Justice of the Peace at Charleston and later Fairbank, and who was downstream of Greene, was responsible. He gunned down Burnett at, of all places, the O.K. Corral in Tombstone, in the summer of 1897. [92] But it all started with disputes over dams, springs and water flow in the San Pedro. Less than a decade later, one man and two perfectly innocent children paid the ultimate price for water issues along the river. [93]

Peter Moore had worked for William Greene at his ranch, and also located a ranch of his own above Greene's location. "I claim what the law allows…160 acres. I think I fenced in about 200 acres between Charles Antschul's place [spelled differently below] and Hereford…or rather my place is next to his and his is next to Hereford…[Pointing to a diagram] Here is the Green and Moore dam right here below Hereford. Here…is the Antschul place. Here is the San Pedro river running down here through my place that I sold to Mr.Packer [sic]…Last year I had on Mr. Green's place about sixty five acres…it might have been over that…I sowed some barley and wheat but it was cut as hay, and the alfalfa came on afterwards…It was sowed with grain…All the land I tilled for Mr. Green was on the east side of the river…I moved on the Green place…somewhere about that time…within a day or two of the fourteenth of December…" Moore had struck a bargain with Green – labor for water. "I took possession and was to do a certain amount of work for one-third of the ditch. I found the ditch in bad condition and the dam washed out, and I went to work and straightened out the ditch and put in a dam and kept it in good condition ever since, and have never been molested while I was in possession till now…I put in 18 acres on my own place, of alfalfa that Green didn't furnish me according to agreement and gave me all I made off his place that year, and I put in about 60 acres all told on Green's place the first year." In his testimony Moore pointed to a diagram that was admitted into evidence. This was one of a number of illustrations used in the case, that did not remain with the testimony.

Moore then sold out to B.A. (Burdett Aden) Packard, who would later partner with nearby neighbor William Greene in vast real-estate holdings. Moore recalled that he had just sold out to Packard in the last ten or twelve days, and "I didn't know [of] any trouble at all, till Mr. Packard came with notice for me to come here as a witness…I never wasted any water. I was always careful with the water. My dam was high and if there was any surplus of water it run off [and] I turned it into the slough and into the river. The water that was used run right direct without standing in holes or ponds, run right in this slough at my place, and on the Greene place it run back into the river. There is a good deal of fall there and it run right back." Moore added, "I consider myself an expert because since 1852 I have had experience in ditching and damming."

By the time of the Hill vs. Herrick case, Moore had sold out to Mr. Packard and moved to No. 24 on the Bisbee Road, making a living supplying wood to the Queen mine. But Moore did recall that he was surprised even before the Hill vs. Herrick case that his use of river water was the source of local controversy. "I should say that I never anticipated any trouble. The Mormons never asked me about the water, but I did when I started in the first year or two, hear of complaints by the Charleston mill people, [Richard Gird's operation that remained after his hasty departure] and I know that the mill companies had the first right and I took particular notice of this water down for thre[e] miles at what is called the Crystal Springs, and I never could see any difference in the water. There was more water at Crystal Springs three miles above than there was where I took it out on the Anshutz place.

"You can see the marks of the water on the banks of the river and you can notice if it falls an inch or half an inch or two, inches, and you can never see any difference in the water; it is always the same. Up there the bedrock is nearer the surface than it was below and nearer the surface the bedrock is[,] the nearer the water comes to the surface, and the deeper the soil the deeper the water sinks and you lose it." Moore noted the dams in the area, including that of former neighbor William Greene who put "a temporary dam right opposite his place. That is a new dam, lately put in since this law-suit. The next dam that I know anything about is the Banning dam…those are all the dams I know anything about."

Moore's prior experiences on the Gila and Boise Rivers and on his own ranch on the San Pedro prompted relevant observations of the general nature of the river and of ranching in his area. Of his former home he stated, "My ground is all laid off like a garden patch and it runs direct into the slough and on the Green place it runs direct into the river. It has a good fall and there is but very little water [that] evaporates, but as you get further down and get to the leveller [sic] land and there is more ponds to hold the water it might evaporate. But as an old experienced hand at it in the Gila, where I never saw any difference, we would go and take the water out a quarter of a mile above one another and I never saw any difference, also on the Boise river in Idaho, the water always appeared to rise below." When asked whether the water naturally seeps into the river again, Moore replied, "Yes sir, I think the San Pedro is the main basin and catches all the water." Moore cautioned against measuring distances for the purpose of testimony using the natural bends in the river "It is a very crooked river. It is one of the crookedest rivers I ever saw…It would be twice as far to go by the courses of the river."

Moore further verified the springs that W.C. Greene had testified to, noting that "Hereford Springs is a big feeder, I think half of the water comes from there…it comes along and there is springs coming out all along the banks of the river till you get down below the Green place and there…is a great many springs coming out and you get to Lewiston Springs and it [is] a third or maybe half of the river." The water at the location of Charleston, which was now on a steep and irreversible economic decline, was also at issue. "I have particularly noticed it crossing at Charleston. There was always a big amount of water there. I haven't been crossing since the water got scarce. A year ago last summer…I always saw plenty of water there. That was along through the summer…the dry season. I have always seen plenty of water flowing there…I have been to Crystal Springs several times on business I did at one time expect trouble with the Charleston Mill Company before their dam went out, and I never could see any difference whether we were using the water or not. That was down about three miles below it. It takes about three miles for the water to come out on the surface again…"

Just as area farmer W.F. Banning had noted, Moore also found challenging soil conditions on his former place, which he described as

"Sand and clay. Part of it is black clay and part of it [is] kind of loamy sand…At the time of the earthquake [May 3, 1887] springs gushed right up on my place."

Moore was asked if others in the area caused him trouble by overusing water, and whether they had been detrimental to his interests. "All I can say is that being they didn't meddle with my family and my property, it is none of my business and" I didn't "meddle with other people's affairs." Instead of using Tombstone as his base for shopping, he chose to travel up and down the San Pedro, as many did who lived along the river. It was its own form of a community, and given that Charleston businesses had mostly gone under and moved on, Moore had to travel to Fairbank. "It was my business to go to Fairbanks, I bought my goods there and I generally went once a week, maybe not so often, sometimes, and I noticed particularly in crossing the road there at Charleston, or a little below, that there was always plenty of water there." He also noted that his horseback rides to shop at Fairbank had now been replaced by the Iron Horse. "…I ride on the railroad." [94]

WHEN QUESTIONING BECOMES AN INTERROGATION

N.W. Storer worked as another agent for one of the defendants, Robert T. Swan, working on mines and also the Boston Mill Ranch. He arrived on May 17th, 1887. "I was sent out here by the Boston Mining and Reduction Co." He was subjected to a number of questioners, but none so aggressive as attorney Goodrich, who demanded to know why Greene, Moore, Banning and Scranton were also brought into the suit as defendants, given they were not named in the original filing by John Hill. Also, they were much further south from the area that was being fought over. It is of course true that all water use on the river was relevant, but even John Hill and those who joined with him in the suit didn't care to bring the de Valle ranchers in. Goodrich would not allow this to go unanswered, and made scant effort to hold back his irritation over the matter. It was only ordered by the court after the initial filing, and Goodrich knew that Storer's counsel had done this, and he demanded to know why. Storer wasn't going to make it easy for him, but Goodrich pursued, asking how it was "that Green and Moore and Scranton and Banning became defendants in that action?"

Goodrich wanted Storer to admit that he was instrumental in bringing into the suit the other named ranchers. He persisted with leads like "I would like to have you tell… You don't know… Didn't you know they were not… That is evading my question… Wasn't it at your instance that your counsel did that?" and "Didn't they advise it at your instance and request?"

Goodrich then demanded, "Wasn't it the action of your counsel produced at your urgent request that something be done to bring these people [Green, Moore, Scranton, and Banning] in?" Goodrich and Judge Berry had little use of Storer's answer: "I think I am dull. I can't understand you." Berry ordered Storer to "Answer the question according to the facts and satisfy him." He went into detail about his path in discussing the case with counsel, who recommended the ranchers further upstream be brought in, but did not offer exact details of those conversations.

But the goading by Goodrich did enhance the record in this matter. It was the latter testimony of Storer that most succinctly told of why John Hill initiated legal proceedings; in fact, he made the case in a far more direct manner that even John Hill himself had, even though Hill sued him as well. "The fact is that the people I represent were sued by Hill and others and I suppose the suit was brought for the same reason…I know it was brought because Hill told me so, because they hadn't sufficient water to irrigate their lands. And I think it is shown by the testimony in this case, that the reason they didn't have water to irrigate with was that the parties above [south] him and between him and the Mexican line had taken out water to irrigate lands subsequent to the time that our parties and Mr. Hill and the Noyes Bros and others had taken out the water, which caused a shortage in the water and caused this suit to be brought. That is the reason that I am here and that is the only grievance I have against the people up the river."

Goodrich was not satisfied: "I will ask you now, to make this whole thing short…if you have not recently through you own instigation and the employment of runners and of hunters and spies obtained an order restraining all these people above from diverting any water from the San Pedro river, for any purpose whatever?" It appears Storer was cool in replying, "No sir." "The main object then of this late restraining order issued upon your affidavit was not for the purpose of bulldozing these parties into helping you out in paying…your expenses of law-suit with John Hill and his associates?" "I just replied to that question. It was not."

Storer further offered testimony that showed that production at the Boston Mill had been affected by the water use upstream. "…I came here in May, 1887 and I have been here since that. I didn't take so much notice of the water in 1887 as I did in 1888, but we had all the water necessary for our purposes to irrigate and there was a good head below, and I think in 1888 we were not in any trouble up to that time when we were enjoined, to get all the water necessary. Since I have been here it has always been necessary in the dry seasons to make the dam a little tighter, but this year I don't think we had half the usual flow…no more than that."

Given that the Boston Mill was just north of Millville, it was geographically and legally caught in the middle in this case. It was an operation that had existed for years, and the mills at Millville no longer were as active as they had once been, so from the viewpoint of the Boston Mill, less water was being used for milling, so why were they dragged into this? Storer also alluded to a fact of life in the desert – the unpredictability of rain – "…this year I don't think we had half the usual flow…"

Storer's many answers indicate that he was not pleased to be known publicly as having forced the ranchers to the south into the suit, which is in itself making the corporate neighbor look like they are picking on the small timers in the area, but at the same time, he did have a legitimate point, and John Hill would have been wise to have included Green, Moore, Scranton and Banning in his original action to make the suit more comprehensive in nature, and also to give a greater fairness to the casual, and serious observer. [95]

> **Notice.**
> Wing Waugh to Yung Lung: This certifies that Wing Waugh has sold to Yung Lung certain real estate and horses and wagons at Boston Mill, for $750, on October 18, 1885.
> o28-4t   YUEN LUNG.

A sale of real estate and wagons is transacted at the Boston Mill. Daily Tombstone, October 30, 1885.

> Mr. Storer, of the Boston mill ranch, reports no rain there yesterday and no signs of high water in the river this morning.

N.W. Storer who was badgered by Attorney Goodrich during the Hill vs. Herrick case, reports no high water in the San Pedro. Tombstone Daily Prospector, August 23, 1890.

> Mr. Storer of the Boston Mill ranch reports very heavy rain and high water on the river last night.

Tombstone Daily Prospector, September 6, 1890.

The Boston Mill photo, located by Richard Bauer and identified as noted by the AHS. The hill shown appears to have been cropped to appear flat.

The foundation of the Boston Mill from a different angle. Note the natural incline of the same hill un-cropped. Photo by Stephanie Rose.

CHAPTER 9

A DISINTERESTED PARTY SPEAKS TO THE COURT

"I don't think they have sufficient water to irrigate for corn now…" –W.W. Woodman

Now it was time for the testimony of a non-combatant. The court had wisely sent its own representative, W.W. (Warren Walter) Woodman, to see for himself the conditions of water flow along the San Pedro, view ranches and farms, and speak with owners involved. He took special notice of the condition of their fields and the crops that they grew there. They also conducted nonscientific water manipulation studies, measuring the water level in a given area of the river, closing down irrigation systems upstream, then going back to the same measured point and remeasuring, to make note of any differences.

At times the differences measured were minimal to say the least, and the findings were occasionally at odds with each other. But he did offer a brief synopsis of the intermittent nature of San Pedro River surface flow. "…one place there will be no water and then you go a little ways further and there you find water that can be taken out, and so on a little further. Everybody knows that that travels up and down the river." He visited ranches further north on the San Pedro, those located on the Union Ditch. Woodman's observations created a temporary fracture between two parties on the same side of the suit, neighbors John Hill and Andrew Summers. One morning while riding along the river, Woodman noticed a head of water coming out of the Summers ranch (above Hill's), running into the river, bypassing the irrigation ditch that fed Hill's and Clifford's places.

Woodman pointed out to Hill that water was running into the river that was being wasted, and given the related controversy and lack of water in general, it was self-evident that this was less than desirable. Summers blamed his horse. Woodman testified, "I told Mr. Hill that under the present condition of the water it would not do to let any run into the river, and he said he would go and give Summers hell about it, and the next time I saw him Mr. Summers explained, or had explained, that the horses in the pasture had forced the top of the board off the gate and let the water down." This wasn't the only case of waste that Woodman observed. "One time from Clifford's place a small stream was running out one morning," running to waste. It's the same water that "…runs down the centre of the slough that runs through the centre of the Hill and Clifford places."

Important to his testimony was Woodman's emphasis to the court that he truly did not want to appear that he was in any way advocating for or against anyone involved. His words do read true to this ethos, and it would appear that his visits gave him an understanding that few court officials in the hearing may have had. It may have surprised him as well, as he spoke eloquently to the water needs of many on both sides of the controversy.

Woodman testified that H.C. Herrick was suffering for want of water. "Well, I haven't seen much waste water on Mr. Herrick's place. He has had very little water…very little water indeed, while I have been there." Woodman was then asked about Mr. Storer, who was so harshly handled by attorney Goodrich, and his water use. "I haven't been through it this year, but I don't think he wastes any water. It is my impression that what water he loses gets back into the creek [San Pedro River]."

He also shared an unusual description about Storer's system at the Boston Mill site, and the source was Storer himself. "…he has a flume that runs right under the river. I haven't seen it, but he tells me about it…in very bad condition, leaks a good deal. I told him it wasn't my fault. From what I know of his ranch there can't be but very little waste on his farm because he has got too much of it…Mr. Storer needs some water more than he has. He has a pasture field that I go by every day that would be benefitted by water."

Woodman was then asked if he took notice of John Hill's oat field. "…it needs water, and he has since given it water, I believe…I don't think they have sufficient water to irrigate for corn now…I don't wish it understood at all in my testimony that I have said or am willing to say that these people down there have had all the water that they need at this time of the year."

Because of Woodman's previous experiences with farming and irrigating, he was able to offer an interesting theory as to how ranchers could most benefit from the limited waters of the river. His testimony indicated that there was a fair amount of water wasted on some of the ranches. He was asked, "From your experience and what you have observed along that river what is your opinion, if the water was properly used, as to there being a supply for them all above Charleston, on that river?" Woodman was tentative in his reply: "…more economy could be practiced in the use of water than there is now." "If that economy was used would there be enough for all practical purposes for ranchers up there?" "I undertake to say that there would be no very great suffering. Of course, at this time of year a man might lose a crop or a portion of it, but if they would begin in the fall…" The court asked, "Suppose people would all saturate their land thoroughly in the winter months, when there was plenty of water—and then economise in April and May?" "Well, there are a great many things to be considered. In the first place the preparation of the land when put down in crops should be most thorough. I have been a good deal over that land and I know the best of the farmers are at fault…the crops can be matured earlier in the season than they are now if proper precautions were taken in the fall and winter and less would be required in the summer. And the theory that I have [,] I have seen it worked out in California to my entire satisfaction…The more water is used on the land, in the event of years it will increase materially from year to year and my theory carried out it would eventually furnish the whole river with all the water they want— certainly for all lands now under cultivation. That is my private opinion." [96]

This closely matches William Greene's observation that there was more water in the river in the three or four years after the dams were put in. However, rainfall amounts over those years do not appear to have been taken into account by Greene. Judge Berry was not completely convinced, pointing out differences between Arizona and California in climate, the soil, and how the springs flowed in the San Pedro, questioning whether Woodman's theory could play out well here. But the court was in no position or authority to adjudicate practical measures that ranchers could take amongst themselves. The court's authority was directed at what could be done at the time of its judgment, given the scarcity of water in the San Pedro at the time. (Warren Walter Woodman was listed as an American born 51 year old Tombstone miner in the 1882 Cochise County Great Register.)

HILL VS. HERRICK HAS CONCLUDED

"On May 25th, 1889, the Plaintiffs rest and the Defendants rest. Rest all. Testimony is closed."

District Court.

The following cases were disposed of during the past week:

Cohn vs. Nardini—Judgment for plaintiff.

W. H. Barnes was admitted to practice.

Hill vs. Herrick—Clerk ordered to pay over to B. W. Tichenor the sum of $351.65, less clerk's costs.

Backus vs. Ewald—Judgment for plaintiff in the sum of $1,018 and costs.

Wilson vs. Chisholm—Taken under advisement.

Williams vs. Williams—Referred to W. F. Nichols to take testimony.

The December 28, 1889 Tombstone Epitaph notes payment to self-described "Legal Stenographer and Type Writer" Byran Tichenor of $351.65.

1116

TESTIMONY CLOSED.

ARGUMENT PROCEEDED WITH.

I hereby certify the foregoing to be a true, full
and correct transcript of my short-hand notes of the
testimony of said witness, taken at the time and place
in this transcript stated, according to the best of my
skill and understanding.

[signature]

Commissioner.

Notice that the testimony of the Hill vs. Herrick case is complete.
Courtesy AHS.

One of the key testimonies in the case had been that of W.W. Woodman, the impartial witness who traveled the San Pedro River visiting its many inhabitants. He listened to their troubles and concerns, observed their fields no longer green, and saw their losses as their crops withered and their hopes declined, due to lack of water. Had the year preceding been of record rain, it is unlikely that the suit would have ever taken place.

The local press even as far away as Tucson took notice of the suit. Such a case could set a legal precedent which could have far reaching effects beyond ranching farmers who called the San Pedro River Valley home, at that time and in the future. It was Tucson resident B. [Bryan] W. Tichenor who took on the massive job of typing all the testimony given. Every word that was spoken in the hearing was his to record. The Tucson Weekly Citizen caught the attention of its readers by leading with "San Pedro Water Troubles. Mr. W.B. [Bryan W.] Tichenor is just completing the work of putting the evidence recently taken at Tombstone into type-written shape. The work has proved a formidable job. He was engaged ten days in taking the testimony and over fifty witnesses were examined. The entire testimony will make over 1,250 pages of type-written matter. The case is one of great importance to every rancher on the San Pedro from Benson to the Mexican line…." [97]

Judge Wm. H. Barnes would soon make his decision, carried by the Tombstone press, whose readership included many wanting to know just what impact this case had on anyone in the area using surface water as part of making a living. It had been a complicated case, which required a complicated decision, but Barnes did well in boiling down all the elements into a clear cut decision. Although H.C. Herrick's testimony was riddled with self-contradictions and some outright falsehoods, he won.

On Wednesday morning, October 23rd, 1889, the Tombstone Epitaph told its readers, "THE WATER CASE DECIDED. Judgment for Defendants—Milling Companies Not Allowed Water for Irrigating Purposes. In the district court of the First Judicial District of the Territory of Arizona, in and for the county of Cochise. John Hill et al. vs. H.C. Herrick et al.

"In this case I find that Hop Kee and Herrick are the owners of the first ditch; that about 1878 their predecessors appropriated as much water as would run through a ditch 18 inches wide on top, 12 inches on the bottom and 18 inches deep, each owning one half of the same and each having the right of use of the same.

"I find that the next appropriation was by what is called the Mason and Cable ditch, now owned by the plaintiffs, who appropriated in 1878 so much water as would run through a gate 4.8 feet wide and 1 foot deep.

"I find that the next appropriation is by the ditch now owned by Noyes and Christianson who, in March, 1879, appropriated so much water as would run through a ditch about three and a half feet wide. The evidence shows that this ditch has not been materially altered since, and they are entitled to the amount which it now carries.

"All of the above water was appropriated for agricultural purposes in irrigation.

"The fourth ditch is the Grand Central ditch, which appropriated water for milling purposes, and the water is – at least eighty-five per cent – restored to the river, and the said company is entitled to continue the use of it; and that the ditch has not been materially increased since the appropriation.

"I find that the next ditch is what is called the Crane Brothers' ditch, who, in 1884, appropriated the amount of water their ditch now carries and which has not been materially increased since 1884. In 1885 Herrick increased his appropriation up to what is now used by him.

"I find from the evidence in this case that the ditches on the Upper San Pedro do not appear to have materially interfered with the uses of the water below and hence this bill as to them, is dismissed without costs, with the privilege that if it shall appear hereafter that their use of the water interferes with the uses of the parties, as found by this decision, that they may file a bill for relief hereafter.

"I find also that the uses of the water coming from the Babacomari creek are not shown by the evidence to interfere with the uses of the water below, and hence the bill, as to those parties using such water, is dismissed without costs, with the same privilege in case such use should hereafter be shown to interfere with the rights of the parties settled by this decision.

"I find from the evidence that the Boston Milling and Mining Company have appropriated water for milling purposes. I find that the articles of incorporation, which are to be treated as the charter of the corporation, shows that the corporation was organized for mining, milling and reduction of ores, and not for the purposes of irrigation, and I find that it was ultra vires [Latin phrase for "beyond the powers"] to the purposes of that corporation to appropriate water for irrigation.

"A decree may be prepared in accordance with the above opinion.

"I have not seen fit to give my reasons at large, through lack of time to do so.

"Costs should be apportioned as follows: All costs equally divided between Herrick, Boston company, or Swan, its successor, and plaintiff, except that Hop Kee, Noyes Bros., Crane Bros. and Christianson to pay their own costs.

"October 21, 1889.

"Wm. H. Barnes, Judge."

In 1891, an appeal against the ruling was dismissed. [98]

But for Robert T. Swan, a trustee interested in the Boston Mill and Mining Company, the case was far from over. The Boston Mill had retained the right to utilize surface flow for its mill, but given that their charter made no mention of irrigating for agricultural uses, Judge Barnes ordered such irrigation be stopped. Swan first made a motion for a new trial, which was overruled. He then appealed to the Supreme Court of the Arizona Territory, and the appellees moved to dismiss the action as they claimed defects in the appeal bond. This technicality would prove to be an effective strategy, as it appeared to them that Swan was not giving up. Chief Justice of the United States Supreme Court, Melville Weston Fuller, wrote the court's finding, noting that the error in the appeal violated section 859 of the Revised Statutes of Arizona. He stated further that "The motion was sustained upon that ground, the appeal dismissed with costs, and Swan, trustee, brought this case to this court...Mr. Chief Justice FULLER, after stating the facts in the foregoing language, delivered the opinion of the court." Swan would learn that drawing the Supreme Court into the matter was not an inexpensive one. Fuller also took note of the following clause in Section 859: "...The appellant or plaintiff in error...shall pay all the costs which have accrued in the court below, or which may accrue in the appellate court." Another portion of section 859 further states that the appellant or plaintiff in error also is liable for a sum "at least double the probable amount of the costs of the suit of both the appellate court and the court below..." [99]

One of the clear differences that the interceding decade shows from Drew vs. Mason in 1879 and Hill vs. Herrick in 1889, is that available water for farms in the area had clearly diminished. The Drew vs. Mason case in centered on access to the water that was available at the time. Nothing in this case indicates that there was a severe lack of water, rather, it was a fight about to whom that water would go. The Hill vs. Herrick case is different in nature. Repeated testimony from a variety of first hand sources, especially W.W. Woodman, indicate that this second lawsuit was not a fight over dividing up a large amount of water, but rather, it was a fight over who had access to a reduced amount of water. It is further clear that as the number of ranching farmers and the demands that they placed on a scarce supply of water increased, the supply of surface water diminished. It was a perfect recipe for conflict, with livelihoods hanging in the balance.

What the Hill vs. Herrick case offers is a brief glimpse into a history of the San Pedro and its people, and that there are times when circumstances can overwhelm individuals in a way that they turn on each other, instead of attempting to find common solutions to their mutual problems. They were, after all, in it together, but little in the way of this approach manifested itself in what occurred along the San Pedro River as the 1880's drew to a close.

A SHORTAGE OF WATER IN THE RIVER

"I also withheld the rain from you when there were yet three months to the harvest… and the field on which it did not rain would wither…" –Amos 4:7

The testimony from Hill vs. Herrick, and its predecessor Drew vs. Mason, makes more than clear that without access to the multiple dams connected to ditches that carried San Pedro water to these farming sites, the land would be worthless as anything more than a home site. The testimony further established that many ranchers at these locations were growing food to eat, feed for their animals, and hay and crops for sale. Attorney Goodrich queried Andrew Wild, one of the early shareholders in the Union Ditch, "Can you successfully irrigate any of these lands under the Union ditch, unless you have a flow of water at the head of the ditch?" Wild replied, "Not successfully."

These lawsuits also offer testimony that even WITH access to these river bottom dams and accompanying network of ditches, if too many used the limited waters of the San Pedro, and rainfall fell short of increased demands, they still couldn't make a living with the ditches running directly to their fields. The vivid descriptions offered in testimony of dried fields and burnt crops verify this amply.

At the time of the suit in 1889 Drew's Station was still the most northern site with direct access to the Mason Cable ditch. Wild stated that if water were coming down the river, the Union ditch did supply his, Summers, Hill, and the old Drew ranch with the necessary amount of water. At the time of the suit, ranchers had the advantage of knowing that the Head Centre Mill at Contention City's northern boundary, as well as the Contention Mill at its southern end, had shut down, removing two more drains on available water from the San

Pedro, but it wasn't enough. "Now state whether or not you had any more supply of water since they [the mills] shut down than you had before they shut down," Goodrich requested. Wild told him, "I don't think we have." "Have you as much?" "Well," Wild said, "sometimes we have as much when it is in the river, and sometimes they don't have as much come down to our headgate." When Goodrich again pressed the issue asking if they now had a greater water supply than they did before, Wild told him, "I don't think we have."

For Wild and those nearby, there was little gain in water from the closing down of the Contention and Head Centre Mills. It may be that additional ranchers south of Charleston in the area of Colonel Greene, W.F. Banning and others may have used up any increase that those suffering downstream had hoped for with the loss of the mills. Making matters worse, the loss of the mills only meant fewer paychecks in nearby declining Contention City, and fewer wage earners to purchase their crops. It was a downward economic cycle in need of a reverse. Hill vs. Herrick was an example of such desperation that the shortage of water had caused.

When pressed for greater details as to water flow and how many inches he claimed he needed for his crops, Wild was on the defensive. "Well, I am like Mr. Hill, I ain't an educated man and don't know anything about figures and never made a calculation. I know from personal experience that it requires our ditch or headgate about a full of water to cultivate the farms that are cultivated under it." But regardless of technical terminology, Wild summed up the situation when he talked about the condition of his crops on June 11th, 1888, the day that the Hill vs. Herrick suit was filed and began. "They were very dry and suffering for the want of water...A considerable extent." At the time of testimony in 1889 little had changed. "...some portions of the field...it is getting pretty dry now and I would say suffering for want of water." [100]

Just a decade after the books were closed on this case, the Kern Land and Cattle Company of California would purchase the vast majority of the area that had been at the heart of the dispute from the estate of George Hearst.

For all his notoriety as a businessman, Hearst had allowed many to live on the grant in violation of his rights. Most of the ranchers on the grant were paying taxes for their homes and improvements. Several do appear as paying taxes on the land as well. Phoebe Hearst, widow of George Hearst, was billed for taxes on 10,000 acres of land in 1897. The grant itself encompassed 17,255 acres. It appears that tax assessors took into account that others were paying taxes on their portions of land. This may also imply that the owners of the grant understood that others had settled upon their grant. As the 19th Century drew to a close, new ownership of an impersonal, corporate nature would bring an end to the life that many had known along the San Pedro, and the era of these small ranches and farms would cease to exist. This way of life, its charms and its challenges, would not be seen again.

The personal account of George Hearst appears in the day book of the Pima County Bank. Courtesy U of A Special Collections.

The Hearst Party Safe.

Frank Lobracco, who went to Baso-chuca with George Hearst, returned last evening, he being one of the musicians at the Knights' ball. He left Basochuca Sunday morning, when the entire party were safe and well and no word of Indian troubles west of the Ajos range of mountains. This is as we assumed in our article upon this subject in yesterday's issue. That the Sumner and Earl party are also safe and sound we do not doubt, from the fact that the hostiles were being hotly pursued by at least 1000 good Indian fighters—men who can follow wherever an Indian dare go. The alarm was given by some irresponsible Mexican, who may have seen or heard his ominous tale in the bottom of a bottle of Senor Elias' good mescal. The great mistake was made in telegraphing the rumor to Haggin & Tevis by some one of Mr. Hearst's friends here in Tombstone. This fact alone was the cause of unnecessary pain to his many friends and political supporters in California.

On February 20, 1882, the Tombstone Epitaph informs its readers that George Hearst and party are not in the hands of the Apaches.

> Southern papers are booming ex-Governor of Utah, Eli Murray for the United States senate in the event of Senator Hearst's death. It strikes us that California is in somewhat of a rush about this senator business, as old Uncle George Hearst is not likely to die right away.

Political buzzards circle over the Senate seat held by George Hearst as he fights for his life. Arizona Weekly-Journal Miner, February 4, 1891.

> **BORNE TO REST.**
>
> **The Remains of Senator Hearst Laid in the Tomb.**
>
> SAN FRANCISCO, March 16.—The remains of the late Senator George Hearst were escorted to Laurel Hill cemetery yesterday afternoon by representatives of national, State and municipal bodies, and over a thousand State militia, in a drenching rain.
>
> The services at Grace Church were conducted by Rev. Dr. Foote, Rev. C. J. Mason and Rev. M. R. Nicholson, and were attended by Governor Markham and staff and many distinguished citizens.

The funeral of George Hearst. Arizona Republican, March 17, 1891.

Notice to Creditors.

Estate of George Hearst, deceased.

Notice is hereby given by the undersigned executrix of the estate of George Hearst, deceased, to the creditors of, and all p rsons having claims against said deceased to exhibit them with the necessary vouchers, within ten months after the first publication of this notice to W H Stilwell, attorney for said executrix at his office, No 117 Fourth street City of Tombstone, Cochise County. the same being the place for the transaction of said business of said estate in Arizona Territory.

PHEBE A. HEARST,
Executrix of the estate of George Hearst, deceased.
Dated Tombstone, June. 12, 1891.

The widow of George Hearst, Phoebe Hearst, advertises in the Tombstone Epitaph on June 28, 1891, that she is in the process of settling his estate.

Phoebe Hearst is taxed by Cochise County for 10,000 acres of the Boquillas Land Grant, even though the actual size of the grant was over 17,000 acres. Courtesy of Kevin Pyles, Cochise County Archives.

"J. H. Jastor, one of the members of the Kern County Cattle company, of California, will be here on or about the 10th instant for the purpose of going over and inspecting the Boquillas land gant [sic] on the San Pedro river, which they have purchased from the Hearst estate. This grant takes in all that strip of country lying between St. David, on the north, to above old Charleston, on the south, a distance of about twelve miles. The intention of the compa[n]y is to fence this tract in and use it for pasturing cattle. A very serious proposition now confronts the people living on this tract of land, the title to which was recently confirmed by the land court, sitting at Tucson, and they now have to make terms with the Kern County Co. or be dispossessed of the homes which many of them have spent the best years of their lives in bui[l]ding up and improving, and which will entail heavy loss to a number of our best citizens." [101]

CHAPTER 10

POST 1889 ERA NORTH OF DREW'S RANCH

Andrew "A.B." Wild's ranch near the San Pedro would later be noted on John Rockfellow's map in 1899, but ten years earlier he was embroiled in the Hill vs. Herrick lawsuit, fighting for his share of the San Pedro's limited water flow. He joined the suit as one of the plaintiffs, having first moved to the area of the river in the spring of 1881. When Wild arrived, Cable was still living on his same place that William Drew had noted on his hand drawn map of 1879. About Cable Wild stated, "I think he gave up farming himself. What land he had under fence he had rented to [a] Chinaman."

At the time of the suit in 1889 Wild was living "on a portion of the place purchased by Mr. Cable" noting that this was not where he stayed when he first arrived in late 1881; he purchased the land from Cable "...It must have been in the fore part of January 1882...I didn't go there until about March 1883...He [Cable] claimed a quarter section of land, a hundred and sixty acres...I have possession of the whole one hundred and sixty acres of land." Wild was partners with S.B. Curtis and a man named Hubbard. Curtis bought out Hubbard and then moved north as documented on the Rockfellow map. Just as Cable had done before, Wild rented the place to a Chinaman until he himself moved to the site. It may have been the same Chinaman that rented from Cable.

Wild was asked a routine question which over a century later, provides a real insight to the site north of the real Drew's Station site that has been incorrectly promoted by some as Drew's Station. Q. "What right did you say you purchased in that ditch?" Wild responded saying "I purchased one third of one forth in the ditch." This amounted to one third of Cable's right. Attorney Goodrich then asked "Well, what other farms were under that ditch [downstream, using it] when you went there?" Wild stated, "Well, that place a[n]d

Summers and the Hill place and the Drew place." [102] He lists no other ranches further north of Drew's.

It has already been proven that the distance from the north side of Contention (the Sunset/Head Centre Mill) to Philpot's wash is approximately one mile (according to Bob Paul); Drew's Station was reported to be another 200 yards beyond this wash. A ground survey today shows that the ruins of Drew's Station are 533 yards to the northwest. According to William Drew, his station was located approximately three miles north of the ruins at Terrenate as one follows the road (2.8 miles as the crow flies). (See *On the Road to Tombstone: Drew's Station, Contention City And Fairbank,* Pages 7-14 and 306-313) The testimony of William Drew (Drew vs. Mason case) and Bob Paul (his telegraph dispatch to Tombstone the night of the attempted Philpot stage robbery) should leave no doubt in the minds of the discerning reader where Drew's was located. The TTR/Sosa site, now also publicly promoted by John Boessenecker, author of *When Law Was in the Holster, The Frontier Life of Bob Paul,* defies the ultimate primary sources in the matter. But Drew's testimony could not possibly resolve the origins of the TTR/Sosa site, as it wasn't constructed during his lifetime, or during the lifetime of Bud Philpot.

The site that the TTR/Sosa group claims is Drew's station is 3.68 miles north of the ruins. The wash where it claims Philpot was murdered is 3.5 miles north of the same ruins, and approximately 1.99 miles from the north side of Contention. Any site or wash too far north or too far south of Paul's measurement is obviously incorrect.

So the question arises again: Upon which ranch further north and in which wash does the TTR/Sosa group claim that the stage robbery took place which took the life of Bud Philpot? Further testimony from John Hill and Samuel "S.B." Curtis helps to clarify this issue. Curtis also appeared on the Rockfellow map as the 19th Century drew to a close, but before that, he would testify at the Hill vs. Herrick suit, on behalf of Hill. "I live on the San Pedro" he told the court. "…about a mile and a half below Hill's place" adding that he was "Farming a little…Well, I am trying to make a living…Our alfalfa…portions of it died out so we had to sow it over again…I lost my potato crop entirely." Attorney Goodrich must have been pleased that unlike some of his neighbors, Curtis knew the water measurements that they did not. "I own two-thirds of the Cable right…Two-thirds of one-fourth…it is supposed to be 144 inches of water." [103]

As mentioned before, Curtis was one of three partners who bought out the Cable ranch, one of six ranches on the Drew map. He himself bought out Mr. Hubbard's share. Wild remained on the Cable place but Curtis moved northward, and retained his water rights to the Union ditch. Curtis had a brother, Joseph, who was farming with him at the northern site. He also alludes to himself and another brother having two parcels of land. "How many acres do you and your brother got now under cultivation?" "We claim 160 acres apiece."

Hill, who was still living on the old Mason ranch at the time of the suit, was asked, "Mr. Curtis lives below [north of] you?" "Yes sir, does now." "Who lived on that land where he now lives, in 1882, when you went there?" Hill answered, "Nobody." Hill further stated that Curtis had between 75 and 100 acres under cultivation. Judge Stillwell then asked, "Did he irrigate this land from this ditch [the Union Ditch]?" "Yes, sir, the termination of the Union ditch goes right to his [Elijah Clifford's] land; it joins right on to my north line…Mr. Curtis had made a distributing ditch from the end of our ditch to his land, and when there is any waste water it runs in that ditch." Hill was asked, "How many miles is it from where that distributing ditch commences to the Curtis place?" Hill wasn't exactly sure, but estimated about two miles. "Is there any cultivation of fields for that distance of two miles before the ditch reaches the Curtis place?" Col. Herring is asking this question as it applies in real time (1889). "No," Hill replied.

This is significant because we do know that on the Drew's place, occupied by Elijah Clifford in 1889, there were "I should think from 20 to 25 acres…" under cultivation. William and Eddie Drew had said that they were cultivating their land from the spring of 1879, and did so until Mrs. Drew left her land, more than one year after the stage robbery. And before Clifford arrived at the Drew ranch, Horne farmed there. So there was continual cultivation at the Drew ranch at least up until the time of the lawsuit. Hill added that Curtis cut his distribution ditch from the termination point in the fall of 1883, and had only grown crops on the Cable ranch prior to that time. So in 1889 there was no further cultivation north of Drew's until Curtis' place. So Drew's Station could not have been located north at the TTR/ Sosa site.

S. Curtis' name appears on the Rockfellow map as the northernmost ranch on the Boquillas land grant. This location is almost exactly 1 ½ miles north of a location on the same map marked "Hill." Although Hill, in 1889, was still living and farming on the old Mason ranch, it stands to reason that he had purchased another parcel of land north of his original location, to which Curtis refers. When Hill was asked during the trial, "Have you bought any land since then [since the purchase of the Mason place]?" he responded, "Yes sir." [104] This land appears to be on the northern border of the old Drew place. And it later appears that Hill purchased more than one parcel. (Records searched do not verify these purchases.)

In 1889, Hill had two sons living and farming on his land (the Mason ranch). "I have got two [sons]. One married son---One left and bought the other out." [105] It appears that both of his sons moved to a more northern location, even further than the Hill location marked on the Rockfellow map, because in 1894 John Hill sold his northernmost site, occupied at that time by his sons, John Hill, Jr. and F.M. Hill, to W.S. (William Sherman) Gray. Gray appears north of Hill on Rockfellow's map. John Hill Jr. had decided to move to the Thatcher area, which may have prompted this sale. This key deed proves that John Hill, in 1894, was the earliest owner of record of this property. Given that Hill had not even moved to this part of the country until January of 1882, it is clearly impossible that this site existed on March 15th, 1881, when Bud Philpot was murdered in the wash south of the real Drew's Station, well south of what would later become the Hill Ranch, with another of Hill's properties becoming the Gray Ranch in 1894.

"This Indenture, made the 19th day of July in the year of our Lord one thousand eight hundred and ninety four, Between John Hill of Cochise County in Arizona Territory, party of the first part, and W.S. Gray of Cochise County, Arizona Territory, the party of the second part, Witnesseth: that the said party of the first part for and in consideration of the sum of One thousand dollars lawful money of the United States of America, to him in hand paid, by the said party of the second part, [W.S. Gray] the receipt whereof is hereby acknowledged, does by these presents, remise, release, and forever Quitclaim, unto the said party of the second part, [W.S. Gray] and to his heirs and assigns forever all that certain lot piece or parcel of land situated in the said Cochise County of Arizona Territory, and bounded and particularly described as follows to wit:
"Beginning at the southeast corner of the said John Hill claim. Thence west across the San Pedro river to the North west corner of said claim, thence south sixty rods more or less to a petition fence, thence east to the east line to said claim, thence north to beginning, said piece of land being now occupied by my two sons J and F.M. Hill. Together with all and singular the tenements, hereditaments and appurtenances thereunto belonging, or in anywise appertaining, and the revision and revisions, remainder and remainders, rents, issues and profits thereof. To have and to hold, all and singular the said premises, second part, and to his heirs and assigns forever. In witness whereof, the said party of the first part has herein set his hand and seal the day and year first above written, John Hill, Signed Sealed and Delivered in the Presence of John Hill Jr. Territory of Arizona County of Graham." [106] This deed wasn't recorded in Cochise County until September 5th, 1895, and at the request of W.C. Stachel. By that time, John Hill Jr. had been living in Graham County, and this is why the filing above refers to him as in that county.

207

John Hill, Jr., has sold his ranch at St. David to W. S. Gray, formerly of Willcox, and will, with his family, leave next week for Thatcher, Graham county, to remain. He has purchased both a home in the town and a farm just outside, where, with the industry that has always characterized him he hopes to build up a fortune. Cochise county is sorry to lose him, but wishes him success.

On August 19th, 1894, the Tombstone Epitaph misinforms its readers stating that "John Hill, Jr., has sold his ranch at St. David to W.S. Gray..." It was actually the property of his father, John Hill Sr., who sold to W.S. Gray in the deed noted on the prior page. Five years later when John Rockfellow made his map of the area he referred to this property as the Gray Ranch, but it is clear that given John Hill Sr. had allowed his sons to occupy the site before selling to Gray, that Hill is the first owner of record of this location.

WHAT WAS THE TTR/SOSA SITE IN REALITY?

There remain two sets of foundations on Hill's northern properties. It is the northern foundation which Nancy Sosa identifies as Drew's station. This foundation is located on the southern area of Gray's. This means that this foundation, prior to John Hill's 1894 sale to W.S. Gray, was without question, on his northernmost site.

The wash which Sosa and author John Boessenecker identify as the robbery site of the Philpot stage is in some areas perhaps five feet wide, and quite steep on its northern side. In fact, Sosa's proposed stage road leads right up the side of a hill. That hill is cut with a graded road, having the appearance of being mechanically worked, most likely constructed in the 20th century, as it does not coincide with any roadways published on the Drew, Solon Allis, and Rockfellow maps.

John and Aubrey Rose stand at the adobe ruins of the Gray Ranch.
Photo by Stephanie Rose.

John Rose and Richard Bauer illustrate the very steep climb that Mrs. Sosa and John Boessenecker believe the Kinnear stage traversed at the point of Philpot's murder. Mrs. Sosa identifies the area where John Rose stands as the road that the runaway team raced down after being frightened by gunfire. This would require the runaway team to make a near perfect ninety degree turn without crashing the stage at high speed. Further, this roadway does not head to Benson as it must to be confirmed by the primary sources. Photo by Aubrey Rose.

The same photo from the previous page, but annotated with the wagon route that the Kinnear stage must have traveled if Mrs. Sosa and Mr. Boessenecker were correct. Bob Paul noted that he did not gain control of the runaway team for one mile after the Philpot shooting took place in the wash, making this site and theory impossible. Photo annotated by Kevin Pyles.

Because of Curtis' and Hill's clear testimony, and the deed above, we now know without question that the TTR/Sosa site was constructed after 1889, at least eight years after Philpot's death, and was part of one of the northern ranches of John Hill that he allowed his sons John Hill Jr. and F.M. Hill to occupy, selling out to W.S. Gray in 1894, as the deed above illustrates. GPS coordinates taken from the Rockfellow map prove conclusively that the W.S. Gray site is the exact location that John Herron of the BLM misidentified as Drew's Station in 1990. (Herron was drawn to this conclusion by the error that Solon Allis had made in 1881. See below for more information.)

This is why it is surprising that, years later, this same site was publicized on the internet as the discovery of Mrs. Nancy Lewis Sosa, who did not acknowledge Mr. Herron, and who also misidentified it as Drew's Station, now commonly known as the TTR/Sosa site. (Ironically, prior to Sosa's discovery of the Herron site, the TTR group had scheduled field trips to the correct Drew's Station, south of the Gray ranch.) Mr. Herron stated to me that he used the notes of Solon Allis to determine the Drew site. Allis was hired in 1881 to survey the San Juan de Boquillas Y Nogales Land Grant for its new owners, James Howard and his wife Janet who were partners with George Hearst.

Sosa site supporter John Boessenecker stated that "The correct location of Drew's Station was ascertained by Tombstone historian Nancy Sosa in 2010. She consulted railroad maps and assessor's records and was kind enough to lead the author and other historians on a tour of the site. Today, nothing is left but part of the slate foundation of the stage station and one adobe corner of Drew's house, located two hundred feet north of the station." [107] It is unfortunate that Mr. Boessenecker was not aware of the original discoverer of the Gray site, John Herron, as this information did not surface in his research before he validated Mrs. Sosa's claims of discovery.

In defense of Mr. Boessenecker, his book was already at the University of Oklahoma's Press and in process of being published, when I published for the first time ever William Drew's testimony and mileage in *On the Road to Tombstone: Drew's Station, Contention City and Fairbank*. Also of note is that Mrs. Sosa has publicly stated that she also has a copy of William Drew's testimony, but has yet to acknowledge that this alone disqualifies hers and Herron's site. But Mr. Boessenecker has yet again reiterated his support of Mrs. Sosa and her Drew's Station site on the internet even after William Drew's testimony was published for the first time in August of 2012.

Another issue with Boessenecker and Drew's Station is the mileage between Contention City and Drew's Station. Of this distance that Bud Philpot traveled on his last journey before being murdered just south of Drew's Station Boessenecker writes the following: "The trip was uneventful as the stage stopped to change horses at Contention, shortly after sundown, then proceeded toward Drew's Station, two miles beyond." [108] Boessenecker offers no source for the statement that Drew's Station was two miles north of Contention City, but in his recent book he does note that "Casey Tefertiller critiqued the section on Tombstone." Whether or not this means that Tefertiller, author of the landmark *Wyatt Earp The Life Behind the Legend*, critiqued material relating to Drew's Station is unknown to myself. But there emerges a common thread between both authors: They both published incorrect mileage when writing about the distance from Contention City and Drew's Station. "Near Drew's Station, two miles from Contention, a man stepped onto the road and yelled, 'Hold.'" [109]

It is curious that Mr. Tefertiller cited this distance as two miles, since he does list as one of his newspaper sources the March 16th, 1881, Tombstone Daily Epitaph article. This key article was based on telegrams by the survivors of the attack, including Bob Paul himself, and is a primary source that is more accurate and definitive than some of the other newspapers that Tefertiller cites, especially by those accounts published by newspapers which were far removed from the locality in which the tragedy occurred. The Epitaph reported,

"As the Stage was going up a small incline about two hundred yards this side of Drew's Station and about a mile the other side of Contention City, a man stepped into the road from the east side and called out "Hold!" (For more analysis of the spatial relationships between Drew's Station and Contention City, see "On the Road to Tombstone: Drew's Station, Contention City and Fairbank" by John D. Rose.)

William Drew knew where he built his home and where he lived. Anyone today wishing to dispute the location of Drew's Station faces a unique challenge. Those who choose to refute Drew's sworn testimony may need to ask themselves what possible proof would ever convince them? Further, if the principal primary source on this subject, William Drew, holds no sway to some researchers in their analysis and deliberations, why pursue such knowledge in the first place if it appears to mean little when it is finally revealed for the first time after 130 years?

Although Mr. Boessenecker refers to Mrs. Sosa's research materials as proof of her claims, he fails to cite what specifically in those materials convinced him of her case even in light of William Drew's definitive testimony. If Mrs. Sosa is indeed correct, as Mr. Boessenecker and Mr. Tefertiller both state, then William Drew, founder of Drew's Station, is wrong. In all other areas of their books, Mr. Boessenecker and Mr. Tefertiller have fully complied with and in many areas far exceeded the publishing standard to provide their sources to their readership. Serious authors such as Boesssenecker and Tefertiller are eager to do so, as this gives their research the credibility to which it is entitled. Yet both authors have bypassed this practice in endorsing Mrs. Sosa.

It should be noted that Mrs. Sosa has promised her readers on the internet a publishing of sources for over two years, and as of this writing, (February 2013) still has not done so. She further states that if others wish to see her sources they can come visit her or attend a lecture. Her credo, "History is best preserved when it is studied, understood & shared with everyone" does not seem to apply in this case. "Everyone" may not be able or choose to go see her or attend a lecture. Why not publish the materials and offer a detailed analysis as to why she believes they prove her point and see if her assertions stand up to the historical scrutiny of all in the field?

This issue aside, Mr. Boessenecker is to be commended for his substantial efforts to bring the remarkable career of Bob Paul to life.

John Rose stands at the exact location that John Boessenecker stood on page 163 of his book *When Law Was in the Holster The Frontier Life of Bob Paul*. William Drew testified that he lived about three miles north of the "old ruins," aka, Terranate. This location is 3.5 miles north of Terranate, disqualifying it as the attempted robbery site near Drew's Station. The GPS coordinates of this location are N 31degrees 47' 58.8"   W 110 degrees 12' 26.7".

CHAPTER 11

CHIMNEYS ON THE DESERT-ANATOMY OF A MYTH

It is an enduring irony that a 19th Century visitor to the San Pedro Valley, with well-versed technical skills, could open the door to a myth that is still being perpetuated over 130 years later. George Hearst had acted in concert with James Howard, who gained control of the Boquillas Grant in the U.S. Courts. He then brought Hearst into the ownership, and his wife Janet Howard would soon hire Tucson surveyor Solon Allis, U. S. Deputy Mineral Surveyor and Civil Engineer from Tucson, to survey this substantial piece of land, over 17,000 acres.

While surveying the boundaries of the grant, he also made mention on the resulting map of key points such as Contention City, the Contention and Grand Central mills, and the old ruins at Santa Cruz (de Terrenate) among others, and the widths of the river at various points. In Allis' notes, he also highlights other landmarks along his line of measure: adobe house (numerous references to these), new hotel, high gulch, old chimney, etc.

Solon Allis began his survey of the Boquillas land grant on February 23, 1881, at the confluence of the Babacomari and San Pedro Rivers and walked south, apparently along the center line of the grant. He made specific mention of the Christianson house, south of the Babacomari. After Allis measured the southern border of the grant, he headed north. When he reached the chimney and house just north of the "Post marked S.J.B.N. No. 9," he identified it as Mason's, and marked it as such on the map. "Chimney of Mason's House bears N 56" 28' E." [110]

The story of Drew's misplaced ranch begins here, in 1881. Allis continued walking north, but found that the trees and brush became too thick to negotiate, so in order to bypass them, he walked a right angle to the east 1,680 feet, then to the north 977 feet. At this point to his west at 300 feet stood some type of structure which Allis identified as Drew's House. It was located between a wash to its east, and the steep decline to the river on its west.

Allis placed Drew's approximately 500 feet from the San Pedro River, when the Eckoff Riecker map of 1880 clearly shows Drew's Station located near, but not this close to the San Pedro. William Drew, on his 1879 map, located his building closer to the eastern border of his property, very close to the stage road, which made a great deal of sense for his business. Drew's seven acres of crop fields fronted the San Pedro River, and he did not build his home/station in the middle of his crop field, as his map illustrates.

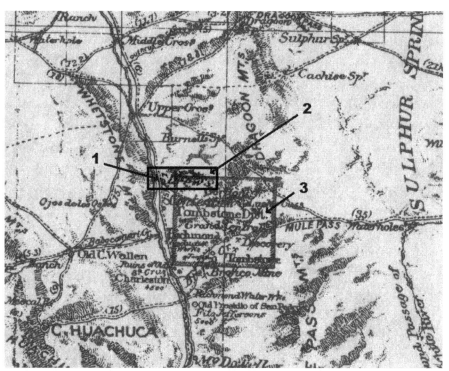

A Cropping from the 1880 Eckoff Reicker map, showing Drew's. #1 points the location on the map that designates Drew's, #2 points to the spelling on the map of Drew's, and #3 points to the letter signifying the Tombstone District. Copy of Eckoff Reicker map from the collections of John D. Rose. Annotated by Kevin Pyles.

Drew not only chose the location of his home site, but also helped lay out the stage road with Robert Mason and H.F. Lawrence. Such decisions do not appear random, but rather, the result of careful thinking by a man looking for opportunities to provide for his family. (See "On the Road to Tombstone: Drew's Station, Contention City and Fairbank," by John D. Rose, pages 3-4.)

On the above 1973 USGS topographic map, information from Solon Allis' survey map has been superimposed. This will give the reader a reasonable idea of how the roads and river ran according to Allis in 1881. The irrigation canal from the hill marked 3818 (center of map) was walked and mapped northward to the large wash northeast of Gray's. Note the location of Gray's ranch (to the east of Allis' Drew's ranch). As stated before, this was the discovery of John Herron in 1990. How did he reach this location? As an archeologist for BLM, Herron was requested by the Drew family to research and find the site of Drew's Station. In my discussion with Herron, he told me how he followed the Allis notes, and that it drew him to that general area, and that he hiked through large amounts of overgrowth until he found the adobe walls. Herron wrote the Drew family and told them of his discovery. "I was recently doing some archaeological research and read the notes of a Mr. Solon Allis who did a survey of the San Juan do las Boquillas y Nogales Land Grant in 1881. I located in his incidental description a 'Drew House.' I plotted his measurements on a USGS topographic map, and went into the field to see if I could locate the house in question. Stumbling through a mesquite thicket at the edge of the San Pedro River I found the corner of an adobe structure. There isn't much left, but I believe this to be the best documented location of the house your family lived in. The location is further north than any of the experts told us it was." [111]

Now there are two sites in question, instead of just one. In analyzing the work of Allis and the discovery of Mr. Herron, a plausible explanation appears. Solon Allis made detailed measurements of his locations. When checking his locations for mills along the river, he is very accurate. So if Mr. Herron had followed the

Allis notes as written, chances are his exploration took him to a site that no longer existed, because it was located close to the San Pedro flood plain. A large amount of erosion has taken place between the 1880's and today, even between the 1970's, when this topo map was produced, to the present. The site Allis identified is now lost in an ever widening river bed, as Charleston has eroded over the decades and is being washed away. A short distance from Allis' Drew's Station, an old tin can was found, but nothing more.

If Herron took the same route as Allis and then exited the river climbing to higher ground, I can confirm the challenge that he faced. Given there was no site near the river as it was already gone, he may have continued to doggedly pursue searching for a site over rough, overgrown terrain, traveling to a point .16 of a mile east until he discovered the Gray Ranch. Given that this is the closest site to the area that Allis identified it may have appeared reasonable that this must be Drew's. What John Herron did find was not Drew's Station, but the Gray Ranch, and he deserves credit for doing so. The Gray Ranch has been proven in this book not to have existed until after the Philpot shooting, and further that it is not Drew's Station.

The adobe that he found is but 43 feet south of an area that has been consumed by the widening of the San Pedro River. This lower area may have once been part of W.S. Gray's crop fields. Both the Gray Ranch and the Allis site called "Drew's House" are indeed too far north. But if one were to use Allis' notes exclusively to measure Drew's location, it would place Drew's Station closer to the TTR/Sosa site.

The following three pages feature the map that I asked Leonard Taylor to create for this book. Leonard's map traces the footsteps of Solon Allis as he made his survey. Further, I have taken Leonard to this area and we have explored these sites together. Notice Allis' survey route from turning post #7 and his detours of east and north right angles to avoid the overgrowth. Allis' "Drew's House" is at the top of the map. The windmill on the map exists today and is noted for those who wish to navigate the area.

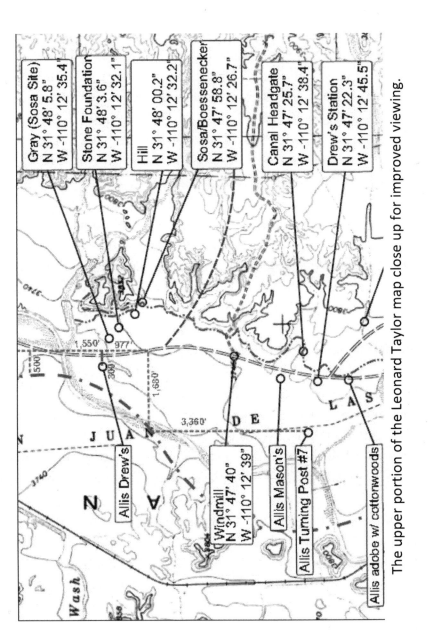

The upper portion of the Leonard Taylor map close up for improved viewing.

Gray (Sosa Site)
N 31° 48' 5.8"
W -110° 12' 35.4"

Stone Foundation
N 31° 48' 3.6"
W -110° 12' 32.1"

Hill
N 31° 48' 00.2"
W -110° 12' 32.2"

Sosa/Boessenecker
N 31° 47' 58.8"
W -110° 12' 26.7"

Canal Headgate
N 31° 47' 25.7"
W -110° 12' 38.4"

Drew's Station
N 31° 47' 22.3"
W -110° 12' 45.5"

Allis Drew's

Windmill
N 31° 47' 40"
W -110° 12' 39"

Allis Mason's

Allis Turning Post #7

Allis adobe w/ cottonwoods

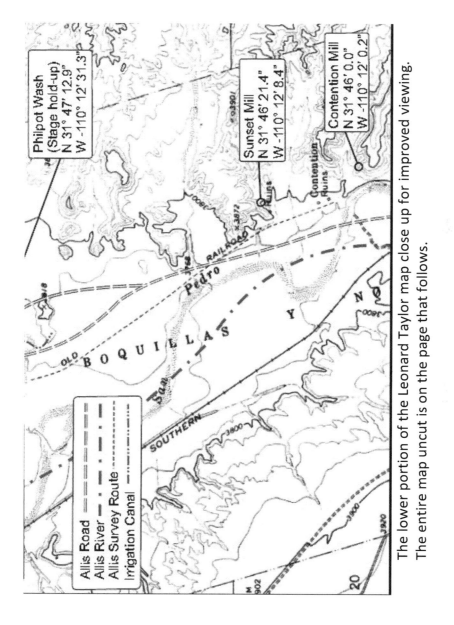

The lower portion of the Leonard Taylor map close up for improved viewing.
The entire map uncut is on the page that follows.

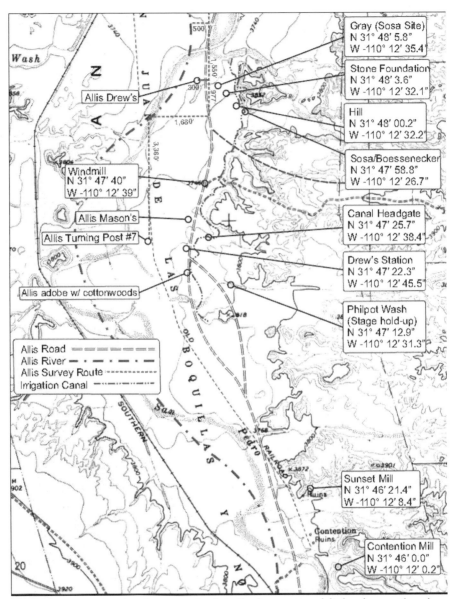

The above map is the most detailed ever published on the key locations at and near Drew's Station, as well as the route that Tucson surveyor Solon Allis traversed as he made is notes for his map of the land grant. Special thanks to Leonard Taylor for creating this map.

So how did Solon Allis conclude that the place he saw was Drew's? Allis' assigned task was the proper survey of this substantial piece of land, so it should not be assumed that Allis would be an expert on who lived in which home, or what life in that area was like on a continuing day to day basis for its long-term residents. Allis was a visitor (his office was in Tucson). As such he was misinformed as to which location was the real Drew's. Keep in mind that by February 1881, when Allis conducted his survey, Contention City had already replaced Drew's Station as the stage stop in this area. Drew's was no longer a place where a high percentage of travelers stopped on their way to Tombstone.

It is interesting that Allis also made the same error regarding Mason's ranch. While they are relationally correct, they are both too far north. Drew himself said that his ranch was about three miles north of the old ruins. Allis places Mason at about this location – 2.98 miles as the crow flies, and 3.2 miles as the road curves north of Terrenate.

Allis' error has had an unfortunate effect, as it has caused some to speculate that we may never know where Drew's Station was. But it is clear that from testimony and foundation stones that we know exactly where it was and still is, regardless of a minor error from a survey conducted over 130 years ago. For Solon Allis to be right, William Drew and Bob Paul would have to be wrong.

William Drew testified as to the dimensions of his ranch - we know that he had 160 acres which measured ½ mile in each direction. It is also clear that Robert Mason's ranch is the same size. Testimony in the Hill vs. Herrick case confirms this. Based on this, the Mason ranch cannot be any further north than 2.5 miles from Terrenate. Drew's testimony and hand-drawn map were not challenged during the Drew vs. Mason case as to their veracity or accuracy, though the map is not to scale. Though it is of interest to speculate as to how Allis made his errors, both of these home sites found their way into his notes approximately .83 miles north of where they should be.

And again, such an error does not indicate that Allis was not competent at his job. His survey did not consist of the duties of a census taker, knocking on doors, verifying the names of those who lived at a given location, etc. However, as we examine the Carlisle Map (see above), Allis may have mistaken the home of a Morgan or another individual who settled on the property north of Drew's. He located a hard site along the river and incorrectly called it Drew's.

CHAPTER 12

HERRICK'S RISE FROM PERJURY TO POLITICS

"Mr. Herrick's heart beat with patriotism as he heard these words..." –Tombstone Epitaph.

Following the closure of the case its participants went back to the same pursuits that brought them to court in the first place- ranching and farming. Judge Barne's decision couldn't control the most important factors, the weak flow of the San Pedro River and the intermittent and seasonal rain fall that could make or break any of their operations. Courts could only adjudicate what was to be done with whatever amount of water existed at any given time, just as was done in the Hill vs. Herrick case.

The summer of 1890 brought with it massive flooding, an ironic event given what had just transpired in court. These events doubtless prompted a humorous statement from rancher Herrick. "H.C. Herrick says that it is a great country where a man has to fight for water nine months in the year and fight against it the other three months." [112]

Maybe a man needed a good sense of humor to endure the trials the river put him through. Intermittent outbreaks of cattle illness plagued ranchers there. At times such incidents had been blamed on diseased cattle brought up from Mexico, and other times those affected where at a loss for an explanation. Given all of his years ranching along the river, Herrick would also suffer from the same. "Reports are coming in that many cattle are dying around the Huachuca Mountains. From Mr. H.C. Herrick, whose ranch is on the San Pedro river, the Prospector learns that a young heifer died in the vicinity of his house last night. She was apparently well a few hours before she was found dead. This morning another was discovered dead in the neighborhood of the railroad track. Both animals were in good condition and probably died from...disease." [113]

The brand of H.C. Herrick as published in the Sunday June 8, 1902. Original Tombstone Epitaph from the collection of Kevin T. Pyles.

Herrick would also see press over an incident that took place with another member of the animal kingdom. It revealed one of Herrick's favorite dinner dishes, as well as the fact that in close quarters, a bobcat was no match for the farmer living near Fairbank. "To retire for rest after a hard day's work and be awakened from a sound sleep by an extra-large bob tail wild cat and a dog above your covering must be a peculiar and not very desirable sensation. If there is one thing in life for which friend Herrick, of the San Pedro, has a penchant, it is young spring chicken, fried to a delicate brown in ranch butter that has just been brought from the spring house, and to that end he has been zealously guarding a few plump birds in a strong box close by the door of his sleeping apartment at home.

"So a few nights ago, being awakened by a noise in the coop, he lost no time in ascertaining the cause. Expecting to find a weasel he unexpectedly encountered a wild cat. Salutations were informal and precipitate, especially on the part of the cat, which, doubtless, deeming the presence of Mr. Herrick an invitation to participate in his hospitality, made a break for the first open door, closely pursued by a watch dog. In this room soundly asleep was one of the workmen attached to the ranch, whose first intimation of trouble was the presence of the wild cat and dog on top of the bed engaged in a vigorous discussion of their respective merits with father Herrick at the door who in calm, unimpassioned tones, advised him [the workman] to scoot. He scooted, and closed the door, the dog following in his wake, and the cat was left in possession. Incensed at the aggression, Mr. Herrick secured his artillery, Mr. Lamb procured a light, and the 'gates ajar' was sung, the door thrown open, and on the first discharge the victim of misplaced confidence was badly wounded, to be finally floored with a single-tree, and Mr. Herrick arrived in the city yesterday with the scalp [of the Bob Cat] attached to his belt." [114]

Herrick would entertain politics, as he was known as one of the staunchest Republicans in the area. But two years after the 1890 floods he also offered a reason as to why he wouldn't run for office, only to do so later anyway. "H.C. Herrick says that water in the river is getting scarce, and that he is not going to run for the legislature next fall." [115]

Just a week following that announcement, Herrick would take up a new line of stock for his ranching operations. "Mr. H.C. Herrick who lives on the San Pedro river, has gone into poultry raising in a scientific manner, having put up another adobe building to hold the incubator, which he has constructed in accordance with his original ideas on the subject. He deserves success." [116]

Considering his treatment of Hop Kee and the other Chinese who were working with him at the time Herrick apprehended twenty pounds of potatoes, it was of little surprise that Herrick would take it upon himself to arrest a group of Chinese. "The nine Chinese who were arrested on a charge preferred by H.C. Herrick, were acquitted last evening in Justice Duncan's court." [117] Whether this arrest was based on an actual charge, or was perhaps a case of harassment, remains an open question.

Herrick came to the aid of a man named Pat Shehe, who was harmed in a buggy accident. "Pat Shehe was brought in town last night from Fairbank by H.C. Herrick, suffering from a broken shoulder, which he sustained being thrown out of a wagon during a runaway. He was taken to the hospital, where he is resting easily." [118]

THE BOYS IS ALL POPULISTS NOW

H.C. Herrick would see press that offered a lighter side to the admitted potato-stealing, Chinaman-punching rancher, known for blaming innocent beavers for building the dams which he "enhanced." In November of 1893, he shared with the Epitaph a story with a bit of humor, and whether it was true or not, he did get his name in the paper talking about his Republican roots. Good press for anyone such as Herrick with political ambitions.

"LEFT THE DEMOCRACY"

"The Tramps Have All Deserted the Ranks of the Great Unwashed. A number of tramps are moving along the N.M. & A. road at present and find a harbor in Bisbee and Nogales. The farmers along the river are called upon daily to furnish food for them.

"Mr. Herrick tells a story of one fellow who stopped for lunch a few days ago at his ranch near Fairbank. The fellow was talkative and answered all questions intelligently. Mr. Herrick is a Republican from the ground up and always branches off onto politics before anything else is thought of. 'They are all of our belief now,' said the tramp. 'They have all left the Democratic party.'"

"Mr. Herrick's heart beat with patriotism as he heard these words. He pulled down all of the good things to eat that the house contained and the tramp knew that he had struck a responsive chord in the bosom of his host. He ate until he was unable to hold another mouthful. He told the reasons why tramps and Democracy would no longer mix.

"Mr. Herrick grew ten years younger in appearance as he realized the great acquisition the Republican party had received by the hard times, and expressed his sympathy for the downtrodden poor.

"After his dinner had settled sufficiently to admit of navigation, his tramp friend concluded to go. Mr. Herrick longed to hear those welcome words once more. 'So you say that the great army of tramps has deserted the Democracy and gone over to the Republican party,' he said as he grasped the tramp's hand with a warmth that reminded him of home. 'Oh, no, yer don't,' said the departing guest. 'Yer can't fool us twice, The boys is all Populists now.' And Mr. Herrick's looks fell off the ten years they had gained an hour before." [119]

Note the depression in the bank above. This is where the wagon road lowered into Walnut Gulch near Fairbank as it crossed the ranch of H.C. Herrick. The widening of Walnut Gulch has eroded the steady descent that wagons once used. Courtesy of Richard Bauer.

Herrick's bid for a seat in the Arizona Territorial legislature was not an easy road for him. His first run in 1892 saw defeat. He ran again two years later in 1894, and this time attempted to gain votes from a broader base, including Democrats, by attending a meeting of speakers. Herrick attempted a new strategy by preparing a speech to praise those in history that he thought his audience would easily approve of: Patrick Henry, George Washington, and other highly eulogized American fathers. But through no fault of his own, the meeting went badly. "Mr. Herrick began his speech without notes, and made an impression, which lasted until he pulled out a bundle of ancient history. The platform was read by Allen T. Bird. Its allusion to the Wilson bill killing the wool industry of Cochise county caused a sensation, and will probably cause the 1300 sheep in the county to eat less hereafter."

But things really took a turn for the worse when a candidate from Bisbee, Wm. Place, "predicted that if Murphy were elected the silver mines would all start up, and cows would have twins…C.S. Fly created a most favorable impression of any speaker by bowing his acknowledgement and taking his seat. G.W. Swain said he had left his speech at home, but he talked for ten minutes telling what he would do if elected. J.V. Vickers said he would, if elected, collect all the taxes and keep his books straight. The chair then introduced Mr. Bird, who paralyzed his audience by relating a story that shocked all of the democrats in the hall, and caused the ladies and children to blush to the roots of their hair." The Epitaph stopped short of details explaining just what was said that "caused the ladies and children to blush to the roots of their hair" but the headline summed it all up best: "Vulgar Tales and Bloody Shirt Stories Take Up the Time for Two Hours." [120] Herrick may have thought better of attending these meetings in the future, but he would later reach his goal of elected office. He may not have carried the votes of John Hill and his neighbors, but it didn't hold him back either.

Herrick had the unfortunate experience of a death in his household, a nearby rancher who stopped for a visit. "John Schneider, a member of the G.A.R., [a fraternal organization known as the Grand Army of the Republic] died of heart disease last night at the residence of H.C. Herrick at Fairbank. He was an old man and kept a chicken ranch on the river. He will be buried tomorrow under the auspices of Burnside Post of this [Tombstone] city." [121]

Other small troubles would hound him from time to time. One of Herrick's teams arrived at Tombstone, and in violation of local ordinance, it was tied to a telegraph pole. The ordinance was for good reason. "A team belonging to H.C. Herrick was tied to the telegraph pole in front of the Western Union office this noon, when they became frightened at something and pulled back, breaking the pole and landing the wires in a limbered position across the street. After some time, the pole was planted again and the young man who drove the team, learned a lesson in team tying. There is a city ordinance against tying teams to awning posts or telegraph poles." [122]

Small clips would document Herrick's activities as a legislator. "A petition, to defeat the Miles county bill, was telegraphed to Wright, Herrick and Cummings, at Phoenix yesterday, with one hundred and forty signatures. Willcox people are very cunning, but it only took a few minutes to get this number of voters to sign a petition to defeat their cunningness." [123]

Herrick also found himself in a key role during an intense debate. Now instead of being besieged by downstream ranchers and their attorneys, it was political friends and foes on both sides of the spectrum. "CORNERED…Representative Herrick of Cochise County Holding The Winning Hand…The Prison removal bill is still absorbing all the attention of the lower house. The feeling on both sides is very bitter and several lively debates have taken place. Wright still continues to take a leading part for its removal. Representative Herrick has the key to the situation in his power and is besieged on all sides by the friends and enemies of the bill." [124] One might wonder if a man like Herrick actually thrived under these circumstances.

At the same time Herrick was fighting it out in the legislature, his wife went on a shopping spree with friends to Tombstone. "Professor Donnelly, of the Copper Glance mine, accompanied by his wife and Mrs. Herrick, paid us a visit, and made an investment in furniture." [125]

Herrick may have also exercised a bit of political muscle while a legislator, possibly using such status to hurry the N.M. & A. railroad to higher speeds than normal on a run from Benson to Fairbank in 1895. "The train on the N.M. & A. road was only two hours and ten minutes making the distance from Benson to Fairbank yesterday a distance of 17 miles. This quick time was on account of Assemblyman H.C. Herrick being aboard. He is fond of fast riding and the N.M. & A. always strives to please its distinguished patrons."[126]

1895 would also bring yet another death to the Herrick Ranch, this time that of a well-liked ranch hand. "Jas. Dobbins, a man who has been working on the ranch of H.C. Herrick on the San Pedro river for the past five months, died yesterday afternoon of consumption. [Tuberculosis] He was in the hands of kind friends, who did everything that could be done to make the dying man's last hours comfortable. The remains were buried this afternoon." [127]

By 1896 Herrick's son, Henry Clay Herrick Jr. would make the press for reasons that no parent would ever want to see. Herrick Sr. had paid a visit to the offices of the Tucson Daily Citizen, offering an interview on the status of his son, as well as his most current venture. "The Citizen is pleased to acknowledge a very agreeable visit, from [the] Hon. H.C. Herrick, who has, until recently, resided in Fairbanks. Mr. Herrick was a member of the last legislature from Cochise county, and by the exercise of the same worthy traits which have characterized his entire life, won merited praise from all with whom he came in contact.

"He is in Tucson, on his return trip from Los Angeles, where he was called by the dangerous illness of his 16 year old son, H.C. Herrick, Jr. Sometime ago, while engaged in play with other boys, young Herrick was struck in the head with a bunch of grass roots, and as a result of the bruise inflicted, a very delicate surgical operation became necessary.

"Dr. Fleming, of Los Angeles, a noted expert on brain diseases, has just completed the necessary operations and the boy is now rapidly improving, there being every probability that his hearing, which it was feared he would lose, will be preserved. Much praise is due the unceasing attention of physicians and nurses.

"Recently Mr. Herrick has formed a mining partnership with Mr. W.T. Cooper an expert on minerals and mineral formations. Together they are developing some extremely promising properties in the vicinity of Dos Cabezas. From extended investigations carried on for some time past, Mr. Herrick gives it as his opinion that the mountains in that particular region are simply vast natural storehouses of mineral wealth. Gold, silver and copper abound in strong, healthy, large and extensive ledges; and the beautiful specimens of gold quartz he exhibits, certainly go far in corroborating his conclusion. There is a strong probability of a sale being consummated very shortly, and in the event it is, no doubt a number of others will follow in rapid succession. Mr. Herrick gives it as his opinion that capital cannot find a more promising field for profitable investment, and predicts a very busy camp at Dos Cabezas within a short time." [128] It was just the kind of press that anyone promoting a new mining venture sought out. Such a report could spur interest and hopefully investment, and a profit to boot.

Herrick's son, H.C. Herrick Jr., or Clay as he was known, made a quick recovery, and would soon be horseback riding along the San Pedro but a few months later, when he had a chance at acquiring a coyote as a pet. Things didn't work out well for the coyote. A dramatic headline led with "THE ENEMY CAPTURED. And After a Short Confinement is Put to Death. H.C Herrick, Jr. had quite an exciting experience a few days since with a prairie wolf. He was out riding over the ranch in close proximity to the river when suddenly his dogs ran onto a coyote which, in its efforts to escape, made for the water with the dogs in hot pursuit and about midway of the stream was overtaken and held until Mr. Herrick came up, when by a little encouragement the dogs took hold of his wolfship and attempted to drown the animal by forcing its head under water and holding it there. An idea struck the young man that here was an opportunity to secure a valuable addition to his menagerie and, putting the thought to action he took his riata and waded into the river; securing the wolf he brought it to dry land but the thing was frightened and vicious and hard to handle, however Clay improvised a muzzle out of [a] piece of wire and after fixing the beast's mouth so that there was no danger from its biting, led and drag[g]ed it home.

"Reaching that haven of rest he tied up his prize and allowed it a little time for meditation on the change [of] affairs [that] had taken place, but the wolf grew more vicious with each passing hour until finally, in self-protection, Mr. H. with a heavy heart was forced to part with his pet by shooting it; and now he is out of the wolf business." [129]

Just after shooting his pet wolf of but a few hours, Clay Herrick and his father Henry Clay Herrick traveled to Tombstone to take in a show. "H.C. Herrick, Sr. and H.C. Herrick, Jr. were up from the river last evening to attend entertainment." [130]

Herrick was still putting a great deal of energy into his claims at Dos Cabezas in 1898, in hopes of a good profit for his efforts. "H.C. Herrick was up from Fairbank today. Mr. Herrick is interested in some valuable mines near Dos Cabezas, which are now under bond for a good round figure. The parties working the property under the option are pleased with the development and in all probability the bond will be taken up at [its] expiration of the time and the patience of the ex-legislator will be rewarded in a substantial manner." [131]

A NEAR TRAGEDY IS AVOIDED

Several months later, Herrick's wife showed great courage in saving the life of a young woman who could have burned to death. "Last week Miss Carrie Williams who resides with Mr. and Mrs. H.C. Herrick on the river narrowly escaped a terrible death. While building a fire in some manner the dress of the young lady became ignited and was soon in flames. But for the presence of mind and the thoughtfulness of Mrs. H.C. Herrick, who extinguished the flames, the consequences might have been frightful. Fortunately the young lady escaped without injury for which she can thank Mrs. Herrick whose heroic action probably saved her life." [132]

James Herrick, H. C. Herrick's oldest son, in late 1899 would inform the Tombstone press that things were going well in their fight to stay on the Boquillas Grant even in the face of determined new ownership that wanted them moved off the property that had been home for so long. "James Herrick came up from his ranch upon the San Pedro. Mr. Herrick is feeling in a very happy mood owing to the news concerning the Boquillos [sic] land grant to which reference is made in another column of this issue." [133]

H.C. Herrick appears above with substantial holdings ten years after the Hill vs. Herrick case in 1899, the year that the Kern Land and Cattle Company took control of the area. Book 1, page 101, courtesy Cochise County Archives.

Fairbank during the historic period. Copy photo from the collections of John D. Rose.

FAIRBANK CELEBRATES, FOR NOW

The other report referred to, published on the same day, read as follows: "A dispatch to several parties living at Fairbank last evening from Tucson stated that the Boquillas Land Grant had been thrown out or rejected by the Land Court at Tucson. Upon the strength of this citizens of Fairbank held a mass meeting and gave full demonstration to their joyous feelings and sentiments in the matter. The ranchers living upon this grant have our sincere congratulations upon the termination of this matter and it comes to them as a regular Thanksgiving offering." [134] But this would not be the last that residents would hear of the Kern Company.

Still busy with his mining claim in 1902, the Bisbee Daily Review reported, "H.C. Herrick returned from Dos Cabezas last evening. He reports business improving and a number of people are doing some development...and have unabated faith in the value of their holdings...The Summit tunnel belonging to Herrick and Cooper is in 130 feet in ore and seems to be in a fine prospect.-Prospector."[135]

That same year, Herrick was traveling back and forth between the Fairbank area and Dos Cabezas, and soon had another title to add, with other duties. The man who had lied so easily during the Hill vs. Herrick case was now, of all things, the new judge at Fairbank. Given that the infamous "Justice Jim" Burnett of Charleston fame had also held this position, it could at least be said that Herrick was an improvement where ethics were concerned. "Petition of the citizens of Fairbank for the appointment of H.C. Herrick Justice of the Peace read. All members voting aye. H.C. Herrick was duly appointed Justice of the Peace Precinct No. 13. Clerk instructed to notify H.C. Herrick to file his official bond." [136]

But just as he had the good fortune to be named Justice of the Peace at Fairbank, his health was also in decline. The Arizona Weekly Citizen referred to him as "the oldest in years" as a reason for his chairmanship of a committee in the legislature, on January 26, 1895. "The many Tombstone friends of H.C. Herrick will be pained to learn that the old Arizona pioneer is rapidly failing, and fears are entertained for his recovery." [137]

CHAPTER 13

JOHN HILL BEFORE AND AFTER THE SUIT
"The delay is occasioned by the transferring of passengers across the
break at Hill's ranch." –Tombstone Daily Prospector, 1890.

Hill's ranch and area was still of importance to the interests of
Tombstone and the travelling public in 1887, just as it had been when
William Drew began laying adobe bricks with son Harrison and two
hired hands. "A petition in accordance with law having been received
asking the division of the Fairbanks road district, it was…ordered that
the roads from Hill's Ranch to the Boston Mill and from Fairbanks
across the San Pedro river, and including each and every of the streets
through and in the unincorporated towns of Fairbank and Contention,
and the country included within three miles of the said roads, are
hereby seggregated [sic] from the Fairbank Road District, and are
hereby declared as composing the Grand Central Mill Road District,
and S.W. Wood is hereby appointed Road Overseer of said Grand
Central Mill Road District and required to give an official bond in the
sum of $500 for faithful performance of his duties." [138]

In 1888 Hill and his neighbors would see a manhunt sweep
through their area. A love triangle turned deadly, and a shooting death
and subsequent pursuit, would place these ranching farmers north of
Contention City on the route of trackers on behalf of justice for a
husband who was gunned down over his cheating wife. Hill's
neighbor, Samuel Summers, actually had the killers cross his property,
and his ranch was part of the topography of the chase. It was the kind
of violent death that harkened back to the March 1881 shooting of
Bud Philpot and Peter Roerig, and in the same general area. [139]

John Hill would suffer a visit from a hungry visitor who
repaid the hospitality by unleashing a tragedy on one of his neighbors,
Andrew Wild. "A Mexican who did not appear to be overly well
balanced in his upper story stopped at John Hill's place last night and
was given something to eat. From there he went on to Wild's ranch

and, whether intentionally or accidentaly [sic], he set the haystack and barn on fire. The latter contained two fine horses, which were burned to death along with the other contents. Sheriff Kelton sent a deputy down there as soon as word was received here [Tombstone] of the fellow's doings. Up to 4 o'clock nothing had been heard of him." [140]

John Hill would see a surprising business opportunity born out of a natural disaster a year following Hill vs. Herrick. Massive flooding so damaged the N.M. & A. railroad that the area of John Hill's farm would have an additional value. The N.M. & A. had become the standard of travel from Benson south to Contention, and Hill's properties were located between these two points. The days of stage coaches filled with passengers had long since passed, and old stage roads were used more for area residents. But because of the flooding, transportation infrastructure was so damaged that changes were required just to keep the local economy moving. Stage travel would return to this area for the first time since Contention City rose from the high desert floor to replace Drew's Station as the key stop when traveling south first from Tres Alamos, and later Benson, on the road to Tombstone. Just as William Drew had foreseen his opportunity for a stage stop in that area, John Hill now saw the same opportunity return, offering him an unanticipated boom in the stage stop business.

The Tombstone Prospector updated its readers on August 5th, 1890, who were affected by such inconveniences. "The mail now leaves Tombstone at 8:15 a.m. and arrives at about 4:30 p.m. There will be but one stage running out and one in until the railroad is repaired to Fairbank from both sides. The stage company run six horses to Fairbank, change there and make the trip to Hill's ranch, where the train from Benson arrives about 11 o'clock. Passengers are transferred across the break to the stage and upon arriving at Fairbank another change is made and six fresh horses carry the passengers to Tombstone. The enterprise shown by the stage company and the obliging disposition of the railroad company is a pleasing contrast with the wash-out days a few years ago, when no mail arrived in

Tombstone for two weeks and passengers were obliged to camp until walking was good."

Other updates from Hill's read, "The stages are running to Hill's ranch, a few miles below Contention, where the trains on the N. M. and A. make close connection." "The stage arrived at 5 p.m. this afternoon. The delay is occasioned by the transferring of passengers across the break at Hill's ranch." [141] It was an enterprise that Hill likely never had envisioned, but once repairs were made to the railroad the status quo would soon return, leaving behind his days operating "Hill's Station."

Just after his loss in the suit against Herrick, Hill himself was on the defensive as a legal action loomed against him, his brother George Hill, and son John Hill, Jr. It started with V.H. Igo who had attained a government contract to provide hay for the hungry army horses stationed at Fort Huachuca. Igo had hired the Hill brothers to cut the grass, to the protest of the owners thereof. The genesis of the issue took place not on the Boquillas Grant, but the nearby Babacomari Land Grant. "The papers filed to show that the Hill brothers entered upon the grant…and have been and now are cutting natural grass, to the damage of the plaintiffs, who have the grant stocked with cattle to its full capacity…The defendants when they heard of the probable suit against them moved off of the grant, and by the time the papers were served on them were not trespassing." [142]

HILL BUILDS TO THE NORTH AND LATER SELLS THE TTR/SOSA SITE

Sometime between 1889 and 1894, John Hill would build further to the north than the old Drew place once had been. He would later be the owner of two homes to the north of Drew's Station, and may have constructed them, or hired out the construction of them himself. One of these two homes listed on the Rockfellow map as "Hill" was his residence, and just to the north of that was another site that was listed as "Gray." But originally, the site north of Hill's was built for his sons, who resided there until 1894 when he sold the property to W.S. Gray. The newspaper of the time was mistaken in stating that the seller was John Hill, Jr., when it was actually his father.

What is also clear is that no record exists or even alludes to these northern homes when Philpot was killed. In fact Hill hadn't even arrived in that area at the time of the shooting, on March 15th, 1881. He arrived months later as he testified, in late 1881 or early 1882, and when he did locate in the area north of Contention City, he lived first at Mason's former ranch. And testimony also proves that as late as 1889, the Drew site, which was now the home of Elijah Clifford, was still the northern most home site with the Mason/Cable ditch extended to it. Curtis' distribution ditch did exist by 1883, and it is likely that when Hill did build further north, he procured a right to that water, or kept his right from the Mason ranch.

"John Hill Jr., has sold his ranch at St. David to W.S. Gray, formerly of Willcox, and will, with his family, leave next week for Thatcher, Graham county, to remain. He has purchased both a home in the town and a farm just outside, where, with the industry that has always characterized him he hopes to build up a fortune. Cochise county is sorry to lose him, but wishes him success." [143]

JOHN HILL THE SPORTING MAN

Hill also loved races horses, and before his lawsuit against Herrick et al he had a winning one that he was partnered in. Perhaps some of his winnings found their way into his initial fees to launch the suit. "John Hill and John Roberts were in town [Tombstone] Thursday. They were exceedingly jubilant over the victory of the little roan pony, which succeeded in defeating the best blooded stock that could be brought against him. The race took place in Phenix [the Tombstone press was known for often intentionally misspelling Phoenix] last Saturday-Hungry John being the loser-distance 600 yards, for a purse of $500. Cochise county is hard to down [beat], when it comes to men, horses or pumpkins." [144] The reference made to the pumpkins may have related to an oft repeated story that an early name for Phoenix was Pumpkinville, given the amount of pumpkins once under cultivation in that area.

On February 14, 1891, the Tombstone Daily Prospector noted that Sheriff Kelton had appointed John Hill as Deputy Sheriff. The appointment was designed to instill greater order in the area that Hill resided in. It was always remote, even when stage traffic flowed through there in the days of William Drew, and so a lawman on the ground was clearly needed. John Hill was a good choice for the job. Harkening back to the free meal that Hill had given to a drunk who then set fire to Andrew Wild's barn, the Daily Prospector told its readers, "The New York tramp who set fire to the Wild barn and was subsequently captured by John Hill, was up before Judge Wolcott yesterday and leaves tomorrow for Phenix, [sic] in charge of Pete Hook, where he will take up his residence as a guest of the Territory."[145]

John Hill Jr. would later suffer a business setback four years after he moved to Thatcher, with losses and a hard lesson about trusting too much as his only compensation. "The experience of John Hill, Jr., as given in the Bulletin, should be a caution to our farmers about shipping hay away from home, and especially to Los Angeles. Mr. Hill sold seventy tons of hay to a buyer from Los Angeles, who was at Thatcher and saw the quality of the hay. When the hay arrived at Los Angeles it was turned over to another hay firm, who paid the freight and unloaded the hay in their hay yards. Then Mr. Hill was notified that the hay was damaged and would not be paid for. Mr. Hill went to Los Angeles, but was unable to arrange the matter satisfactorily. It seems the hay was of the first cutting and was really first-class hay here at home and could have been sold here for as much or more than was offered by the California buyer. Hay, however, is rated different in California. Mr. Hill lost $200.00 besides the expense of a trip to Los Angeles, receiving only half of the agreed price, with the understanding when hay sells for more than he has received he is to receive the difference." [146]

W. S. GRAY IMPROVES UPON HIS RANCH

W.S. Gray would waste little time in getting to work on his newly purchased land. The following year, 1895, he made a point of visiting the office of the Tombstone Epitaph and telling them of his progress. Key to his advances was access to irrigation water. Although wells were often dug in his area with success, pumping in the late 19th Century was expensive and rarely seen on such types of small family farms. William Drew had dug a well on the Drew's Station site, but still risked Robert Mason's wrath in laboring long and hard to first extend the Upper San Pedro Ditch to his property. Then after Mason literally shot at him over it, and also pointed his shotgun at Drew's son Edward, Drew was then willing to pursue the matter through the courts. He fought for the water as he knew he had to have it to irrigate the seven acres of mostly corn that he had planted. Given the amount that W.S. Gray was planning on irrigating, 75 acres, the idea that he would attempt to water such a large piece of land while dragging a bucket from his well is clearly untenable.

The ample testimony of Hill vs. Herrick further makes this clear. All of the river ranchers/farmers told of their hard and long labors to build dams in the river and dig ditches to feed water from the dam across their land to reach their crops. None told of installing pumping systems. The mills had such devices, but these were well funded operations, and could support such substantial purchases and the accompanying maintenance that they demanded. These farmers simply couldn't make the money back on such outlays of needed capital.

"W.S. Gray came up the river yesterday and spent a few hours in town. He has 75 acres in alfalfa this year, which will be ready to cut next month. He also has a fine lot of hogs which he believes are destined to become a valuable class of live stock to raise in this section. Mr. Gray is one of the most enterprising and consequently one of the most prosperous on the river." [147] Articles in the local press stop short of specifying how Gray was able to irrigate his 75 acres; Curtis still had his distribution ditch which reached his place to the north; it is possible that both Hill and Gray were able to access this ditch.

By 1897 Gray was after additional water, and hoped that an artesian well he was sinking would be of use. Such a well would also mean that if fights arose over surface water again as they had in the Drew vs. Mason and Hill vs. Herrick cases, an underground water source was at least harder to sue against since its impact on others was more difficult to determine, especially in light of the technology existing at the time. But even today artesian well owners find the need to add pumping to their systems. "W.S. Gray is up from the river today. He is having an artesian well sunk on his ranch and has already attained a depth of 225 feet. Mr. Gray expects to drive his well down 600 feet to secure a strong flow." [148]

But Gray also had other talents, and joined a group of performers united by their common bond of living on or near the river. "W.S. Gray was up from Fairbank today. Mr. Gray is a star performer with the San Pedro Thespians and it is understood the company will come to Tombstone during court and show one or two nights at Schieffelin Hall." [149] Note that the Epitaph says Gray is from Fairbank on May 28, 1899. Given that the Rockfellow map shows Gray at the site just north of John Hill's place, the reporter is likely referring to the nearest thriving town to Gray, since Contention did not survive into 1899 to the extent that Fairbank did. Gray also filed a notice of Homestead on this property. [150] In addition to being a bit of an area celebrity as a member of the San Pedro Thespians, Gray also served as Clerk of the Board of Trustees, for San Pedro District Number 10. [151]

CHAPTER 14

THE PARTY IS OVER-EVICTION NOTICES

"Sheriff Lewis last week by order of the court removed all the old residents..." Bisbee Daily Review, 1904.

Rallies and mutual confidence in the ranchers' cause to stay on their homesteads soon proved to be of little consequence, as The Kern Land and Cattle Company continued its legal victories, and news in 1902 reflected the inevitable. "Another batch of papers was distributed along the San Pedro river Tuesday by the claimants of the alleged Boquillas grant, notifying the settlers 'to get off the earth.'" [152] That the Epitaph would call into question the validity of the grant was more a function of sympathy than reality. The era of small time ranching farmers was closing, and nothing could be done to stop the loss of homes that many thought they had legal right to, and had often paid for, as well as paying taxes on such lands. The harsh reality was that they had always been little more than squatters, albeit it well intended ones.

On February 14, 1899, the Court of Private Land Claims decreed that the right to the Boquillas Grant had indeed been lawful, and that its foundational authority was derived from the State of Sonora Mexico in 1833, which was further enforced by the terms of the Gadsden Purchase. (Nine months later John Rockfellow would begin his mapping of this area.) Following up from this ruling, a patent was issued for the Grant on December 14, 1900. With the issuing of this patent, the right to the entire grant was legally verified, giving credence to earlier legal rulings on the matter and making clear the ownership would not fall in favor of the settlers, but rather to Boquillas Land and Cattle Company. Only by purchasing these lands from the earlier verified owner, George Hearst, and later his estate, could a legal verifiable claim have been established and maintained. It was simply a lost cause that these homesteaders could never win. It is an enduring irony that had Hearst been more aggressive about his grant claim and held new coming residents accountable to either purchase a parcel or stay as temporary renters, ranchers may not have lost so much in financial and emotional investment. [153]

Herrick gave a candid assessment of his feeling regarding the pending loss of his home and business. "H.C. Herrick was at the county seat today [Tombstone] from his ranch at Fairbank. Mr. Herrick states the confirmation of the Boquillas [land] grant by the land court has made the many settlers upon this land, himself included, feel rather blue, but thus far none of the settlers have moved. It is believed a final effort will be made to overthrow the legality of the grant and permit the undisputed possession of the buildings by the settlers." [154]

NEVER COUNT A HERRICK OUT

In 1904 James Herrick would continue the fight following his father death, showing much of the same pluck, with issues that involved the land grant, and (perhaps characteristic of this family) a Chinese farmer. "James L. Herrick eldest son of the late Hon. H.C. Herrick, who died at the age of 72 years, several months ago at the family home at Fairbank on the San Pedro, is in the city on legal business in connection with the case of the Chinese farmer who lived near Mr. Herrick's home and whose case was recently heard before [the] United States Commissioner Culver, deportation being ordered and appeal taken. Mr. Herrick said that the settlers on the San Pedro, those living on the Hearst grant, hope to settle matters very soon with the widow and her son the candidate for the Presidency." It was noted at the time that the Hearst estate did indeed have a clear right to the Boquillas Grant, as ruled by the court of private land claims. "The Herricks and others now desire to obtain a good and sufficient title to these valuable lands. Both James and Clay Herrick, brothers, are energetic young citizens of Cochise county. Clay Herrick has been a very successful real estate dealer at Douglas." [155]

Just over a month later, on July 21st, 1904, the Bisbee Daily Review would publish the inevitable and painful news. "Ousted From Homes-Sheriff Lewis last week by order of the court removed all the old residents, with the exception of one, from the Boquillos [sic] land grant…J.N. Curtis refused to leave his place as he has a patent given him by the United States to the ground he occupies. Many of those who had taken up their homes in this grant did so thinking that it was on government land, and have been in possession of the ground for many years. The contestants to the ground will carry the case to the Supreme Court of the United States." [156] J.N. Curtis may be related to S.B Curtis whose ranch is named on the Rockfellow map. Recollect that a Joseph Curtis was farming with his brother at the same northern location. [157]

This further diminished the fading hopes of settlers along the river, but in the case of Herrick's son, H.C. Jr., his family name and long presence along the San Pedro meant one more try at victory in the courts, and this time a Herrick would be the plaintiff, and not the key defendant. The suit initiated by young Herrick would also travel upward through the courts and onto the Supreme Court of the United States, in 1906. Herrick v. Boquillas Land & Cattle Company is still a formative case that has been cited in other cases where land use and water utilization are as deeply intertwined as they were and are along the San Pedro. On January 2, 1906, the U.S. Supreme Court decided in favor of the Boquillas Land and Cattle Company. Lawsuits and the San Pedro River would remain well acquainted with each other well into the 20th and 21st Centuries.

"U.S. SUPREME COURT DECIDES IMPORTANT ARIZONA CASES

"Boquillas Land Co. Wins Contest With Settlers—Decision of Territorial Court Upheld in Coconino County [This is misstated and should read "Cochise County"]

"Washington, Jan. 2—The U. S. Supreme Court today affirmed the decision of the Supreme Court of Arizona in the case of

H. C. Herrick and others versus the Boquillas Land and Cattle Company, decision being in favor of the latter.

"This case involved a controversy over the Boquillas Land grant in Cochise county, embracing 17,255 acres. The action was brought by about thirty settlers who claimed twenty years occupancy before the cattle company took possession. They asked for restoration of the lands, $1,000 damages, and $10,000 a year rental since 1901. In opinion by Justice Brewer, the Supreme Court of the U. S. today affirmed the decision of the Supreme Court of Arizona in the case of Howard vs. Perrin, involving title to certain land within the Atlantic and Pacific railroad grant in Coconino county, Arizona.

"The case involved the Arizona statute of limitations and the right to use seepage water for irrigation." [158]

Even in the 20th Century lawsuits indirectly related to the San Pedro were launched against the strategic Fort Huachuca Army installation. Over the decades, whether it was one Native American tribe fighting another, or rancher against rancher, farmer against farmer, or environmental groups against the U.S. Army, the San Pedro has never long been the peaceful location that its serene physical appearance implies, and it likely never will be.

The End.

APPENDIX A
Solon Allis notes and newspaper clippings, and his map.

On the pages that follow, the field notes of Solon Allis are published in quantity for the first time. I am doing this so that other researchers can have access to the materials that I have acquired over many years of study and collecting. Although there are gaps in my copy of the Allis notes, this offers the reader a great deal of information about the San Pedro River in 1881. Regardless of the fact that Allis misidentified the location of the Mason and Drew Ranch, one can learn what the width of the San Pedro was in varying places, and find a glimpse of the river from a surveyors view. When I began my research of this area I was not aware of the existence of some of these materials. By sharing them in this book, it allows the reader to see first-hand some of the materials that are required to do such research, as well as the opportunity to utilize the same for their own discoveries. References in period newspapers that mention Solon Allis will be seen in the pages that follow his notes.

BOOK 1712

Preliminary
Survey of the

San Juan de las
Boquillas y Nogales
Private
Land Claim
Cochise Co.
Arizona

Survey Commenced Feb 23d 1881
under instructions from Surveyor Genl
John Wasson dated Feb 22nd 1881
and
Contract of Feb 1st 1881 —
N° 61
Preliminary Survey Completed
March 5. 1881

Solon M. Allis U. S. Dep Surveyor.

BOOK 1772

Preliminary Oaths of Assistants.

We, *Samuel K Van Pelt*
and *Charles W. Weeks*
do solemnly swear that we will faithfully execute
the duties of Chain Carriers; that we will level the
chain upon uneven ground, and plumb the tally
pins, whether by sticking or dropping the same;
that we will report the true distance to all notable
objects, and the true length of all lines that we assist in measuring, to the best of our skill and
ability.

Saml K Van Pelt
Chas W Weeks

Sworn to and subscribed before me, this 23d
day of *February*, 1881.

Solon M. Allis
Notary Public
Pima Co A. T.

We, _William W. Dodd_
and Charles W. Platt
do solemnly swear that we will well and truly perform the duties of _Oxeman_
and "Flagman
according to instructions given us, and to the best
of our skill and ability.

Wm W. Dodd
Charles W. Platt

Sworn to and subscribed before me this 23ᵈ
day of _February_ 188!

Solon M. Allis
Notary Public
Pima Co. A. T.

253

IC

BOOK 1772

Index.

'D

San Jaun de las Boquillas y
Nogales Private Land Claim Cochise Co. A.T.

Survey commenced Feb. 23d 1881

First proceeded to the point
where the Babacomori Creek
enters the San Pedro River
and opposite what were once
known as the Mule Mts.
Here I set a post of
Mesquite 14 by 14 inches sq,
five feet long marked
S.J.B.N. No. 1. Two feet in
the ground and built a
mound of Earth around it.
This Post is set quite
near the bank of the San Pedro
River on its East bank and
distant from the mouth of the
Babacomori Creek which
enters the San Pedro from
the West, 46 feet bearing

BOOK 1772

San Juan de las Boquillas y

Nogales Private Land Claim broken los A.J.

N 52° 33' W –

Var 11° 28' E by obs
on Polaris

From this Post the
S.W. Cor of an Adobe House
bears S 58° 10' East dist 4.30
feet.

Edge of River, dist 10 feet.

Steep Banks.

Having thus established
the Initial Point of the Survey
I proceeded to run the Center
Line South.

As by my instructions
this line is to be run 245
Cordeles to correspond with
the distances mentioned in
the original grant Papers. I
find that it equals 33680.45
feet as by reference to

BOOK. 1772

San Jauu de las Buquillas y Nogales

Brief Land Claim Pockies Co N Y.

Feet	printed instructions from the General Land Office at Washington — One Cordell contains 50 Varas and as by the same instructions one Vara equals 32.9931 inches
	Taking the general course of the Valley from this point I run
	Var 11°28'6 by obs on Polaris at this point S10°03'E
500	In a point opposite Adobe House which is 300 feet left
1100	Crossed Road to Fort Wallen running S W
3000	Crossed San Pedro River feet wide running N W
4700	Crossed Road which runs up the Valley to Charleston

257

San Juan de las Boquillas y Nogales

Private Land Claim Cochise Co A.T.

Feet	
5125	Adobe House. 100 ft. left occupied by Chinamen who have about 20 Acres under Cultivation
7050	Top of flat Mesa here making a steep point crossing the line from the West.
8500	Crossed Charleston road running S.W.
9500	Crossed San Pedro River running N.E. here 10 ft wide
10500	Opp Christianson House. 200 ft left at foot of Mesa
	Feb. 24th
13000	Top of Steep rocky Ridge crossing line in a S.E. & N.W. direction
13400	Bottom of Ridge
14200	Top of 2nd Rocky Ridge

BOOK 1772

San Juan de las Boquillas y Nogales

Private Land Claim Cochise Co A.T.

	N.E. & S.W.
	N.E. & S.W.
15000	Opp Empire Mill also called Boston Mills 600 ft left.
15100	Crossed Ditch
15300	Empire Mill Office 1600 ft left.
15700	Boarding House 1100 ft left.
15800	Crossed San Pedro River 15 ft wide running N.W.
16000	Small Wooden House about 300 ft Right —
19600	A Point 10 ft Right of the upper end of Mill Ditch where it commences to run straight. Direction of same from this point N 4° 13' E
19700	Crossed ditch.
19900	„ San Pedro River 15. Get wide running N.E.
21500	Same running N.W.

b

BOOK 1772

San Juan de las Boquillas y Nogales

<u>Private Land Claim Course by A. J.</u>

21400	Crossed ditch running N. W.
25800	" " " N. E.
35700	" " River " N. E. 10 ft wide
26300	Crossed road to Charleston running S.E. at foot of cliff Hill
27200	Crossed high pt. of ridge
29300	Bottom of ravine which here is a steep rocky cliff
39500	Cross River running N W 15 ft wide
	Give Mods pass left
29850	Opposite Corbin Mill 100 ft left
30200	Opposite large new block with hipped Roof near the Center of the Village of Charleston and distant about 500 feet to the right

260

San Jaun de los Boquillas y Nogales

Private Land Claim _____

Feet

30680   Cross the San Pedro River
        running N 16 ft wide —

33353   Crossed South Wall of the
        ruins of old Corral of San
        Rafael.

36680.45 Reached the South East Corner
          of the Claim where I set a
          Mesquite Post 4 ½ ins × 4 ins,
          of 5 ft long marked
          _____; Set Post
          2 ft in the ground and
          built a monument of Stone
          2 ½ feet high from which
                    Var 12° 21' E at this
          Point by comparison with
          Transit line,
                    U.S. Mineral Monument
          on ____ Hill bears S 57° 31' E
          A Large Cottonwood tree
          on bottom near the River bears

San Juan de las Boquillas y Nogales

Private Land Claim locaties by A.J

Post   A 74° 47' W dist 168 ft —

February 25th

Returned to Initial Point of survey at Batocomori Creek, and starting at ceule as established proceeded to run across the claim to set Post No 2 at corner where side lines intersect, the direction of Valley from this point northward makes, an angle of 5°37' West or to the left.

     Turning 90° plus the deflection angle I ran —
Var 11° 28' E
N 77°11' E —

550   To a point opposite House
190 ft to Right

700   To Road to Fort Wallen

San Jaun de las Boquillas y Nogales

Private Land Claim by his Ex X X
feet

running South

1200   To Charleston Road running
        South

5851.40 To Corner where I set a post
        of pine 3 x 3 inches sq. 1 ft long
        marked S J B N X 5 R one
        foot in the ground and
        built a mound around
        it from which

                A small Knoll about
        30 ft high bears S 61° 05' W
        dis 300 ft

        Ind of deep bank of Mesa
        50 ft ast bears W

        Ajax Hill bears S 65° 05' E

Returning to center or initial
Point I now there

            Var 11° 38' E

20   S 77° 10' W to opposite or West
        bank of San Pedro River —

BOOK 1772

San Juan de las Boquillas y Nogales

Private Land Claim Locating by A.I.

Feet	hence 10 ft wide
400	To point opposite House 600 ft left
500	To Batocomori Creek 5 ft wide running N.E.
2600	Crossed same running S.E. 10 ft wide
3500	" Same running N.E. 10 ft wide
8700	Crossed road running N.E.
11600	Crossed sharp spur of high Klofs of Mesa coming down from the right.
8745	Steep tank of Steep gulch and dry wash 50 ft wide
585120	Set Post 99 feet North of true place as corner could in bottom of Arroyo. Set Post of Mesquite 8 x 3 inches sq. 5 ft long

San Juan de las Boquillas y Nogales

__Private Land Clo in Cochise Co. A.T.__

Jer

    marked S.J.B.N. Nº 3.
3 ft from the East Bank
2 ft in the round and
built a monument of stone
2½ ft high from which
    A Mesquite Tree 16 inches
    in dia bears N. 32° 28′ E.
    dist 78 ft.
    A Mesquite Tree 16 inches
    in dia bears N 11° 32′ W
    dist 65 ft.

Returning to center or Initial
Point I ran down the Valley
According to my instructions
this line is to be 300 chains
or 41241.38 feet in length
to center line of Claim — Var 12°
1800   N 15° 89′ W to road
running S.W.

BOOK 1772

San Juan de las Boquillas y Nogales
Private Land Claim Cochise Co. A.J.

ft	
4900	Crossed San Pedro River running N.E. 10 ft wide.
4900	Adobe House about 2000 ft right.
5500	Foot of Mesa Adobe House about 2200 ft Rt.
7300	Adobe House about 2200 ft right.
8000	Opposite Grand Central Quartz Mill about 2600 ft right
8500	Office of same 2700 ft Rt.

February 26

| 12200 | Crossed North Wall of ruins of old Santa Cruz Corral and buildings on summit of steep bluff facing N. & E. — |
| 12500 | Foot of steep bluff and commencement of flat — |

San Juan de las Boquillas y Nogales

<u>Private Land Claim. Cochise Co A.T.</u>

Feet

13600	Crossed San Pedro River running West – here 15 ft wide –
14900	crossed same running N.E.
17600	Opp Contention Mill 1900 ft Right Also New Hotel 1900 ft Rt.
20000	Crossed Road running N. W.
20500	Opp Sunset Mill about 2100 ft Right
21700	Crossed San Pedro River running N. W. 15 feet wide steep banks.
22800	Opp Adobe House 500 ft Rt
23200	" " " 700 " "
23700	" " " 500 " "
24850	" Old Chimney 15 ft Rt –
26700	" Adobe House with row of Cottonwoods 800 ft Rt –
27813	Set post for turning point

BOOK 1772

San Jacin de las Boquillas y Nogales

<u>Private Land Claim Cochise Co A.T.</u>

feet

as Valley here turns to the R^t
Post of Mesquite 3 x 3 inches
5 ft long marked <u>S.J.B.N.N°7</u>
Set ten feet in the ground
and built a mound around
it From which

Chimney of Mason's House
bears N 56°28' E dist 1500 ft
Willow post (blazed) of
wire fence 6 inches in
dia 6 ft dist bears N
7°02' W
San Pedro River nearest
point bears S 83°09' W
Dist 2125 feet.
Thence I ran down the Valley
Var 11°28' E

3360   N 1°58' E To bank of San
Pedro River - Bank very
Steep and high -

San Juan de las Boquillas y Nogales

Private Land Claim Cochise Co A.T.

feet

As river bottom was very much
broken with steep banks
and full of trees and brush
I turned right angle to
Course to the right and
run 1680 feet. Here I
turned right angle to left
and run on this offset line
N 1°58' E

       Var 11°28' E

and at

3887   Crossed road to Tombstone
      running S.E.

4337   Drew's House 300 ft left

5887   San Pedro River 500 ft left

6687   Crossed Tombstone Road
      running South

8887   Crossed same running S.E.

11987   "   "   "   N.E.

13+28.38   Reached North End of Claim

San Juan de las Boquillas y Nogales

Private Land Claim Cochise Co A.T.

Feet	
	of steep high Mesa forming a narrow tongue
3100	Summit of 2nd High Mesa forming a narrow steep ridge
3560	road in flat running E.&W.
5280	Set Mile post of Pine 1x3 inches marked <u>S.J.B N. 1 Mile</u>
10560	Set Mile Post N° 2 on summit of high ridge
14201.38	Set temporary post for Corner or turning point at intersection of side lines

March 1st

Returned to Post N° 7 already described and ran across the Claim to set post on intersection of East Side lines I ran from Center

San Juan de las Boquillas y Nogales

Private Land Claim Cochise Co. A.T.

feet

           Var 11°28' E

      N 83°09' E   across flat

1220 To wire fence running

      N & S at foot of Mesa.

5104.94 To Cor where I set a pine

      post 3×3 inches marked

      <u>S.J.B.N N° 9</u>. Post 4 ft

long drove one foot in the

ground and built a mon-

-ument of stones around

it 2½ feet high. This post

is on North Slope of a flat

Mesa 400 feet North of a

steep Gulch —

      Returning to center or

Post N° y I ran thence

      Var 11°28' E

Towards intersection of West

side lines S 83°09' W

1080 To West edge of plowed ground

San Juan de las Boquillas y Nogales

Private Land Claim Cochise Co A.T.

feet

1250   To Gulch N + S.

1950   To Steep bank of San Pedro
       River running N.W. here
       15 feet wide

2000   Cross road running N.W.

2275   Bottom of Mesa and Steep bank

2400   Sharp ridge of detached Mesa
       facing the South. Small
       Adobe House about 700 ft
       left.

5104.94 Set post for Corner finding
        my temporary post set
        45 feet too far East and
        92 feet too far South
        making the distance from
        post No 11 to this post

14109.38 ~~14109.38~~ feet as measured
         and 92 feet less than
         Calculated distance 14201.38 ft.
         This error of 92 feet in

San Juan de las Boquillas y Nogales

Private Land Claim Cochise Co A.T.

fet

measurement is allowed for
in running the next mile —
    Post of Mesquite 3×3
inches sq 5 ft long marked
S.J.B.N. No 8 Set two feet
in the ground and
build Mound from
which
        Rincon Peak bears N 37°28′W
        Sharp Peak of Whitstone
    Mts bears N 78° 30′W
Thence I ran from Post No 8
        Var 11° 28′E
Along West boundary of Claim
            S 15° 89′ E

1639   Set 3d Mile post from N. W.
       Cor— in flat 12 ft north
       of Road—

1651   Crossed Road running N.E.
       & S.W. —

BOOK 1772

San Juan de las Boquillas y Nogales

Private Land Claim Cochise Co A.T.

feet	
3750	Top of steep bank of Mesa
6919	Set Mile Post No 4
8200	Crossed road E & W
12199	Set Mile Post No 5
17479	" " " No 6
22759	" " " No 7
24800	Opp large flat hill about 1500 ft left
28039	Set Mile post No 8 Country from 3750 ft to here rolling Mesa covered with good grass and much brush

March 2nd

| 28450 | Struck 15 ft et or west of Post No 3 already described as being set 29 feet north of true place or point — This makes my line as |

BOOK 1772

San Jaun de las Boquillas y Nogales

Private Land Claim Cochise Co A.T.

feet

measured 209.21 feet longer
than calculated distance 28240.79
As the middle line rran through
comparatively level ground
and free from obstructions I
concluded the error to be
in measuring and assumed
the corner to be correctly
established as described
heretofore and allow error g
209.21 feet in measuring
the next mile—

Thence Iran
Var 11°28' E
Along West side g Claim
from Post No. 3.   S 10°02' E
125 To South side g steep bank g
Arroys—and foot g steep bluff
500 Summit g steep bluff
1500 Opps Cienga and pond

BOOK 1772

San Juan de las Boquillas y Nogales

Private Land Claim Cochise Co A.T.

Feet	
21120	Set Mile post N° 4
26200	Opp Adobe House in Valley
	2700 ft left

March 4th

26400	Set Mile post N° 5 on Steep ridge
26800	Opp new Wooden House in Valley dist 1500 ft left approx
28700	Crossed Steep Gulch 100 ft wide
31680	Set Mile Post N° 6
33586	Crossed Gulch 100 ft wide
33986	Struck point 43 ft left of post N° 2 already described

As this line is by calculation 33926.66 feet long error in measurement amounts to 59.34 ft Said error I allow for in measuring the next mile

From this post I

BOOK 1772

San Juana de las Boquillas y Nogales

Private Land Claim Cochise Co A. T.

pan

Var 11° 28 E

N 15° 39 W

600	To road running N, W.
2263	" bottom y Mesa and end y wide flat—
2600	Top y high ridge
3034	Set Mile post N= 7—
3900	Top y high hill
	From here to 8290 cross series y small hills and hollows full y brush
8290	Crossed Road from Grand Central Mill to Mine—
8314	Set Mile post N= 8

March 5th

10900	Cross Gulch and road—
13594	Set Mile Post N= 9.
17250	Cross Road from Contention

34

BOOK 1772

San Juan de las Boquillas y Nogales

Private Land Claim Cochise Co A.T.

feet

	mile to Tombstone S.E.
17800	Cross high and sharp ridge
18874x	Set Mile post No 10
24154	" " " 11
27356	Struck point 37 ft left of
	Post No 9 already described
	As my line should be (by
	Calculation) but 27286.21
	feet I find this line has
	69.79 feet error in
	measurement which I allow—
	for in measuring next mile.
	Thence I ran from Post No 9
	Var 11° 28' E
600	N 1° 58' E to bottom of hill
1400	To road to Tombstone running
	E, W—
1500	Bottom of hill and end of
	flat—

BOOK 1772

San Juan de las Boquillas y Nogales

Private Land Claim Cochise Co A.T.

feet	
2148	Set Mile post No 12 - From here a Succession of Gulches Ravines + Sharp ridges g forth hills g Mesa -
7428	Set Mile Post No 13
8080	Crossed Old road to Tombstone in flat running a little N y E.
9000	End g flat and bottom g high Steep bluff —

Offset here 400 ft left right angle to line then turned right angle to rts to avoid Steep bluffs and ran

Var 11°28'E

N 1°58'E

9150	Opp pt g Bluffs 100 ft Rt
9800	" " " 250 " "
9900	" " " " 280 " "
12000	Offsett to right, 400 ft into line and ran N 1°58' E and at

BOOK 1772

San Juan de las Boquillas y Nogales

Private Land Claim Cochise Co A.T.

feet

12615	Struck a pt 15 feet left of Post No 12 already described

As this line is by calculation 12655
feet long error in measurement
equals 40 feet
As this line was over
extremely rough ground I
assume the post as set to be
correct —

This Closed the Survey

General Description

This Claim is found in
the San Pedro Valley 60
miles S.E. of Tucson at
its Lower end —
Initial Point being at
Babacomori Creek, where

San Juan de las Boquillas y Nogales
Privat Land Claim Cochise Co A.T.

it empties into the San
Pedro River and opposite
what used to be called the
Mule Mts now called
Tombstone Hills Ajax hill
being the highest point. By
Original Grant papers
this grant contains 4 sq
leagues and as the center
line was measured south
from opp mouth of
Babacomori Creek 245
Cordeles ó 33680.45 feet
and northward 300 cordeles or
41241.38 feet thus making the
center line 545 cordells
or 74921.83 feet long, and
as the Grant calls for 4 sq
leagues. I make the
width 10090.8 feet and

San Jacm de las Boquillas y Nogales
Private Land Claim Cochise Co A.J.

one half width to be consequently
5045.40 ft

The Grant therefore
Contains 4 sq Leagues or
17355.856 Acres.

The Initial Point
is in a wide Smooth Valley
which gradually narrows
towards the South end
until at a point one or
one and a quarter miles
north of south end o the
Valley. becomes a narrow
gorge between high hills for
one half a mile then the
Valley widens and the
Town of Charleston is found
to be about 3/4 of a mile
north of South end of
Grant

San Jaun de las Boquillas ytogales
Private Land Claim Cochise Co A.T.

Going south from Initial
Point a number of farmers
have taken out water from
the San Pedro River and
are getting one or two
Hundred acres under
cultivation.
            Going north from
Initial Point the Valley
maintains a width of over
a mile for about one
and three quarters of a
mile + or a little above,
the Grand Central Mill
where it rapidly narrows
to a gorge two miles from
Initial point and
opposite the ruins of old
Santa Cruz.

San Juan de las Boquillas y Nogales
Private Land Claim Cochise Co A.T.

After passing the gorge
northward the Valley widens
to a point about 3 miles
out where it becomes
nearly as wide as the Plains
and is bounded on each
side by high and Steep
Bluffs intruding in Sharp
steep points upon the plain

The Mesas upon
the West side are comparatively
smooth and much fine
grass is found
On the East side
the Country is much
cut up by ravines and
hills covered with cat
claw and other thorny
bushes. No timber is

San Jaun de las Boquillas y Nogales
Private Land Claim Cochise Co A.J.

found except a few scattered
trees along the bottom of the
San Pedro at its lower end
At the S.E. Corner of
the Grant The End and
side lines cross several
mining claims and the
Needle is quite materially
affected. Crystals of Selenite
and Some Gypsum of
the Fibrous variety are
found on the bluffs on the
N.W. Side of the Claim
but I saw no Gypsum
beds in place,
The bottom lands
between the Mesas are of
the finest description
and many acres are
under cultivation. North of

San Juan de las Boquillas y Nogales
Private Land Claim Cochise Co A.T.

the Grand Central Mill
Upon this claim is
found the Towns of
Charleston and Contention
City and the following named
quartz mills all all
obtaining their ore from
Tombstone Mines. At
Charleston the Gird and
Corbin Mills. At Contention
City the Contention and
Sunset mills. A little
above the Contention mill is
found the Grand Central
Mill about two miles
dist. and about six miles
dist the Empire Mill
also called the Boston
Mill.
The Mill ports

BOOK 1772

Lindaun de las Boquillas y Nogales
Private Land Claim Cochise Co. A.T.

are all of pine 3 X 1 inches
and all marked
S.J.B.N & Numbered consecutively
from N.W. & S.E. Corners.
Respectively

Survey finished
March 5th. 1887

Solon M Allis
U.S. Dep. Surveyor

List of Names.

A List of the Names of Individuals employed to assist in running, measuring, or marking the lines and corners described in the foregoing Field Notes of the survey of _the San Jaun de las Boquillas y Nogales Private Land Claim_

Cochise County, Arizona

Showing the respective capacities in which they acted.

Samuel K. Van Pelt Chainman.

Chas W. Weeks Chainman,

Wm W Dodd. Axeman.

Charles W Platt Flagman.

Final Oath of Assistants.

We hereby certify that we assisted *Solon M Allis* U. S. Deputy Surveyor, in surveying *The San Juan de los Boquillas y Nogales Private Land Claim Cochise Co Arizona Territory*

and that said Survey has been in all respects, to the best of our knowledge and belief, well and faithfully executed, and the boundary monuments planted according to the instructions furnished by the Surveyor-General.

Chas R Van Pelt Chainman.

Chas W West Chainman,

Wm W Dodd Axeman.

Charles W Platt Flagman.

Sworn to and subscribed before me, this *Fifth* day of *March*, 189!

Solon M Allis

Notary Public
Pima Co A.T.

Final Oath of Deputy Surveyor.

I, *Solon M Allis*

U. S. Deputy Surveyor, do solemnly swear that
in pursuance of a contract with John Wasson,
United States Surveyor-General for Arizona, bearing date the *first* day of *February*

188*1*. I have well, faithfully and truly, in my
own proper person, and in strict conformity with
the instructions furnished by the Surveyor-General,
al, ~~the Surveying Manual,~~ and the laws of the
United States, surveyed all those portions of *the*
San Juan de las
Baquillas y Nogales
Privat Land Claim
Cochise County Arizona

_____ as are repre-
sented in the foregoing Field Notes as having
been surveyed under my directions; and I do
further solemnly swear that all the corners of
said surveys have been established and perpet-
u ated in strict accordance with ~~the Surveying~~
~~Manual and printed~~ instructions, ~~and also in ac-~~
~~cordance with the additional requirements con-~~

~~tained in circular instructions from the U. S. Surveyor General for Arizona, dated September 1, 1873, regarding the establishment of corner boundaries of public surveys~~, *and that the foregoing are the true and original Field Notes of such surveys.*

Solon M. Allis
Deputy Surveyor.

Sworn to and subscribed before me, this 26th *day of* March, 188*1.*

John Wasson,
U. S. Sur Genl.

U. S. Surveyor, General's Office,

Tucson, Arizona, *April 26*, 1881.

preliminary

The foregoing Field Notes of the survey of

the Exterior boundaries of the

San Juan de las Boquillas y Nogales

Private Land Claim,

Cachise county, Arizona.

~~of the Gila and Salt River Base and Meridian~~, Arizona

executed by *Solon M. Allis*,

D. S., under his contract of the *first* day of

February, 1881, having been critically ex-

amined and the necessary corrections and explanations

made, the said Field Notes and the surveys they de-

scribe, are hereby approved.

Jhn Wasson

Surveyor General.

292

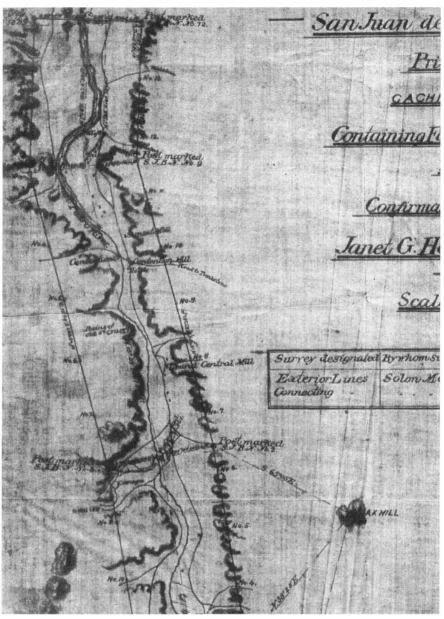

A portion of Solon Allis' map, from the collections of John D. Rose.

> Deputy United States Mineral Sur-
> veyor Solon M. Allis returned Thurs-
> day from an extended professional
> tour through Tombstone District and
> the Dragoon Mountains.

On January 8, 1881, the Arizona Weekly Citizen informs its readers that Tucson surveyor Solon Allis will be making a professional visit to the Tombstone District. This is just six weeks before he commenced his Boquillas Land Grant survey.

> Mr. Solon M. Allis will take a trip
> to Boston about May 1st.

Nearly two months after his preliminary survey was complete, Allis travels to Boston. His busy schedule may have caused him to delegate additional duties to his staff. Arizona Weekly Citizen, May 1, 1881.

> N. D. Anderson, Esq., Attorney at
> Law, has located his office with Mr.
> Solon Allis, corner of Church Plaza
> and Congress street.

Arizona Citizen, December 27, 1879.

SOLON M. ALLIS,

U, S. Deputy Mineral Surveyor and Civil
Engineer,

Tucson, - - Arizona.

Office with James Buet. Congress Street
Opposite U S. Internal Revenue office.

is prepared to do any work in his line
with promptness and dispatch.

Making Topographical Maps and Section-
al drawing of mines a specialty.

Arizona Citizen, February 1, 1879.

SOLON M. ALLIS,

CIVIL ENGINEER AND U. S. DEPUTY MINERAL
SURVEYOR AND NOTARY PUBLIC.

HAS REMOVED HIS OFFICE TO CORNER
of Pennington and Meyer streets. Topographical Maps a specialty. All business en-
trusted to him will be attended to with promptness and dispatch.

Arizona Weekly Citizen, April 28, 1883.

APPENDIX B

The following pages are the 1990 public recording of John Herron's discovery. Though he did not locate Drew's Station, he made a new discovery, now correctly identified as the Gray Ranch.

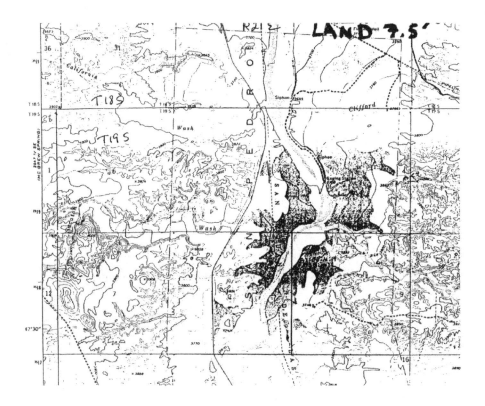

UNITED STATES DEPARTMENT OF THE INTERIOR
BUREAU OF LAND MANAGEMENT
ARIZONA STATE OFFICE
CULTURAL RESOURCE SITE RECORD   Page 2 of 8
Site Number AZ EE : 4 : 14 (BLM)

Phys Province (DESERT   MOUNTAIN   PLATEAU   (TRANSITION) ; % Slope _____0_____ ;
Elev (ft) 3720 _____ ; Exposure (N NE E SE S SW W NW (OPEN) UNKNOWN) ;
Drainage NEAREST-NAMED; Drainage Name _____San Pedro River_____ ;
Other Water Sources__springs_____ ; Distance to Closest Sources_300 M_ ;
Topo Feat _Flood-plain_ ; Topo Loc (BASE EDGE (IN/ON) NEAR SIDE RIM/TOP);
Topo Feat _River_ ; Topo Loc (BASE (EDGE) IN/ON NEAR SIDE RIM/TOP);
Topo Feat _Terrace_ ; Topo Loc ((BASE) EDGE IN/ON NEAR SIDE RIM/TOP);
Topo Feat_____ ; Topo Loc (BASE EDGE IN/ON NEAR SIDE RIM/TOP);
Environ Desc Brown, Lowe, and Pase: 224.52

_____SHS-BLM: Mesquite Bosque_____
_____ ;

- - - - - - - - - - - - - - - COMPONENT INFO - - - - - - - - - - - - - - -
#1
Component Time   (HISTORIC   (PREHISTORIC)   PROTOHISTORIC   UNKNOWN) ;
Component Function (AGRICULTURAL CEREMONIAL COMMERCIAL COMMUNICATION DEFENSIVE
                     HABITATION HERDING RESOURCE-EXPLOIT OTHER (UNKNOWN))
Component Basis   (FUNCTIONAL   SINGLE-COMPONENT   SPATIAL (TEMPORAL)) ;
Culture (ANASAZI ANGLO APACHE ARCHAIC CASAS-GRANDES EASTERN-PUEBLO HAKATAYA (HOHOKAM)
          HOPI MEXICAN-SPANISH MOGOLLON MORMON NAVAJO ORIENTAL PAI PAIUTE-UTE PALEO-INDIAN
          PIMAN PLAINS SALADO SERI TARAHUMARA TRINCHERAS UNKNOWN WESTERN-PUEBLO YAQUI
          YUMAN ZUNI);
Period _____ ; Phase _____ ;
Begin Date _____ ; End Date _____ ;
Date Method (ARCHAEOMAG ABSOLUTE ARCHITECTURE ARCHIVAL CERAMIC C14 DENDRO
              HISTORIC-ARTIF INFORMANT LITHIC OTHER RELATIVE UNKNOWN);
Feature _artifact scatter_ ; Feat Count _1_ ; Feat Desc _artifacts eroding from_ ;
Feature _____ ; Feat Count _____ ; Feat Desc _area South of the ruin._ ;
Feature _____ ; Feat Count _____ ; Feat Desc _____ ;
Feature _____ ; Feat Count _____ ; Feat Desc _____ ;
Component Desc _Mixed artifacts from badlands area. Site probably subsurface._
_____ ;

- - - - - - - - - - - - - - - ARTIFACT INFO - - - - - - - - - - - - - - -
Sample Artifact ((CERAMIC) CHIPPED-STONE EXOTIC-STONE FAUNAL FIRECRACKED-ROCK
                  FLORAL FOSSIL GROUND-STONE HISTORIC-ARTIF HUMAN-BONE OTHER
                  POLLEN SHELL SOIL);
Sample Method (EXCAVATED SUBSURF-TEST (SURFACE-ARBIT) SURFACE-COMPLETE
                 SURFACE-RANDOM SURFACE-SYSTEM SURFACE-UNKNOWN UNKNOWN);
Sample Coll Made (YES (NO)); Sample Size _____ .
Category _plainware_ ; Cat Count _999_ ; Category _R/Brown_ ; Cat Count _-1_ ;
Category _____ ; Cat Count _____ ; Category _____ ; Cat Count _____ ;
Category _____ ; Cat Count _____ ; Category _____ ; Cat Count _____ ;
Category _____ ; Cat Count _____ ; Category _____ ; Cat Count _____ ;
Sample Info_ Hohokam in appearance. 20+

- - - - - - - - - - - - - - - - ARTIFACT INFO - - - - - - - - - - - - - - - - -

Sample Artifact (CERAMIC (CHIPPED-STONE) EXOTIC-STONE FAUNAL FIRECRACKED-ROCK
                  FLORAL   FOSSIL GROUND-STONE HISTORIC-ARTIF HUMAN-BONE OTHER
                  POLLEN SHELL SOIL);
Sample Method (EXCAVATED SUBSURF-TEST (SURFACE-ARBIT) SURFACE-COMPLETE
                SURFACE-RANDOM SURFACE-SYSTEM SURFACE-UNKNOWN UNKNOWN);
Sample Coll Made (YES (NO)); Sample Size _____;

Category _flakes_____ ; Cat Count 999; Category _____ ; Cat Count _____ ;
Category _____ ; Cat Count ____; Category _____ ; Cat Count _____ ;
Category _____ ; Cat Count ____; Category _____ ; Cat Count _____ ;
Category _____ ; Cat Count ____; Category _____ ; Cat Count _____ ;
Sample Info_ 20 +,black, salicified limestone like material._____ ;

- - - - - - - - - - - - - - - - ARTIFACT INFO - - - - - - - - - - - - - - - - -

Sample Artifact (CERAMIC CHIPPED-STONE EXOTIC-STONE FAUNAL FIRECRACKED-ROCK
                  FLORAL   FOSSIL GROUND-STONE HISTORIC-ARTIF HUMAN-BONE OTHER
                  POLLEN SHELL SOIL);
Sample Method (EXCAVATED SUBSURF-TEST SURFACE-ARBIT SURFACE-COMPLETE
                SURFACE-RANDOM SURFACE-SYSTEM SURFACE-UNKNOWN UNKNOWN);
Sample Coll Made (YES NO); Sample Size _____;

Category _____ ; Cat Count ____; Category _____ ; Cat Count _____ ;
Category _____ ; Cat Count ____; Category _____ ; Cat Count _____ ;
Category _____ ; Cat Count ____; Category _____ ; Cat Count _____ ;
Category _____ ; Cat Count ____; Category _____ ; Cat Count _____ ;
Sample Info_____ ;

- - - - - - - - - - - - - - - - ARTIFACT INFO - - - - - - - - - - - - - - - - -

Sample Artifact (CERAMIC CHIPPED-STONE EXOTIC-STONE FAUNAL FIRECRACKED-ROCK
                  FLORAL   FOSSIL GROUND-STONE HISTORIC-ARTIF HUMAN-BONE OTHER
                  POLLEN SHELL SOIL);
Sample Method (EXCAVATED SUBSURF-TEST SURFACE-ARBIT SURFACE-COMPLETE
                SURFACE-RANDOM SURFACE-SYSTEM SURFACE-UNKNOWN UNKNOWN);
Sample Coll Made (YES NO); Sample Size _____;

Category _____ ; Cat Count ____; Category _____ ; Cat Count _____ ;
Category _____ ; Cat Count ____; Category _____ ; Cat Count _____ ;
Category _____ ; Cat Count ____; Category _____ ; Cat Count _____ ;
Category _____ ; Cat Count ____; Category _____ ; Cat Count _____ ;
Sample Info_____ ;

- - - - - - - - - - - - - - - - ARTIFACT INFO - - - - - - - - - - - - - - - - -

Sample Artifact (CERAMIC CHIPPED-STONE EXOTIC-STONE FAUNAL FIRECRACKED-ROCK
                  FLORAL   FOSSIL GROUND-STONE HISTORIC-ARTIF HUMAN-BONE OTHER
                  POLLEN SHELL SOIL);
Sample Method (EXCAVATED SUBSURF-TEST SURFACE-ARBIT SURFACE-COMPLETE
                SURFACE-RANDOM SURFACE-SYSTEM SURFACE-UNKNOWN UNKNOWN);
Sample Coll Made (YES NO); Sample Size _____;

Category _____ ; Cat Count ____; Category _____ ; Cat Count _____ ;
Category _____ ; Cat Count ____; Category _____ ; Cat Count _____ ;
Category _____ ; Cat Count ____; Category _____ ; Cat Count _____ ;
Category _____ ; Cat Count ____; Category _____ ; Cat Count _____ ;
Sample Info_____ ;

Component 2

- COMPONENT INFO - - - - - - - - - - - - - - -

Component Time   ((HISTORIC)   PREHISTORIC   PROTOHISTORIC   UNKNOWN)

Component Function (AGRICULTURAL   CEREMONIAL   (COMMERCIAL) COMMUNICATION   DEFENSIVE
               (HABITATION)   HERDING   RESOURCE-EXPLOIT   OTHER   UNKNOWN)

Component Basis   (FUNCTIONAL   SINGLE-COMPONENT   SPATIAL   (TEMPORAL))

Culture (ANASAZI (ANGLO) APACHE ARCHAIC CASAS-GRANDES EASTERN-PUEBLO HAKATAYA HOHOKAM
         HOPI MEXICAN-SPANISH MOGOLLON MORMON NAVAJO ORIENTAL PAI PAIUTE-UTE PALEO-INDIA
         PIMAN PLAINS SALADO SERI TARAHUMARA TRINCHERAS UNKNOWN WESTERN-PUEBLO YAQUI
         YUMAN ZUNI);

Period _____ ; Phase _____

Begin Date _____ ; End Date _____ ;

Date Method (ARCHAEOMAG ABSOLUTE ARCHITECTURE (ARCHIVAL) CERAMIC C14 DENDRO
            HISTORIC-ARTIF INFORMANT LITHIC OTHER RELATIVE UNKNOWN);

Feature House _____ . _____ ; Feat Count _-1 ; Feat Desc Adobe ruin remnant

Feature Pit _____ ; Feat Count _-1 ; Feat Desc structure?, Barrow pit?

Feature ARTIFACT SCATTER _____ ; Feat Count _-1 ; Feat Desc historic artifacts

Feature _____ ; Feat Count _____ ; Feat Desc _____

Component Desc Most of the artifacts are buried in the duff around the adobe
The pit may contain trash.

- - - - - - - - - - - - - - - - - - - ARTIFACT INFO - - - - - - - - - - - - - - - -

Sample Artifact (CERAMIC CHIPPED-STONE   EXOTIC-STONE   FAUNAL   FIRECRACKED-ROCK
            FLORAL   FOSSIL   GROUND-STONE (HISTORIC-ARTIF) HUMAN-BONE   OTHER
            POLLEN   SHELL   SOIL);

Sample Method (EXCAVATED   SUBSURF-TEST (SURFACE-ARBIT) SURFACE-COMPLETE
            SURFACE-RANDOM (SURFACE-SYSTEM) SURFACE-UNKNOWN   UNKNOWN);

Sample Coll Made (YES (NO)); Sample Size _____ ;

Category Soldered cans ; Cat Count 999 ; Category Glass bottle frag Cat Count 999

Category Crockery frags. ; Cat Count 999 ; Category Sq. cut nails ; Cat Count 999

Category _____ ; Cat Count ___ ; Category _____ ; Cat Count _____

Category _____ ; Cat Count ___ ; Category _____ ; Cat Count _____

Sample Info Glass: purple, green, aqua, brown

- - - - - - - - - - - - - - - - - - - ARTIFACT INFO - - - - - - - - - - - - - - - -

Sample Artifact (CERAMIC CHIPPED-STONE   EXOTIC-STONE   FAUNAL   FIRECRACKED-ROCK
            FLORAL   FOSSIL   GROUND-STONE HISTORIC-ARTIF HUMAN-BONE   OTHER
            POLLEN   SHELL   SOIL);

Sample Method (EXCAVATED   SUBSURF-TEST SURFACE-ARBIT SURFACE-COMPLETE
            SURFACE-RANDOM SURFACE-SYSTEM SURFACE-UNKNOWN   UNKNOWN);

Sample Coll Made (YES NO); Sample Size _____ ;

Category _____ ; Cat Count ___ ; Category _____ ; Cat Count _____

Category _____ ; Cat Count ___ ; Category _____ ; Cat Count _____

Category _____ ; Cat Count ___ ; Category _____ ; Cat Count _____

Category _____ ; Cat Count ___ ; Category _____ ; Cat Count _____

Sample Info _____

UNITED STATES DEPARTMENT OF THE INTERIOR
BUREAU OF LAND MANAGEMENT
ARIZONA STATE OFFICE
CULTURAL RESOURCE SITE RECORD
Site Number AZ:EE: 4 :14 (BLM)

- - - - - - - - - - - - - - - -SUMMARY- -

Site Discussion (include temporal and spatial relationship to other sites or districts; relationship between features, components): At present only the ruin remnant and the pit (about 15M to east of adobe) are visable. Corrals and probable field and irrigation system are yet to be located and identified. There are several historic ranches in this general area.

Site Significance (National Register qualities including integrity, justification of local, state or national importance): Integrity appears good. Site has significance in several areas- local history (Benson Stage robbery), State history in the development of transportation systems, ranches, and farms. This is also true of the Nations early colonization of the southwest.

Site Evaluation (assess and explain use potential according to the Use Categories defined in Arizona BLM Manual Supplement 8111): Site potential is excellent for both scientific study and public interpretation in that order. Site is in a sensitive to erosion area. However access is somewhat difficult at present because of vegetation cover.

Management Recommendations: Recommend excavation and mapping and public interpretation while the site is still observable.

- - - - - - - - - - - - - - - - -ACCESS INFO- -

Access (explain how to reach site, include mileages, reference well-known landmarks, key to attached sketch map and location map:

Contact Name:_____ Phone: (___) _____
Contact Address:_____

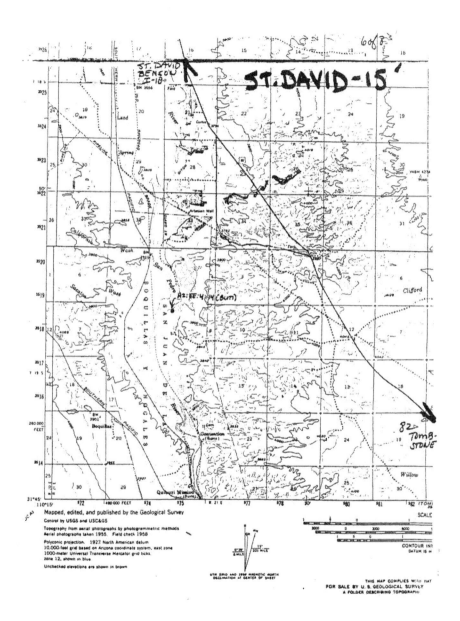

St. DAVID -15'

Mapped, edited, and published by the Geological Survey

Control by USGS and USC&GS

Topography from aerial photographs by photogrammetric methods.
Aerial photographs taken 1955. Field check 1958

Polyconic projection. 1927 North American datum
10,000-foot grid based on Arizona coordinate system, east zone
1000-meter Universal Transverse Mercator grid ticks.
zone 12, shown in blue

Unchecked elevations are shown in brown

SCALE

CONTOUR INT
DATUM IS M

THIS MAP COMPLIES WITH NAT
FOR SALE BY U. S. GEOLOGICAL SURVEY
A FOLDER DESCRIBING TOPOGRAPHIC

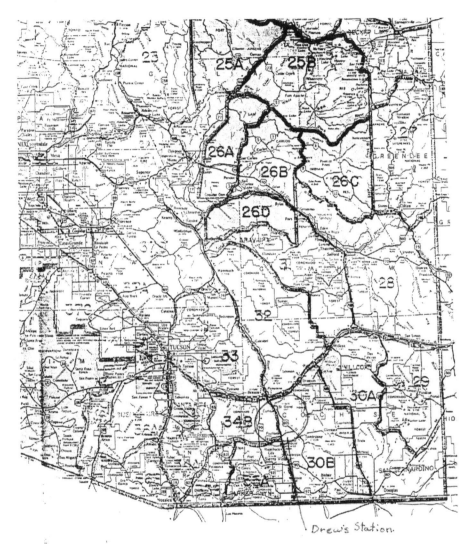

Drew's Station

COURTESY OF ARIZONA GAME AND FISH

- - - - - - - - - - - - - - - -SITE SKETCH/LOCATION- - - - - - - - - - - - - - - - - -

scale: _None_ ; _____ ; drawn by: _Herron_ _____ date: _10-15-1990_

(include key for symbols used, provide North arrow, clearly label elements)

N

SAN PEDRO RIVER   WASH

AZ:EE:4:14
(BLM)

/// Artifact Scatter
☐ Adobe Ruin Rumina
⊕ Pit depression

Badlands
Looking
Area
Containing a
Low density sherd & chipped Stone Scatter.

FORM AZ-8111-1

303

APPENDIX C

DEEDS

Although some of the following deeds have been transcribed and or cited in the pages above, I am publishing them in original form so that the reader can view them for themselves.

This Indenture, Made the 19th day of July in the year of our Lord one thousand eight hundred and ninety four, Between John Hill of Cochise County in Arizona Territory, party of the first part, and W.S. Gray of Cochise County, Arizona Territory, the party of the second part. Witnesseth: That the said party of the first part for and in consideration of the sum of One thousand dollars lawful money of the United States of America, to him in hand paid, by the said party of the second part, the receipt whereof is hereby acknowledged, does by these presents, remise release, and forever Quitclaim, unto the said party of the second part, and to his heirs and assigns forever all that certain lot piece or parcel of land situated in the said Cochise county of Arizona Territory, and bounded and particularly described as follows, to wit: Beginning at the south east corner of the said John Hill claim, thence west across the San Pedro river to the north west corner of said claim, thence south sixty rods more or less to a partition fence, thence East to the East line

John Hill Sr. sells the home that his sons John Hill Jr. and F.M. Hill had lived in until the sale of the property in 1894 to W.S. Gray. This property has been incorrectly publicized as Drew's Station, known commonly as the TTR/Sosa site. This deed, combined with the extensive Hill vs. Herrick testimony and further sources herein, prove that this site was part of John Hill's latter northern ranch, before he sold it to W.S. Gray and it then became known as the Gray Ranch. It was never Drew's Station, and did not exist when Bud Philpot was murdered near Drew's Station on March 15th, 1881. Book 12 of Deeds, page 135. Courtesy of Christine Rhodes, Cochise County Recorder.

to said claim, thence North to beginning, said piece of
land being ~~~ ~~~ by my lot ~~~ J E & M Hill.
Together with all and singular the tenements, hereditaments
and appurtenances thereunto belonging, or in anywise
appertaining, and the reversion and reversions, remainder
and remainders, rents, issues and profits thereof.
To have and to hold, all and singular the said premises,
together with the appurtenances, unto said party of the
second part, and to his heirs and assigns forever.
In Witness Whereof, the said party of the first part has hereunto
set his hand and seal the day and year first above written,

John Hill, [SEAL]

Signed Sealed & Delivered
in the Presence of
John Hill Jr.
Territory of Arizona } ss
County of Cochise }

On this 19th day of July AD 1894 before
me Thos E. Williams a notary Public in and for the
County of Graham, Territory of Arizona personally appeared
John Hill, whose name is subscribed to the annexed
instrument as a party thereto, personally known to me
to be the person described in and who executed the
said annexed instrument as a party thereto; who
acknowledged to me that he executed the same
freely and voluntarily, and for the purposes and
uses therein mentioned,
In Witness Whereof, I have hereunto set my hand and
affixed my official seal the day and year in this
certificate first above written,

[SEAL]   Thos E. Williams
                Notary Public.

Filed and recorded at request of W. C. Stacker
Sept 5th AD 1895 at 11 a.m.

A. W. Dutworth
County Recorder,

The final page of the Hill to Gray deed. Book 12 of Deeds, page 136.
Courtesy of Christine Rhodes, Cochise County Recorder.

[Handwritten:]

Filed March 6 1883 at 9.30 W M o

A P Jones

County Recorder

J H Hoops

To

D P Kimball

Sept 15 1882

This indenture made the fifteenth day of September in the year of Lord one thousand eight hundred and eighty two: Between John Hill Hoops the party of the first part and David P Kimball the party of the second part both residence in County of Cochise Arizona Territory. Witnesseth that the said party of the first part for and in consideration of the sum of Five hundred dollars lawful money of the United States of America to him in hand paid the receipt whereof is hereby acknowledge has granted bargained sold remised released and conveyed and quit claimed and by these presents does grant bargain sell remise release convey and quit claim unto the said party of the second part and to his heirs and assigns forever all the right title and interest estate claim and demand both in law and equity as well in possession as in expectancy of the said party of the first part of in or to that certain water right and interest in the dam and ditch Known as the Mason ditch lying and being in cochise county of the Territory of Arizona and more particularly described as follows to wit:

All the surplus water in said Mason ditch and canal after the necessary supply is given for

John Hill used his complete name (John Hill Hoops) above when selling surplus water to David P. Kimball from the Mason ditch. Deed book 4, page 495. Cochise County Recorder's office.

the cultivation of about one hundred
and twenty five acres of land now occupied
by the the party of the first part and under
fence and known as the Mason farm
or that portion thereof lying East side of the
San Pedro River with the right in common
to an enlargment of said ditch to the dam
on the San Pedro River and located 300 yards
north of the Old Ruins and all other rights
thereto pertaining. To have and to hold all
and singular the said premises together
with all the rights and privileges thereto incident
unto the said party of the second part his
heirs and assigns forever. In witness whereof
the said party of the first part has hereunto
set his hand and seal the day and
year first above written.
Signed sealed and delivered John Hill Hoops (seal)
in presence of B.F. Johnson
Ed Sessions

Territory of Arizona
County of Cochise

On this six day of
Febry A. D. John Hill Hoops personally
appeared before me a Justice of the Peace
in and for the said County of Cochise known
to me to be the person described in and who
executed the foregoing instrument who acknowledged to me that he executed the same
freely and voluntarily and for the uses and
purposes therein mentioned.
                    N. P. Butler
                    Justice of the Peace

Deed book 4, page 496. Cochise County Recorder's office.

APPENDIX D

The 1902 Philip Contzen map of the San Rafael Del Valle.

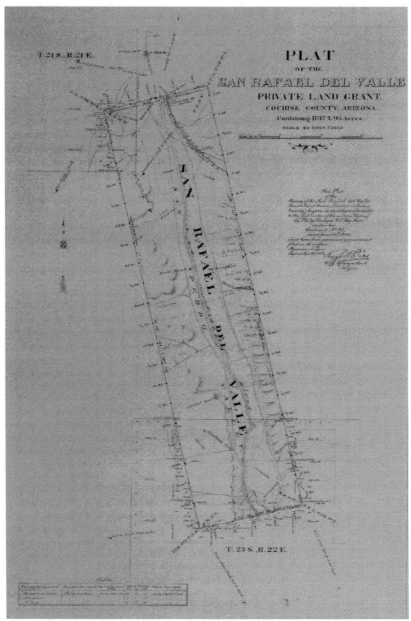

Copy of map from the collections of John D. Rose.

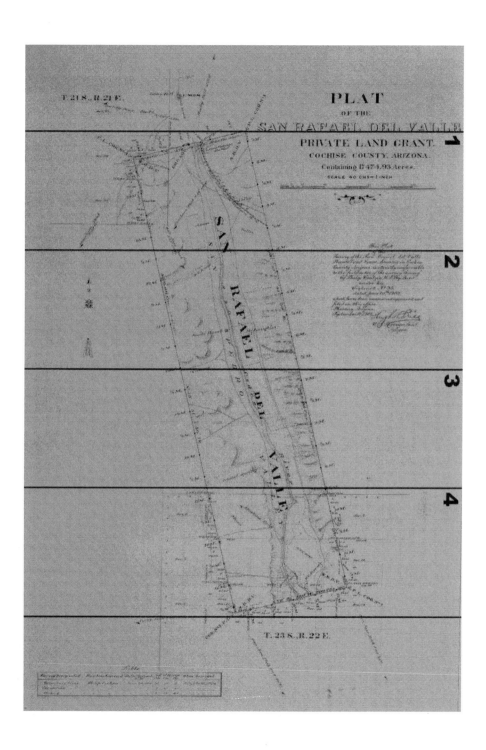

PLAT
OF THE
SAN RAFAEL DEL VALLE
PRIVATE LAND GRANT.
COCHISE COUNTY, ARIZONA.
Containing 17474.93 Acres.
SCALE 40 CHS=1 INCH

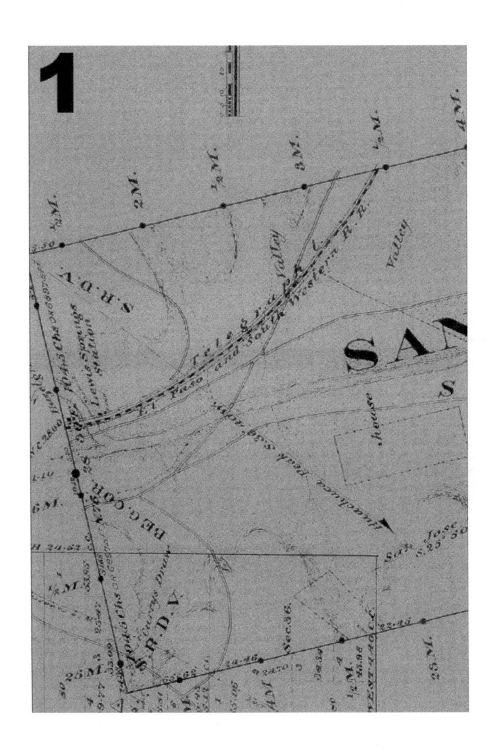

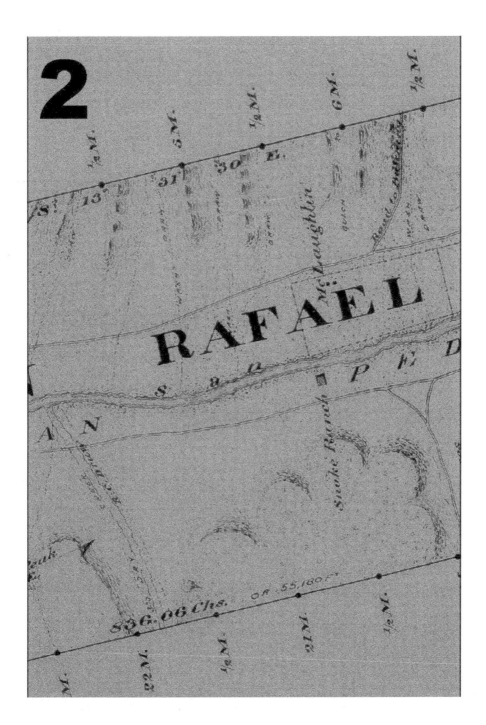

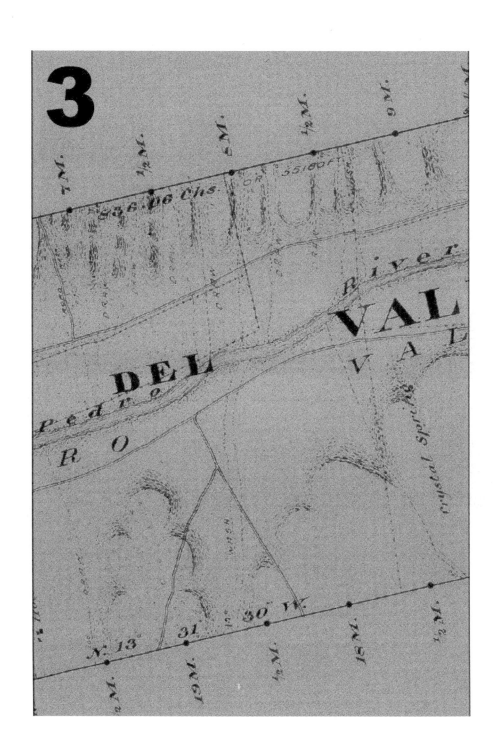

312

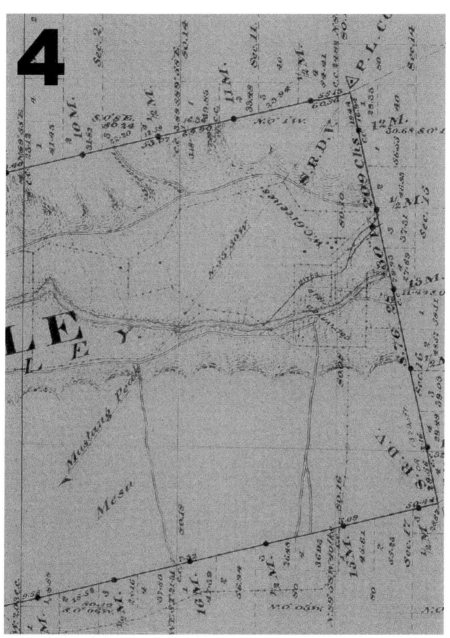

The southernmost portion of the Del Valle map above shows the
W.C. Greene Ranch.

APPENDIX E

A DISCUSSION OF THE RANCH LOCALES

"I went down there and Mr. Mason called my attention to his place…" –T.S. Harris

In the effort to determine how the parcels on the Boquillas land grant were laid out, area maps were used in concert with testimony from those who lived on these sites. Drew's hand-drawn map of 1879 gives an accurate view of the succession of ranches beginning at his place and moving south to their dam and ditch. Because of testimony as to the size of Drew's ranch, the relationships on his map may not be to scale. In the Drew vs. Mason case of 1879, Drew testified of his tract of land "…about three miles North of the old San Pedro ruins…commencing at a point 20 rods East of irrigating ditch…and east from the North line of the defendants ranch, and running North 880 yards, then West 880 yards, then South 880 yards, then East 880 yards along the North line of Masons ranch…containing 160 acres." [159] 880 yards measures ½ mile in each direction (1/2 mile square).

According to John Hill's testimony, the Mason ranch also included 160 acres, as did Davis' [Summers in 1889] and Cable's. "…Mr. Wild, Hubbard and Curtis bought out the Cable right, 160 acres of land there…" [160] 160 acres appears to be a typically sized parcel on both the Boquillas grant and the San Rafael de Valle grant to its south. H.C. Herrick bought land adjoining Landis' land on his north side, "160 acres more or less…" [161] T. S. Harris judged that it was close to half a mile when walking across the Mason place. [162] Bertolomeo Avancino stated that when Herrick fenced off his original road which passed "in the middle of the ranch…I was passing outside of the fence…about half a mile along-side of his fence…" [163] So Herrick's ranch apparently measured about ½ mile square. Landis himself had 160 acres and specified that from south to north his ranch spanned "About half a mile. It is 160 rods and it was just near the line [southern border of Herrick's property]." [164] A rod is 16.5 feet in length. 160 rods equal 2640 feet, or ½ mile. Hop Kee purchased 160 acres from Landis, [165] and P. W. B. Crane said he owned 160 acres. [166] Mr. Christianson owned 160 acres, and was cultivating about 100 acres.

W.F. Banning had a ranch in the Crystal Springs area on the de Valle grant. When asked how much land, he replied, "160 acres." His next door neighbor, Levi Scranton, claimed 160 acres as well. [167] Peter Moore, south of Greene's place, claimed "…what the law allows…160 acres." [168] If in fact these ranchers were claiming lands under the Homestead Act, there was no incentive to claim less than what the law allowed, 160 acres.

While it cannot be proven from testimony or deeds for all the ranches, William Drew, Robert Mason, H.C. Herrick, and Jacob Landis had ½ mile square parcels. Many of the ranches spanned both sides of the San Pedro River, as testimony indicates that several owners were farming on both sides. William Drew's map shows this as well. Given this information, it is possible to speculate how the original ranches on the Mason Cable ditch were laid out. Below is a speculative drawing showing how the ranches stretched further south than Drew's drawing shows, if each parcel is indeed ½ mile in length from north to south. Compare to Drew's 1879 map. There is more evidence in testimony to estimate the north/south boundaries than there is the east/west boundaries; consequently, those have been left open. Drew's map gives the reader an idea, but since then the river may have changed, and the topo map used is from 1973.

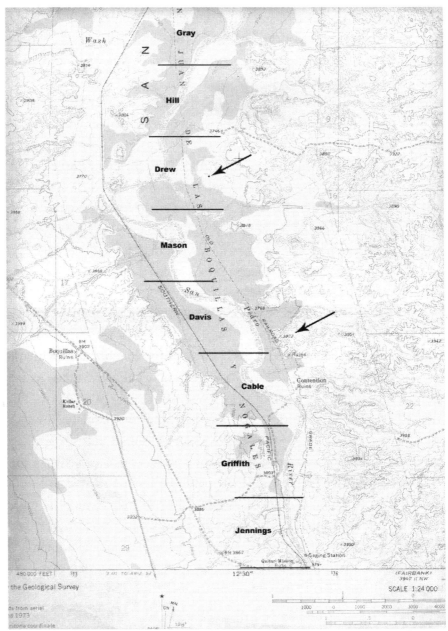

The USGS Quadrangle with overlaid estimations of the north/south boundaries of ranches in the Contention area. Special thanks to Stephanie Rose for the draft that this is based on. Annotated by Kevin Pyles.

Based on this topographic map, a discussion follows concerning the actual sites of the ranches along the river, from Drew's moving south, and the Union Dam and Ditch. The drawing of Drew's boundaries is based on GPS coordinates taken by Richard Bauer of Drew's foundation, Drew's testimony of his distance from the ruins, and his positioning of his station/home on his hand-drawn map. All other boundaries are based on this location.

Hill stated that the original dam and the head gate of the Mason Cable ditch were located about ¾ of a mile above Contention. [169] Christianson said the 1st dam was built in 1877 and 1878. It washed out in '78 and was rebuilt in 1879, "higher up." [170] It is possible that the original dam washed out in the summer of 1878 as a result of flooding from monsoonal rains. But the Jennings boys would not have benefited from the first dam and ditch because it was constructed at the very north side of their property. The second dam and ditch was built further south, "higher up" the river; as John Hill testified, "I should think the present dam is a mile and a half or a mile and three quarters, as near as I can judge it…" below the point where the Babacomari empties into the San Pedro River. [171] The deed from Mason to Kimble states that the dam was 200 yards north of the old ruins (Terrenate). [172] This means Hill's estimate of 1 ¾ miles is the more accurate; it was actually closer to two miles.

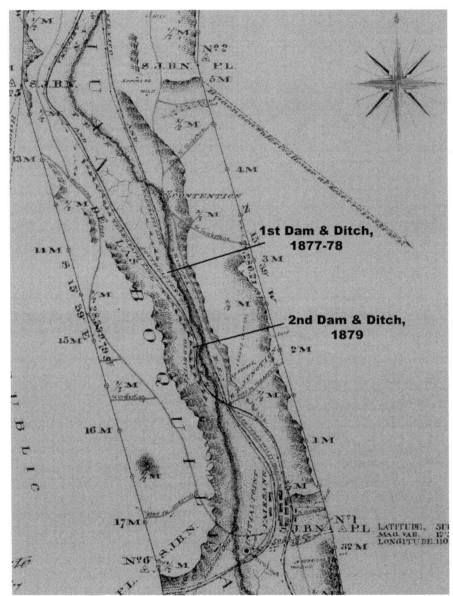

A portion of the Rockfellow map noting the location of the dams that created the reservoir feeding the Mason/Cable ditch. Annotated by Kevin Pyles.

So the new dam was located just above, or south of, Jennings' place. But by the time Hill arrived in the area, neither Griffith nor the Jennings boys were there any longer, as testimony confirms only four ranch sites using the Union ditch. No records of sales were found from Griffith or Jennings to new owners of their sites. Using ½ mile as the north to south standard for each ranch, Contention was built on Cable's ranch, or directly adjacent to it.

T.S. Harris was questioned extensively concerning cultivation of the ranches along the road. "These parties that you speak about, if they cultivated lands at all, they lived down back of the road. The road makes a bend up kind of through the hills there after it leaves this place where Mason is, it makes a bend up around and don't go to the river again till it comes to Contention, consequently there may have been people living down in there that I never saw." [173] He testified that a man named Gale lived off the road below Contention, but could not see how much land he was cultivating because "the road didn't pass that way." Gale lived and farmed on the old Davis place, owned later by T.C. Merrill who sold to Summers.

Harris also gave the location of the Wild ranch. (Wild bought from Cable.) Mr. Goodrich cross-examined Harris and stated, "The first place south of the Mason place is the Summers place and the place right on up the river is the Wild place… [is there] cultivation there now on those tracts?" "Yes sir…after you pass around the hill you can see down on Wild's place, I think, that is on his furthest place…After you get around the hill pretty near Contention you can see in there and see those particular fields." [174] Wild's place, according to Harris, was very near Contention. Of Wild's place, Hill testified, "it is an out-of-the way place, away in below the railroad, and I haven't any business in there and don't go there very often. I have been up through there with Mr. Wild." [175]

Wild's cultivated fields were probably tucked in between the railroad and the river. It is reasonable to assume that Harris' testimony has him travelling from north to south, upstream, along the river, since Mr. Goodrich asked, "Did the road run where it runs

now...the road that comes **up** from Benson to Contention?"
(Emphasis supplied) Harris replied, "...there was one road run
around the hill to the right as **you come up**, and the other road runs
over the hill to about where it runs now." (Emphasis supplied.) This
means that the hill to which Harris refers, "After you get around the
hill pretty near Contention..." is the last large hill on the east side of
the river, marked 3,872 feet, containing the ruins of the Head Center
Mill. (See topographic map below.)

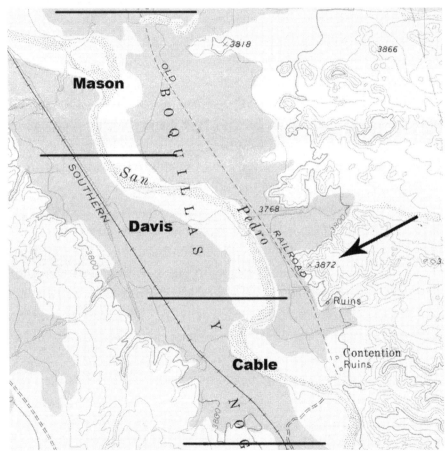

The arrow above marks the hill that T.S. Harris referred to. Special
thanks to Stephanie Rose for the draft that this is based on.
Annotated by Kevin Pyles.

A deed of sale from Cable to Wild and Curtis, dated January 30, 1882, states, "Being a tract of land about 160 acres in area known as 'Cable" Ranch on the San Pedro River about one half mile below Contention City commencing about 1 ½ miles below and north of the Old ruins on the San Pedro River..." [176] The deed also confirms that his ranch is ½ mile square. 1 ½ miles below the old ruins is on the north line of Cable's ranch, just north of Contention City. (Note that there is a variance in these two measurements of ¼ of a mile, as measured on the topographic map. When measured on the Rockfellow map, the one and one half mile measure places the southern end of his ranch one quarter of a mile south of Contention City. That matches perfectly with the other evidence that Cable's ranch was adjacent to Contention City, as shown on page 320. It is possible that variances occur on the Rockfellow map, and/or on the deed document.

Locating the ranches ½ mile apart does present some other contradictions as measured against the Rockfellow map (made in 1899). Summers and Wild are named on his map, but they are only ¼ mile apart, and too far north of the locations they occupied up to the Hill vs. Herrick suit of 1889. By the time of Rockfellow's survey, Clifford has moved north above Curtis, and Hill is north of his original location on the old Mason place. Rockfellow does not name another occupant on Mason's or Clifford's place (originally Drew's). But he is accurate at locating Curtis' place 1 ½ miles below, or north of, Hill, as testimony verified. It is likely that Hill's ranch was located directly north of and adjoining the old Drew place. His sons' occupation would be directly north of him.

SUMMARY OF SUCCESSION OF OWNERSHIP

Drew's ranch and station was next sold to Horne by the summer of 1882. Horne sold out to Clifford, who lived and farmed on the Drew ranch through the time of the lawsuit in 1889. Clifford then moved north to the site annotated on the Rockfellow map, just above the Curtis place. There are no further records of sale or ownership of the Drew ranch after Clifford.

Robert Mason sold his ranch to Kimble who sold it to Hill. There are no records of sale or ownership of this land after Hill moved north. He may have retained ownership of it, even if to secure his right to the Union Ditch.

Fred Bruener owned the next ranch up the river. Drew bought from him and sold to Johnny Davis. According to testimony, the Gale Brothers occupied it next. But according to John Hill, Summers bought it from T.C. Merrill, also known as Old Man Merrill. It is possible that Merrill had purchased it, rented it to the Gale brothers, then sold it to Summers.

Cable sold to Wild, Hubbard and Curtis, and Wild ended up occupying a portion of it by himself. A man named Claflin owned the parcel above, or south of, Cable, then sold it to Griffith, who did not stay there long. Claflin ended up moving up river close to the Noyes brothers.

A TABLE OF DISTANCES AND KEY SITES

Distance from S. Curtis's house to Hill is 1.5 miles
Distance from Hill to Drew's is 0.78 miles
Distance from Drew's to Gray is 0.86 miles
Distance from Terranate Ruins to Drew's is 2.8 miles
Distance from Drew's Station to the N.M. &A. railroad is 0.17 miles
Distance from Drew's Station to the San Pedro River is 0.36 miles current river, 0.56 miles to Allis river
Distance from John Hill's ranch to the N.M & A. railroad bed is 0.51 miles

ENDNOTES

1. *Man and Wildlife in Arizona: The American Exploration Period 1824-1865*, Goode P. Davis, Jr. Edited by Neil B. Carmony & David E. Brown, published 1982, page 130

2. Parsons Journal, as published under the title "A Tenderfoot in Tombstone" by Lynn Bailey of the Westernlore Press, Tucson Arizona, page 67

3. The Private Journal of George Whitwell Parsons, edited by Carl Chafin, page 360

4. Weekly Arizonian, March 31st, 1859

5. *Man and Wildlife in Arizona: The American Exploration Period 1824-1865*, page 125

6. Ibid, page 36

7. Ibid, page 28

8. Ibid, page 126

9. Ibid, page 124

10. Ibid, page 64

11. Ibid, page 108

12. Ibid, page 107

13. Ibid, page 75

14. Sierra Vista Herald Dispatch, December 29, 2012

15. See Transcript, William Drew vs. Robert Mason, 1879, Courtesy AHS

16. Hill vs. Herrick, testimony of H.M Christianson, pages 1083-1086, courtesy of the Arizona State Archives, a complete copy of this case in the collections of John D. Rose

17. Ibid, testimony of Richard Parks, pages 1014-1017

18. Ibid, testimony of Peter Rufly, pages 1017-1022

19. Ibid, testimony of S.B. Curtis, page 470

20. Ibid, testimony of John Hill, page 380

21. Tombstone Epitaph, April 2, 1882

22. Hill vs. Herrick, testimony of John Hill, pages 427-428, 446

23. Ibid, testimony of Col. Herring, pages 997-999

24. Ibid, testimony of John Hill, pages 418-420

25. Tombstone Daily Epitaph, March 16th, 1881

26. Hill vs. Herrick, testimony of Charles Noyes, pages 297-383

27. For further details on this pivotal proceeding see "On the Road to Tombstone: Drew's Station, Contention City and Fairbank" by John D. Rose

28. "My Life in the Early West," by Cora Drew Reynolds, copy in the collection of John D. Rose

29. Hill vs. Herrick, testimony of Ed Drew, pages 884-893

30. See "On the Road to Tombstone: Drew's Station, Contention City and Fairbank" by John D. Rose, page 103

31. Hill vs. Herrick, testimony of John H. Martin, pages 661-778

32. For more on the Charleston career and shooting of Deputy Sheriff Milton McDowell, see *Charleston & Millville A.T. Hell on the San Pedro,* by John D. Rose

33. Hill vs. Herrick, testimony of William Bell pages 802-851

34. For more on Appolinar Bauer see *Cochise County Stalwarts* by Lynn Bailey and Don Chaput Volume 1, page 19, published by the Westernlore Press, P.O. Box 35305, Tucson Arizona, 85740. Bauer's testimony from the Spicer Hearing is found in *The O.K. Corral Inquest* edited by Al Turner, pages 122-124. For further information on Bauer see *Tombstone A.T.* by William B. Shillingberg

35. Hill vs. Herrick, testimony of Henry P. Schultz, pages 354-367

36. Ibid, testimony of Robert Upton, pages 286-296

37. Ibid, testimony of Charles Noyes, pages 297-383

38. Ibid, testimony of Elijah Clifford, 453-463

39. The Corbin Mill would not begin operations until Wednesday January 14th, 1880. Among the many setbacks and controversies that attended its progress was a false rumor of an early sale of the mill, as well as issues with the foundation of a hard rock nature. For more of this key Millville stamp mill see *Charleston & Millville A.T. Hell on the San Pedro* by John D. Rose.

40. Hill vs. Herrick, testimony of T.S. Harris, pages 697-721

41. Ibid, testimony of John Hill, pages 381-383

42. Ibid, testimony of John Martin, P. 668-669

43. Ibid, testimony of John Hill, pages 392-394

44. Ibid, page 416

45. Arizona Weekly Citizen, May 11, 1889

46. Hill vs. Herrick, testimony of John Hill, pages 396-399

47. Ibid, page 386

48. Ibid, pages 391-392

49. From the 1882 Great Register of Cochise County, a complete transcription of which is in the collections of John D. Rose

50. Hill vs. Herrick, testimony of John Hill, pages 399-407

51. Ibid, pages 407, 496

52. For more on the McMenomy murder see *On the Road to Tombstone: Drew's Station, Contention City and Fairbank* by John D. Rose, page 189.

53. Deed Book two, page 518-520, courtesy of Christine Rhodes, Cochise County Recorder's Office, Bisbee, AZ

54. Deed Book four, page 350

55. Ibid, page 495

56. Hill vs. Herrick, testimony of John Hill, page 413

57. Ibid, pages 418-420

58. Transcribed Deed Book two, page 58, courtesy of Cochise County Recorder Christine Rhodes

59. Hill vs. Herrick, testimony of John Hill, page 421. For more information on such outbreaks of illness along the San Pedro see *Charleston and Millville A.T., Hell on the San Pedro,* by John D. Rose.

60. Ibid, testimony of Charles Noyes, page 486

61. Ibid, testimony of John Hill, pages 388-389

62. Ibid, testimony of W.C. Greene, page 875

63. From the 1882 Great Register of Cochise County

64. Ibid, testimony of John Martin, pages 661-778

65. Ibid, testimony of Frank C. Perley, pages 972-982

66. Ibid, testimony of Samuel Sweetman, pages 1000-1003

67. Ibid, testimony of T. [Thomas] Gribble, pages 1023-1026

68. Ibid, testimony of S.W. Wood, pages 1087-1089

69. Ibid, testimony of E.W. Perkins, pages 1090-1091

70. Ibid, testimony of C.M. Bruce, 614-622

71. Ibid, testimony of I. Nicholson, pages 367-377

72. Ibid, testimony of John Montgomery, pages 371-374 and 1008, 1009

73. Ibid, testimony of Jacob Landis, P. 550, 551

74. For more on L.W. Blinn see *Charleston and Millville A.T. Hell on the San Pedro* and *On the Road to Tombstone: Drew's Station, Contention City and Fairbank,* both by John D. Rose

75. Hill vs. Herrick, testimony of John Martin, P. 673

76. Ibid, testimony of H.C. Herrick, Pp. 623 – 802 and 1010-1013

77. Ibid, testimony of Hop Kee, pages 517-536, and 1054

78. Court reporter Tichenor misspells the name of this firm as Maulton & Lynn. For more on this key firm see "*On the Road to Tombstone: Drew's Station, Contention City and Fairbank*" by John D. Rose. For additional information on Charles Lind, of Malter & Lind, see "Cochise County Stalwarts, by Lynn Bailey and Don Chaput, Volume Two, pages 9-10, published by the Westernlore Press, Tucson Arizona.

79. Hill vs. Herrick, testimony of John H. Martin, pages 661-778

80. Ibid, testimony of Jacob Landis, pages 537-613

81. Ibid, testimony of John H. Martin, P. 674

82. Ibid, testimony of Paul De Martini pages 1029-1048

83. Ibid, testimony of Bertolomeo Avancino, pages 256-285

84. Ibid, testimony of Godfrey Tribolet, pages 499-517

85. Ibid, testimony of V. Kimble, page 1062

86. Ibid, testimony of P.W.B. Crane, P. 852

87. Ibid, testimony of Charles Noyes, Pp. 303-304

88. Ibid, pages 297-383

89. Ibid, testimony of Robert Todd, pages 860-867

90. Ibid, testimony of William C. Greene, pages 868-884, courtesy of the Arizona State Archives, a complete copy of this case in the collections of John D. Rose. Also, the Hereford that Greene referred to was not the original location of this once remote stage stop. In

1889 as the Hill vs. Herrick suit was taking place, a new location for Hereford had been established by the Arizona and Southeastern railroad, which ran a line from Fairbank through Hereford and onto Bisbee, for the Phelps Dodge Company, under the leadership of Dr. James Douglas. The original location of Hereford is part of the Earp story as it was between that location and Bisbee that Frank Stilwell and Pete Spence[r] robbed the Sandy Bob Stage Line on September 8th, 1881. The original Hereford location is southwest of the railroad ruins on present day Hereford Road. Many mistakenly believe this second site, built by the railroad and host to Col. Greene's store in later years, to be the original Hereford site. The site known today as Hereford is the third location, which was originally Nicksville.

91. Ibid, testimony of W.F. Banning pages 988-997

92. For more on this incident, as well as the life of Col. Greene, see *Colonel Greene and the Copper Skyrocket*, by C.L. Sonnichsen. For more on the life of Jim Burnett, *see Charleston & Millville A.T. Hell on the San Pedro* by John D. Rose.

93. Hill vs. Herrick, testimony of Charles Otto, pages 897-922

94. Ibid, testimony of Peter Moore, pages 924-943

95. Ibid, testimony of N.W. Storer, pages 894-1074

96. Ibid, testimony of W.W. Woodman, pages 1092-1116

97. Arizona Weekly Citizen, May 11, 1889

98. Tombstone Daily Prospector January 26, 1891

99. See 155 U.S. 394 15 S. Ct. 178 39 Led. 197 Swan v. Hill et al. No.

101. December 17, 1894. This finding can be viewed online at Public. Resource.Org,Inc.

100. Hill vs. Herrick, testimony of A.B. Wild, pages 478-484, and 1078-1079

101. Weekly Orb, Bisbee, March 5, 1899

102. Hill vs. Herrick, testimony of A.B. Wild, pages 478-484

103. Ibid, testimony of S. B. Curtis, pages 463-477

104. Ibid, testimony of John Hill, P. 380

105. Ibid, Pp. 432

106. Deed Book 12, pages 135-136

107. *When Law was in the Holster, The Frontier Life of Bob Paul* by John Boessenecker, published by the University of Oklahoma Press, page 429

108. *When Law was in the Holster The Frontier Life of Bob Paul,* page 161

109. *Wyatt Earp The Life Behind the Legend* by Casey Tefertiller, page 76

110. "Field Notes of Preliminary Survey San Juan de las Boquillas y Nogales private land claim Cachise [later written and pronounced "Cochise] County by Solon Allis dated February 23rd 1881, Page 14, Drew family archive, copy in the collections of John D. Rose. Also on page 285 of *On the Road to Tombstone: Drew's Station, Contention City and Fairbank* by John D. Rose, the following label was misworded. Instead of reading "A portion of Solon Allis' map of the Boquillas Land Grant, showing its boundaries. Note that Drew's Station is not mentioned, but Mason's Ranch is mentioned," this label read that Mason's Ranch was not on the map, which of course it was.

111. See *On the Road To Tombstone: Drew's Station, Contention City And Fairbank*, page 309

112. Tombstone Prospector, August 6, 1890

113. Tombstone Daily Prospector, March 3, 1890

114. Tombstone Epitaph, June 19, 1892

115. Weekly Tombstone Epitaph, May 8, 1892

116. Tombstone Epitaph, May 15, 1892

117. Tombstone Weekly Epitaph, June 18, 1893

118. Tombstone Weekly Epitaph, June 3, 1893

119. Tombstone Epitaph, November 12, 1893, Sunday Edition

120. Tombstone Epitaph, October 14, 1894

121. Weekly Tombstone Epitaph, March 4, 1894

122. Tombstone Daily Prospector, July 10, 1894

123. Tombstone Epitaph, March 24, 1895

124. Ibid

125. Ibid

126. Weekly Tombstone Epitaph, February 24, 1895

127. Weekly Tombstone Epitaph, June 2, 1895

128. Arizona Weekly Citizen, May 23, 1896

129. Tombstone Prospector, December 11, 1896

130. Weekly Tombstone Epitaph, December 13, 1896

131. Tombstone Epitaph, Sunday Edition, December 11, 1898

132. Weekly Epitaph, March 19, 1899

133. Tombstone Epitaph, December 3, 1899

134. Ibid

135. Bisbee Daily Review, August 21, 1902

136. Tombstone Epitaph, August 24, 1902

137. Prescott Evening Courier, January 21, 1904

138. Tombstone Epitaph, October 1, 1887

139. For more on this event see "On the Road to Tombstone: Drew's Station, Contention City and Fairbank" by John D. Rose, pages 252-253

140. Tombstone Epitaph, February 15, 1891

141. Tombstone Daily Prospector, August 4, 1890

142. Tombstone Daily Prospector, September 10, 1890

143. Tombstone Epitaph, August 19 1894

144. Tombstone Epitaph, May 5, 1888

145. Tombstone Daily Prospector, February 17, 1891

146. Tombstone Epitaph, July 17, 1898

147. Tombstone Epitaph, April 7, 1895

148. Tombstone Prospector, August 7, 1897

149. Tombstone Epitaph, May 28, 1899

150. See Tombstone Epitaph, February 16, 1896

151. Tombstone Prospector, October 18th, 1899

152. Tombstone Epitaph, February 16, 1902

153. See 213 U.S. 339 1909 Boquillas Land and Cattle Company v. Curtis. No. 133 Supreme Court of the United States Argued April 7, 1909, and decided ten days later on April 19, 1909

154. Tombstone Daily Prospector March 4, 1899

155. Tucson Daily Citizen, June 8, 1904

156. Bisbee Daily Review, July 21st, 1904

157. Hill vs. Herrick, testimony of S.B. Curtis, P. 466

158. Bisbee Daily Review, January 3, 1906

159. For more on this pivotal case see "On the Road to Tombstone: Drew's Station, Contention City and Fairbank" by John D. Rose. William H. Drew vs. Robert Mason, testimony of William Drew, Courtesy AHS

160. Hill vs. Herrick, testimony of John Hill, page 418-420

161. Ibid, testimony of H.C. Herrick, page 624

162. Ibid, testimony of T. S. Harris, page 719

163. Ibid, testimony of Bertolomeo Avancino, page 273

164. Ibid, testimony of Jacob Landis, page 540

165. Ibid, testimony of Hop Kee, page 521

166. Ibid, testimony of P.W.B. Crane, page 852

167. Ibid, testimony of W.F. Banning, pages 988, 989

168. Ibid, testimony of Peter Moore, page 925

169. Ibid, testimony of John Hill, P. 387

170. Ibid, testimony of H.M. Christianson, P. 1086

171. Ibid, testimony of John Hill, Pp. 387, 391

172. Deed Book two, page 518-520

173. Hill vs. Herrick, testimony of T. S. Harris, page 711

174. Ibid, P. 721

175. Ibid, testimony of John Hill, P. 398

176. Deed Book two, pages 546-547

INDEX

Alfalfa being raised along the San Pedro. 3, 9, 24, 58, 69, 74, 135, 142, 168, 179, 205, 244.

Allis, Solon; Allis notes, Allis map. Tucson based surveyor who was hired by Janet Howard to survey and map the Boquillas Land Grant. xi, 81, 212, 216-219, 222-224, 250-294, 322.

Avancino, Bertolomeo . Neighboring farmer of H.C. Herrick, who once threatened to burn his fence posts. 135, 155-158, 314.

Ayles, T.W. (Thomas Webb) Contention City cattle dealer who was visited by Ed "Eddie" Drew with news of Philpot's shooting death. 38.

Babacomari River. A tributary of the San Pedro, draining into the San Pedro near Fairbank. 12, 44, 74, 94-96, 132, 150, 155-156, 159, 162, 164-165, 194, 216, 317.

Banning, W.F. San Pedro farmer who lived in the general area of W.C. Greene, noted on maps as just south of Lewis Spring. 68, 171, 175-178, 180-183, 185, 197, 315.

Barnes, Wm. H. The Judge who wrote the final decision in the Hill vs. Herrick case. 68, 144, 192, 194.

Bartlett, John. Made note of the San Pedro River in 1851. 14.

Bauer, Appolinar. Tombstone butcher who testified at Spicer Hearing re Gunfight near the O.K. Corral, who may have employed Henry P. Schultz. 49-50.

Bauer, Richard. Present day Tombstone resident and field research historian who located the W.C. Greene Ranch. v. vii, viii, ix, 46, 174, 186, 210, 229, 317.

Beans raised along the San Pedro. 148.

Carlyle Bridge, constructed by William Carlyle. 75, 81.

Cattle illness. 225.

Cattle. vi, 1, 38, 49-50, 94-95, 135, 137, 153, 156-157, 159, 178, 202, 225, 241.

Charleston A.T. 3, 5, 8-10, 12-13, 42, 45, 47-48, 52-53, 55-57, 67, 84, 92-93, 129, 150, 155, 158-161, 163-167, 171, 177-178, 180-182, 189, 197, 202, 219, 237.

Chiricahua Mountains of Arizona. 12, 133.

Christianson, H.M. Arrived north of where Contention would later be built in 1877, labored on the Mason/Cable ditch and partnered with Fred Bruener. 21, 22, 158, 162, 165, 193, 194, 216, 315, 317.

Cienegas along the San Pedro River. 1, 17, 163-165, 168-169.

Claflin, C. First owner of the location marked on William Drew's map as "Griffith," 29, 322; aided in the construction of the Mason/Cable Ditch, later known as the Union Ditch. 22, 39, 149, 162; owner of ¼ interest in the Mason Cable ditch, 41; moved south to a second location, 162, 322

Clifford, Elijah. Third owner of what was originally known as Drew's Station. 32-34, 36, 40, 54-55, 73, 122-123, 187-188, 205, 206, 242, 321-322.

Contention City. 20-21, 25, 42, 46, 48, 55-58, 77, 87, 89-93, 120, 123, 131, 167, 196-197, 213-214, 216, 218, 223, 239-240, 242, 321.

Contention Mill. 22, 35, 46-47, 87, 89, 196.

Contzen, Philip. Surveyor of the San Rafael de Valle land grant. 308.

Corn being raised along the San Pedro. 3, 22, 33, 52, 74, 142-143, 148-149, 177, 187-188, 244.

Cosmopolitan Hotel located at Tombstone. 150.

Cottonwood Trees along the San Pedro River. x, 8-14, 16, 18-19, 53.

Court of Private Land Claims. 246.

Crane, P.W.B., also Crane Brothers Ranch, noted on the Rockfellow map. The Crane Brothers Ranch was located on the former ranch of D.T. Smith, shooting victim of the Bisbee Massacre. 42, 67, 69-70, 157, 159, 161-162, 194, 315.

Crystal Spring, located on the San Pedro south of the Snake Ranch which is south of Charleston. 315.

Curtis, S.B. 23, 35, 69, 71, 203-206, 212, 242, 245, 248, 314, 321-322.

Dams along the San Pedro. 3-5, 11, 16, 21-24, 31, 33, 35-36, 41, 55, 67, 74, 78-80, 83, 88-90, 92, 95, 136-138, 140, 143, 147, 148, 151, 158, 160-161, 163, 165-166, 168-171, 175, 178-181, 184, 189, 196, 228, 244, 314, 317-319.

Davis, Johnny, also Davis Place, Davis Ranch. Purchased the former ranch of Fred Bruener from William Drew after Drew had purchased it from Bruener. This is why Davis, and not Bruener, is noted on William Drew's map. Davis also worked for Drew. 24, 29, 39-40, 44, 53, 58, 67, 314, 319, 322.

De Martini, Paul. Lived on the ranch of H.C. Herrick in 1880, later becoming a long-term merchandising success at Fairbank. 12, 133, 149, 150, 152-156, 158.

Donnelly, Professor Donnelly. Known for the Copper Glance mine, and knew H.C. Herrick and his wife. 232.

Dos Cabezas, A.T. 237.

Douglas A.T. 247.

Drew Family Archive. 37, 43, 100-102, 118.

Drew family located in Tombstone (not the Drew family of Drew's Station). 119.

Drew family. v, vii, 24, 42, 44, 110, 118, 218.

Drew Farm, another name for the site of Drew's Station, aka Drew's Ranch. 54.

Drew Place, another name for the site of Drew's Station, aka Drew Farm, aka Drew Ranch. 34, 36, 40, 54, 71, 74, 204, 206, 241, 321.

Drew Ranch, another name for the site of Drew's Station, aka Drew Farm. 32, 33, 44, 73, 196, 206, 250, 321-322.

Drew, Anne, aka, the widow Drew. 21, 33, 40, 45-46.

Drew, Cora. vi, 42, 110-114.

Drew, Ed, Edward, Eddie. 38-42, 44, 50, 57, 115-117, 119.

Drew, William. Founder of Drew's Station, buried at the Contention Cemetery in 1879. vii, 20, 24, 25, 27, 33-34, 40, 43, 46, 50-52, 57, 77, 84, 100-101, 123, 135, 203-204, 213-215, 217, 223, 239-240, 244, 315.

Drew's Station. vi, vii, viii, ix, xi, 10, 20, 24-25, 32-33, 35, 39-40, 43, 50, 54, 56-57, 71, 81, 100, 110, 115, 119, 122-123, 131, 141, 196, 203-204, 206-207, 209, 212-215, 217-219, 222-223, 240-241, 244, 296, 304, 322.

Dry conditions for crops and dry season along the San Pedro. 13, 55, 68-69, 95, 136, 164, 168-169, 175, 181, 184, 197, 234.

Duncan, Judge Duncan. Dismissed the charge of smoking opium against nine Chinese defendants. This charge was preferred by H.C. Herrick. 227.

Earthquake which occurred on May 3rd, 1887, in the San Pedro River Valley. 55, 175, 182.

Emory, William, Lt. Noted his impressions of the San Pedro from his 1848 and 1857 visits. 13, 16.

Empire Ranch. 148.

Evaporation of irrigation water from the San Pedro. 169.

Herring, Howard, aka, Colonel Herring. One of the attorneys in the Hill vs. Herrick case. 23, 34-36, 47-48, 52-53, 55, 132, 136, 142-143, 156-158, 163, 205.

Herron, John. BLM Archeologist who, while utilizing the Solon Allis field notes, discovered and misidentified the Gray Ranch as Drew's Station. 212-213, 218, 219, 296.

Hill vs. Herrick lawsuit. ix, x, 4, 17, 21, 25, 33, 39, 44, 53, 69, 77, 92, 96-97, 115, 125, 130, 144, 146, 155, 167, 180, 185, 190-191, 195-197, 203-204, 223, 225, 235, 237, 240, 244-245, 304, 321.

Hill, F.M, son of John Hill Sr. Lived in the adobe building that their father owned with his brother John Hill Jr. until his father, John Hill Sr., sold it to W.S. Gray in 1894. This home has incorrectly been identified as Drew's Station, and has also been referred to as the TTR/Sosa Site. 141, 206-207, 212, 304.

Hill, John Jr. Lived in the adobe building that their father owned until he sold it to W.S. Gray in 1894. This home has incorrectly been identified as Drew's Station, and has also been referred to as the TTR/Sosa Site. 141, 206-207, 212, 243, 304.

Hill, John Sr. His full name which he rarely used was John Hill Hoops. Initiated the Hill vs. Herrick lawsuit. He purchased the Robert Mason Ranch acting in concert with D.P. (David) Kimble, and loaned H.J. Horne the funds to buy out the Widow (Anne) Drew. 20, 24-25, 30, 32-36, 39-40, 42, 50-51, 53-54, 66-71, 73-75, 77, 79-80, 82, 84-85, 94-95, 120, 123, 127-129, 132, 138, 141, 149, 160, 161, 182,-185, 187, 188, 197, 204-209, 212, 230, 239-245, 304-306, 317, 319, 321-322.

Hill, Rose, daughter of John Hill Sr. 127.

Hop Kee. Farming neighbor of H.C. Herrick with whom he had many conflicts, and was punched by Herrick as well as having potatoes taken from him by the same. 48, 68, 93, 132, 134, 139-146, 149, 151, 155, 158, 160, 162-163, 193-194, 227, 315.

Howard, James. Gained control of the Boquillas Land Grant and quickly brought George Hearst into ownership as well. x, 212, 216, 249.

Howard, Janet. Wife of James Howard noted in the entry above. 212, 216.

Huachuca Mountains of Arizona. 9, 11-12, 56, 225.

Hubbard. Settler who joined with S.B. Curtis and Andrew Wild to buy the ranch of Daniel Cable. 71, 203, 205, 314, 322.

Hunting along the San Pedro. 47, 91, 146, 160.

Irrigating crops along the San Pedro. 24, 36, 40, 52, 57, 68, 74, 84-85, 136, 143, 164-165, 171, 175, 177, 183-184, 187-188, 196, 205, 244-245.

Jastor, J. H. Official with the Kern Land and Cattle Company sent to the San Pedro to inspect the Boquillas Grant which they had purchased. 202.

Jennings, also, Jennings Ranch, Jennings place, Jennings boys. Early settlers noted on the map by William Drew who left their ranch by the spring of 1882. 24, 30, 45, 58, 317, 319.

Kelton. Sheriff who appointed John Hill Deputy. 243, 240, 243.

Kemble, D. P. See Kimble.

Kern Land and Cattle Company of California. Purchased the Boquillas Grant from the estate of George Hearst, and evicted many settlers who had remained on the grant. 197, 202, 235, 237, 246.

Kimble, D.P. Also spelled Kemble. Purchased the Mason Ranch from Robert Mason, along with John Hill who was a silent partner on the purchase, later deeding the same to John Hill. In addition to his farming, he was also a Mormon Bishop until his death. 35, 44, 74, 75, 77-80, 82, 143, 148, 159, 160, 162, 164, 317, 322.

Kimble, V. Owned a ranch located at the confluence of the Babacomari and San Pedro Rivers. 44, 159, 162.

Kinnear, John D. Also Kinnear and Company Stage. 25, 35, 210-211.

Millville A.T. ix, 5, 8, 10, 55, 93, 124, 161, 163, 184.

Montgomery, John. Owner of Tombstone's O.K. Corral, who testified on behalf of John Hill in the Hill vs. Herrick case. 129, 132.

Moore, Peter. Ranched near W.C. Greene, and received a one third interest in a spring owned by Greene in exchange for labor. 68, 164, 170, 177, 179-183, 185, 315.

N.M. & A. (New Mexico and Arizona railroad.) 24, 33, 95, 102, 228, 232, 240.

Navoni. Italian ranchers (along with a Mr. Rossi) who leased a portion of the Herrick ranch. 133, 150.

Nicholson, I. Testified on behalf of John Hill and other plaintiffs, having worked for H.C. Herrick and lived in Fairbank in 1884. 95.

Noyes Bros., which included Charles Noyes. 70, 183, 194.

Noyes place. 50.

Noyes Ranch. 162.

Noyes, C.A. (Charles) Ranched south of H.C. Herrick who was just south of Fairbank. Testified in detail regarding the Drew Family. 21, 40, 51, 53, 68, 84, 158-165, 193.

Ochoaville. 176.

Ohnesorgen, Billy. 8, 55-56, 77.

Otto, Charles. Stock tender who had worked cattle for John Slaughter. 178.

Pantano, A.T. 164.

Parke, John H. Lt. Participated in an early expedition noting the San Pedro as well as creating a map. 8, 14-15.

Parks, Richard. Laborer on irrigation ditches in the Contention City area, and knew Robert Mason and Daniel Cable. 22.

Parsons, George. Tombstone diarist. 5-6, 52.

Paul, Robert H., "Bob." Boldly squared off against the murderers of Bud Philpot and Peter Roerig in the wash just south of Drew's Station. 25, 204, 211, 213, 215, 223.

Perkins, E. W. Lived and worked at the Grand Central Mill. 94.

Perley, Frank C. A brick maker who arrived in Contention City in May of 1880; worked on the construction of the Head Centre Mill. 90, 91, 130.

Philpot, Eli, "Bud." Driver for Kinnear and Company on March 15th, 1881, when murdered just south of Drew's Station. vii, 25, 35, 38, 116, 204, 206, 209-213, 219, 239, 242, 304.

Phoenix, A.T. 231, 242-243.

Potatoes raised along the San Pedro. 3, 139-140, 142-143, 159, 163, 227.

Rockfellow, John, also the Rockfellow map, of which is he the author, 42, 53, 60, 66, 70-74, 159, 162, 174, 203-204, 206, 208, 209, 212, 241, 245-246, 248, 318, 321.

Roerig, Peter. Shooting victim from the March 15, 1881 attack on the Kinnear and Company Stage which took place just south of Drew's Station. Philpot died on the scene, and Roerig died later that night in Benson. 239.

Rossi. Italian rancher who leased a portion of the Herrick ranch. 133, 150.

Rulfly, Peter. Amalgamator at the Contention Mill. 23.

San Ignacio del Babacomari Land Grant. Commonly referred to as the Babacomari Grant. 94, 241.

San Juan de Boquillas y Nogales land grant. Commonly referred to as the Boquillas Grant. x, 24, 131, 168, 201-202, 206, 212, 216, 218, 235, 237, 241, 246-249, 294, 314.

St. David, aka, St. Davids. Unlike today, the St. David area was sometimes used to designate ranches just north of Contention City, as was the term McDonalds. 6, 57, 75, 95, 123, 148, 202, 208, 242.

Stillwell, Judge Stillwell. One of the questioners in the Hill vs. Herrick case. 45-46, 178, 205.

Storer, N.W. Worked as an agent for Robert Swann at the Boston Mill, assuming key management of the mill and its accompanying 640 acre farm in 1887. 48, 68, 69, 182-185, 188.

Summers, Samuel. Spelled Sommers on the Rockfellow map. Neighbor of key plaintiff John Hill, as well as Andrew Wild, moving onto his land in the spring of 1882. 54, 66-71, 73, 89, 149.

Sunset Mill, aka, Head Centre Mill. 20, 44, 59, 87, 89-91, 130, 146, 196,-197, 204.

Swimming along the San Pedro. 5, 88.

Tamblin. early San Pedro River settler whose ranch later became the property of H.C. Herrick. 133, 148.

Tefertiller, Casey. Author of the landmark *Wyatt Earp The Life Behind the Legend,* the most comprehensive book on the life of Wyatt Earp to date. Supports wrong distance between Contention City and the Philpot hold-up site, 213-214.

Terranate, aka, Santa Cruz de Terranate. Commonly referred to during the historic period as the "old ruins," and also the "San Pedro ruins." William Drew testified that he lived about three miles north of this location, proving definitively where Drew's Station was. 204, 216, 223, 317.

Tevis & Co. Although they ranched on the Babacomari River, they were drawn into the Hill vs. Herrick suit. 94, 96.

Tichenor, Bryan W. The self-described "Law Stenographer and Type Writer" from Tucson who compiled the extensive Hill vs. Herrick case. 97, 167, 190, 192.

Water from the San Pedro and the issue of whether or not a portion of that water sinks into the riverbed. 8, 164, 180.

Water Melon raised along the San Pedro. 59, 89, 122, 142, 146-147.

Western Union office, located at Tombstone, A.T. 231.

White, Josiah Howe. Owner of the Contention Mine at Tombstone and the Contention Mill at Contention City. 35, 43, 46-47.

Wild Ranch, aka, Wild's place. 71, 203, 239, 319.

Wild, Andrew B. Bought out Daniel Cable of the Cable ranch, and later joined with neighbor John Hill in the Hill vs. Herrick lawsuit. 25, 35, 54, 71, 73, 123, 196-197, 203, 205, 239, 243, 314, 319, 321-322.

Williams, Carrie. Saved by Mrs. H.C. Herrick from potentially severe burn injuries. 235.

Williams, Walk. Purchased D.T. Smith's ranch from him, but defaulted. 42, 44, 89, 159, 161, 235.

Willow Trees along the San Pedro River. 3, 10, 12-14, 53, 57, 150.

Wood, S.W., husband of Mary Wood known for her detailed recollection of life at Charleston. Served as Superintendent of the Grand Central Mill and road overseer over the Grand Central Road District. 92, 93, 239.

Woodman, W.W. (Warren Walter). Conducted a water study of personally visited ranches and farms along the San Pedro at the behest of the court in the Hill vs. Herrick case. 187-190, 192, 195.

Made in the USA
Las Vegas, NV
15 February 2025

18210459R00197